FROM TRENCH AND TROOPS

David Kent was born in London in 1942 and educated at Dulwich College and the Universities of Cambridge and Edinburgh. After seven years' lecturing in higher education in Britain he emigrated to Australia. He is currently an Associate Professor at the University of New England in Armidale where he teaches courses on the social history of eighteenth and nineteenth-century Britain. Personal interest (both his grandfathers were casualties of the First World War) led him to explore the rich literary field of *From Trench and Troopship* for several years before finally feeling compelled to write about it. All of his work, including many scholarly articles on both Australian and British history, displays his preference for writing history 'from below'.

FROM TRENCH AND TROOPSHIP

The Experience of the Australian Imperial Force, 1914–1919

David Kent

© David Kent, 1999

This book is copyright. Apart from any fair dealing for the purposes of study, research, criticism, review, or as otherwise permitted under the Copyright Act, no part may be reproduced by any process without written permission. Inquiries should be made to the publisher.

First published in 1999.

Typeset by
Midland Typesetters Pty Ltd
Maryborough, Victoria 3465

Printed and bound by
Southwood Press Pty Ltd
76–82 Chapel St, Marrickville, NSW 2204

Published by
Hale & Iremonger Pty Ltd
PO Box 205, Alexandria, NSW 2015

National Library of Australia
Cataloguing-in-Publication entry

Kent, David, 1942–.
   From trench and troopship: the experience
of the Australian Imperial Force, 1914–1919

   Bibliography.
   ISBN 0 86806 669 9.

   1. Australia. Army. Australian Imperial Force (1914–1921).
2. World War, 1914–1918 – Participation, Australia. 3.
World War, 1914–1918 – Press coverage. 4. Periodicals. I.
Title.

940.483

This project has been assisted by the Commonwealth Government through the Australia Council, its arts funding and advisory body.

Front cover: The cover of *Homeward on H.M.T. A14* a souvenir magazine published in Sydney in March 1918. The cover illustration was by Penleigh Boyd. (*Australian War Memorial Printed Records*)

Back cover: *Billjim at Sea* was the souvenir magazine for the troops who travelled to Egypt on the *Ormonde* in 1918. (*Australian War Memorial Printed Records*)

CONTENTS

	Preface	7
1	Outward Bound on the 'Great Adventure'	11
2	*'A life on the ocean waves'*	24
3	Gallipoli, Egypt and Palestine	47
4	*'We're off to the sand and the sin tra-la'*	71
5	The Western Front	109
6	*'We're here because we're here'*	130
7	Going Home	165
8	*'There's a long, long trail a-winding'*	184
	Appendices	210

(Australian War Memorial Printed Records)

PREFACE

From Trench and Troopship deals with the experiences of the men who served in the Australian Imperial Force (A.I.F.) during the Great War, but it is not a conventional military history. This book examines the soldiers' writings contained in their trench and troopship papers and magazines, but it is not shaped by literary theory. It is principally a work of social history and my intention has been to illuminate an aspect of Australian popular culture.

I have always believed that until we recover the lived experiences of people in the past we cannot begin to attach meaning to their behaviour or write their history. Much has been written about the battles fought by the A.I.F. and it may be thought that the soldiers' experiences have been fully explored. In fact, this is far from the case. Apart from his time in action, the Australian soldier during the First World War spent long periods on troopships and in camps, and shorter periods on leave or in hospital. These episodes are generally neglected by military historians and as a result we acquire a fairly narrow understanding of the soldiers' lived experience. But the times spent out of the fighting were always treasured and often the best remembered, and they should form a vital part of any history of the A.I.F. during 'the war to end all wars'. It is with some trepidation, however, that I make this foray into Australian social and military history. As a historian who normally works on eighteenth- and early nineteenth-century Britain, I know only too well the penalties facing the unwary trespasser in other scholars' fields. I have ventured into the closes of military history and literature, however, in an attempt to make good a significant deficiency in the historiography of the A.I.F. and to lay a very personal ghost.

First I must declare my hand. I am not a devotee of military history as it is generally written. I find the topic of warfare disheartening, depressing and distasteful. I find it vaguely disturbing that military history is so popular, the more so when that history is often little more than food for nationalistic prejudices. Try as I may, I cannot bring myself to think that any war should be glorified. There are occasions when war is undoubtedly necessary, but it is not, and never has been, glorious, except perhaps in the minds of those who have never been required to risk their lives at their country's bidding. In particular, I have no patience with those who enthuse about strategy and tactics and wax lyrical in battle-analysis while forgetting the human cost paid by the front-line soldiers. I have the same feeling about that type of military history as I have about the history of high politics; neither tells me what I want to know about the lived experience of the ordinary soldier or citizen. For the same reason I have never found a Commander's account as informative as that of a Private. I have learned more about the Gallipoli misadventure from Private Albert Facey than from General Sir Ian Hamilton and more about the Second World War from Gunner 'Spike' Milligan than from Field-Marshal Bernard Montgomery. I have always tried to write and teach history 'from below', to recover the history of the neglected majority, and in this book I hope to show how the trench and troopship publications can add to our understanding of the essentially anonymous men of the A.I.F.

For a quarter of a century Australia lived in the shadow of the Great War. The European struggle drew over three hundred thousand Australians away from the peace and tranquillity of their island continent. Nearly half the eligible male population enlisted in the A.I.F. and almost sixty-five per cent of those who left their home shores became casualties of the conflict. One man in five from the enlistment queues was killed on active service. A loss of this magnitude would have been traumatic for any nation but coupled with the permanently crippled, the maimed, the blind, the gassed and the shell-shocked it was impossible to forget the terrible price the young Commonwealth had paid for its membership of the Imperial club. It was only the summons in 1939 to a new conflict and new dangers that laid to rest, at least temporarily, the spectre of 1914 to 1918.

Like most of the combatant nations, Australia showed no desire to forget the Great War. The magnificent multi-volume *Official History of Australia in the War of 1914-18* occupied its editor and principal author, C.E.W. Bean, for more than two decades with volumes appearing every few years from 1921 to 1942. During the same period, many regimental and battalion histories were published to fill in the fine detail for particular units. The war histories reminded survivors of their achievements and the price that the nation had paid and, together with the spate of memoirs and novels that appeared in the 1920s and 1930s, they allowed the non-participants and those who had grown up after the war to share in the experience. While these works kept the memory of the A.I.F. alive, they did little to advance historical understanding of the impact of the war on the men who enlisted. The fact that the literature was overwhelmingly 'official' meant that the fate of individuals was necessarily ignored. There is little in the *Official History* or the unit histories which brings the reader to a closer understanding of the attitudes and sentiments of the ordinary serviceman. This is not an indictment of this body of historical literature, simply an acknowledgement of its inevitable limitations.

There was, however, a neglected body of material that offered the perspective lacking in the military histories. Australian soldiers wrote about every facet of their war experience in the broadsheets, newspapers and magazines they produced on the troopships, in the trenches and at the bases. Similar material was created by each national force, but the Australians were unusually prolific in the number and variety of their publications. Over two hundred and fifty titles have been examined in the preparation of this book and undoubtedly there were many titles that are lost to us. Ranging from handwritten sheets compiled under fire to professionally printed souvenir issues, the field publications tell the modern reader a great deal about the war experiences of the A.I.F. They were written by participants for others in similar circumstances and they dealt with those aspects of service life that other participants would appreciate. As a record of service life, this material has a richness of detail, an immediacy and a spontaneity that cannot be found in any official history.

The trench and troopship papers and magazines also tell us something about the attitudes and values of those who enlisted. Nothing can rival the intimacy of a private diary or letter, but it must be remembered that only a minority kept extensive diaries. In a sense, the field publications became the corporate diaries of tens of thousands of servicemen. These publications allowed them to recall and share experiences among themselves while also, in many cases, transmitting that experience to the people at home. Using this material it is possible to examine the motives of the early volunteers, to see the gradual transformation of their ideas and the development of a new set of attitudes as the war dragged on. Furthermore, as souvenirs and communications from a distant war, this literature was important in forming Australian perceptions of the conflict on the other side of the world.

The service papers and magazines were first and foremost intended to amuse the men in a closed community. The community could be as small as a company, battery or technical unit, or as large as an Army Corps, but in every case the publications were introspective and reflective. Consequently, they allow us to see another side of the men in the A.I.F. We can begin to understand what made them laugh and what provoked a sigh; we can learn what they really thought about the task they were committed to; above all else we can hear their 'voices'. Until now the 'voice' of the ordinary soldier has been heard only in the letters, diaries and memoirs of the more literate and communicative. The enormous volume of material in the trench and troopship literature increases the number of the voices we can listen to, and we might be surprised by what we hear. In particular, the reader of this book will probably be astonished by the deep vein of sentimentalism found in all publications at every stage of the war. Equally surprising will be the extraordinary variety of literary sources and models the soldiers drew upon. Indeed, the reader might derive some quiet amusement from identifying the popular songs, hymns, poems or prose sources that provided the soldiers with the structure for their contributions. The fervent Australian nationalism and disenchantment with Britain and the British which features in most of the publications from 1916 onwards may likewise surprise those readers who think that a sense of a separate Australian identity is a relatively recent phenomenon.

Another surprise is that this significant and valuable body of material has been ignored by scholars for so long. Perhaps the essentially ephemeral nature of these publications has led to their neglect in the past, but today scholars are more sensitive to varieties of discourse. The trench and troopship publications offer exciting prospects for future research in many areas, and scholars are fortunate that such a comprehensive collection exists in the archive of the Australian War Memorial. I must place on record my thanks to the War Memorial for a grant in the earliest stages of this book and for the expert advice and encouragement invariably provided by its staff. The extracts from the service publications which form a substantial part of this book are reproduced with the permission of the War Memorial.

Finally there is the matter of my ghost, or rather ghosts. I first discovered the treasure-house of trench and troopship literature when I got to know a Great War veteran who had served in the Middle East. He possessed an unbroken run of *The Kia-Ora Coo-ee* and kindly allowed me to arrange a facsimile publication of that remarkable magazine. In the course of many conversations about his role as a horse-breaker in the Remount Unit, he told me what the war had meant to a young man from up-country New South Wales. He also talked about the absurdity of war, the remoteness of the decision-makers who sent men to their death, and the non-military activities in Cairo and elsewhere which are tactfully omitted from most histories. That encounter set me thinking about my own grandfathers: one killed in action in 1916; and the other, broken by the war, who died long before I was born. What might they have told me about their personal experiences of war on the Western Front? Would they have shared the gut-wrenching fear so many others wrote about? How might they have reacted to the orders that sent men to their death for no apparent purpose? What did they get up to in the villages behind the lines or when they were on leave? Of my grandfathers' war I know nothing, but the trench and troopship writings of the men of the A.I.F. allow us to recover something of their lived experience. I hope that this small book adds a personal, human perspective to the better-known history of their military exploits.

The start of the adventure. Infantry embarking on the *Hororata* and the *Benalla* at Port Melbourne in 1914. (*Australian War Memorial, Neg. no. C02793*)

By 1917 farewells were quieter and sadder occasions. Families and friends watch soldiers embarking on the *Beltana* at Brisbane. (*Australian War Memorial, Neg. no. H02219*)

CHAPTER ONE

OUTWARD BOUND ON THE 'GREAT ADVENTURE'

During the First World War virtually every troopship leaving Australia published a shipboard newspaper or magazine. Indeed, it was almost unimaginable that a voyage would be completed without at least one issue of a newsheet of gossip and jokes. The custom of the troopship paper was established very early in the war and the first recorded publication, *The Latrine Leader and W.C. Chronicle*, was produced on the *Kanowna* by members of the A.N.M.E.F. bound for Rabaul in August 1914. At least two troopship papers were issued while the first convoy was gathering at Albany in October and several other vessels produced some form of publication during the crossing of the Indian Ocean. In the course of the war many troopships left Australia and most printed some sort of paper, though few could equal the three different newsheets produced on H.M.A.T. *Runic* during the voyage to England in 1916. Many have not survived, which is scarcely surprising given the ephemeral nature of such publications. What is remarkable is that over seventy titles of papers and magazines generated on troopships leaving Australia are held in the archive of the Australian War Memorial. They offer an unrivalled insight into life on board and into the frame of mind in which many went off to war.

Troopship papers, as opposed to souvenir magazines, appeared in several forms. The overwhelming majority were duplicated typescript copies run off on spirit or jelly copiers, but duplicated handwritten copies were produced where the editors could not obtain a typewriter. The editor of *The Kan-Karoo Kronickle*, one of the papers in the first convoy, lamented his lack of proper printing facilities, yet still managed to produce eleven twice-weekly editions with 'an ancient typewriter, a Herbert roll, a few sheets of foolscap, and a gum-pot'. The editor of a troopship paper was lucky to have unrestricted use of a typewriter. *Persique*, the paper of the troopship *Persic*, was produced on the orderly room typewriter, but the editor of the *Beltana Bugle*, though he obtained a typewriter, was frustrated by a lack of ribbon. When it proved impossible to produce a paper at sea, material was usually collected in manuscript form, edited for publication, and printed at the next port of call. *The Pepper Box* and the *Seang-B-Liar*, for example, were both printed in Colombo by the *Ceylon Observer* and the *Ceylon Examiner* respectively.

Very occasionally editors had access to a printing press. The purser of the *Ascanius* put the vessel's printing press, which was normally used to print the liner's menus and notices, at the disposal of the troops to produce their paper. The limitations of this generous gesture were soon realised when the printer ran out of full-stops on the last page and only one number of *The Ascanian* ever appeared. The troops on board the *Marathon* were better served; some men who had been in the printing trade in Sydney approached Sir James Fairfax and the general managers of two leading newspapers to obtain the loan of a press and gifts of paper, ink, type and other printing needs. Although most troopship papers were ad hoc productions a few, like *Honk*, were simply the shipboard issues of a unit magazine. The Australian Heavy Siege Battery, which left Sydney in 1914, took with it a printing press with the fixed intention of producing a record of its activities on active service and the first issue of *Honk* printed at sea contained an account of the sinking of the German cruiser *Emden*. In whatever form they appeared, troopship papers and magazines quickly became an established feature of the outward voyage.

There was no guarantee that a shipboard publication would flourish. For every successful paper that maintained some regularity of production, and perhaps gave rise to a souvenir edition, there was a venture that died after only one or two issues. Usually the failure was attributable to a lack of material. It was almost obligatory for editors to request contributions in the first issue and remind the troops that the success of the paper depended upon their willingness to volunteer copy. Humorous incidents, personal comment and, above all, gossip were the mainstay of soldiers' papers throughout the war; the editor of *The Kanowna Lament* made it clear that 'matters religious, patriotic, or jingoistic' would receive short shrift. Gossip and personal comment were so important that the editor of *The Innocents Abroad* doubted if a single paragraph was printed which did not have fun at someone's expense, though he claimed there was no vindictiveness in the magazine. There was a strong correlation between the manner of production and the quality of the material submitted: typescript and duplicated papers rarely contained serious material, whereas printed papers usually had a mixture of gossip and literary items. Souvenir editions, of course, invariably went beyond the trivia of the voyage to include accounts of most aspects of the trip, as well as serious verse and prose.

The routines of troopship life soon became frustratingly monotonous and the ship's paper with its gossip, in-jokes, news snippets, literary gems, and complaints was a welcome diversion. Actual circulation or sales figures were rarely recorded, but there is clear evidence that the papers were much in demand. During the voyage of the *Osterly* from Australia to Egypt in 1917 over £100 worth of papers were sold at a penny-halfpenny each. The first edition of *The Kanowna Lament* sold out its 360 copies in thirty minutes, while *Shrapnel* usually ran to over 500 copies per issue. The factor which most effectively limited the number of copies produced was the acute shortage of paper, and many editorials noted that only a limited number of copies could be printed. Ordinary lined paper was frequently used even though the duplicated typescript looked ugly on the page and the master copy of *The Ballarat Lyre* was written on leaves torn from an account book.

The paper shortage showed up in other ways too. Papers were usually single sheets, often folded to create extra pages, or printed in a port of call when there were no resources on board. Because there had been an 'excessive demand for copies' the editor of *The Kan-Karoo Kronickle* announced that all shipboard copies would be reprinted in a single edition on arrival in England and this solution was adopted by many other editors who had been unable to print enough copies on board. Another commonly used device was to select the best items from the ship's paper and publish them on arrival in a special souvenir edition. In some cases only the professionally printed souvenirs remain as evidence of the troopship papers which spawned them: no copies of *The Barambah Battler* seem to have survived, but in *The Barambah Souvenir* we have a reminder of the contents and style of the paper.

Many troopship publications took the form of souvenir editions and it is clear from the inscriptions on many of the magazines in the Australian War Memorial that they were sent home to loved ones. The sharing of an experience seems to have been one of the first objects of all troopship souvenir editions. The editor of *Dragropes* made it clear that the magazine was aimed as much towards 'relatives and friends at home' as to members of the

quota. The aim and object of *The Innocents Abroad* was to provide a 'treasured memento' which could be 'sent back to sunny Australia', and the editor of *The Pepper Box* expressed the hope that the troops would consider the magazine 'worthy to be in the list of souvenirs to be sent home to those left behind'.

There seems little doubt that the ship's paper and the souvenir edition were intended to cement unit loyalty and esprit de corps. The foreword in *Aeneasthetic*, published in 1916, envisaged a day when children and grandchildren turning the pages of the magazine would cause the old soldier to summon up 'the faces of comrades with whom we stood in the Great War'. *The Barambah Souvenir* aimed to preserve the 'camaraderie that arises between men thrown together in such circumstances', while *The Book of the Ballarat* hoped to fix 'the golden memories of the comradeship that is born of mutual endeavour'. It is virtually impossible to prove that these magazines had an effect on collective morale, but it is worth noting that many of those sent home bore numerous signatures of men in the sender's unit. Some souvenirs printed the names of all those in the quota while others included a blank page, which was frequently used specifically for recording the names and addresses of newly acquired friends. It seems reasonable to conclude that these troopship publications played a part in forging the men on board into solidary communities bound by common circumstances, interest and purpose—because of this, their role in morale building must be acknowledged.

While the principal purpose of the outward-bound, troopship publications was to entertain, most contained some reflection on why Australia was at war. Even though all the troops were volunteers, who presumably had already decided why they wanted to enlist, virtually every ship's paper and certainly every souvenir magazine held at least one morale-boosting justification or exhortation. In 1914 and 1915, but with diminishing regularity thereafter, Australia's involvement in the war was justified as a natural consequence of her place in the British Empire. The other dominant theme, which appeared increasingly from mid 1915, was the responsibility of Australians to carry on the struggle begun by the original Anzacs, to preserve their sacred memory by defending Australia's name. An interesting feature of these justifications is that, with the exception of editorial comment or an O.C.'s address, they were nearly always expressed in verse. In the entire body of trench and troopship literature serious topics were usually tackled in verse form. Perhaps this reflected the feeling that the contrivance required by verse somehow dignified or intensified the sentiments expressed, or perhaps it was a measure of the familiarity most Australians had with simple balladic verse forms of the sort popularised by the *Bulletin*.

The ties which bound Australia to Britain were often seen as 'chains of blood' which made it inevitable that Australia would share the same ideas and interests as the mother country. The editor of the *Seang-Bee Sea Breezes* argued that Britain had to fight to protect Belgium and the integrity of treaties and that Australia as a member of 'the British Nation' had to do likewise. The plight of the motherland moved Corporal Arthur Hough to pour out his fervent loyalty in this contribution to *The Berrima Souvenir* which appeared in January 1917:

> Oh Britain! Blessed by those sons
> Who guard your shores and man your guns,
> Whenever you call, wherever they be,
> Ready ever to answer thee,
> From every corner of the earth,

> Back to the land which gave them birth,
> Willing and eager for the fight—
> Knowing that thy cause is 'Right'.
> They do not ask what it is for
> When Britain's sons go out to war,
> It is no time to question when
> The Motherland has called for men.
> That latent spirit of the past
> Rises within them like a blast,
> And calls them Home—a noble band
> To fight or fall for dear Homeland.

The notions of homeland, kinship and justice in Hough's poem were repeated in countless similar pledges in which the variable quality of the verse was more significant than the sentiments. The following verses form the first third of a poem about the transport vessel *Suevic* which was printed in the euphoniously named paper *The Heavic:*

> Homeward bound for England,
>   Round the Otway light,
> The big grey transport "29"
>   Stands out across the Bight.
>
> She was a Cape route liner—
>   One of the Queens of Trade—
> A shuttle in that mighty loom,
>   World-wide by Britain made.
>
> But now she's on the Empire's work,
>   Along the L.O.C.,
> That links the dear old motherland,
>   With her children oversea.
>
> Packed with men for the Western front
>   To fight in Humanity's cause—
> True knights of Peace, they take up arms
>   In a war to end all wars . . .

The importance of the imperial connection never totally disappeared from the troopship literature, but it was certainly more evident in the early years of the war. The soldier who sent two poems to *The Clan News* in March 1915 entitled 'The Empire's Call' and 'For Empire' left his readers under no illusion about their purpose. 'Britons afar who are Britons still/In the lands beyond the sea' were to 'List to the call that comes today' and then as 'Sons of the empire speed away'. *The Port Lincoln Lyre* was actually subtitled *The Great Imperial Journal* and although the pretentiousness was unconscious the choice of words was deliberate. It was certainly no less pretentious than the suggestion in the last verse of 'The Pride of Australia' in *The Ballarat Lyre* that the Empire's fate rested on Australian shoulders:

> So Boys of the Southern Cross, when the Empire's at a loss
> To find some sturdy lads her hardest work to do,
> Go give your lives to old England, Australia's pride renew.
> Australia asks, Australia gives—Australia needs but you.

From the middle of 1915 a self-conscious pride in Australia and the achievement of the Anzacs struck a new note in many troopship publications. Lieutenant-Colonel H.A. Goddard, who commanded the troops on the *Miltiades,* reminded his men that they had in their keeping 'the honour of Australia and the maintenance of the reputation gained by . . . gallant comrades on the battlegrounds of Gallipoli'. The editor of *The Ayrshire Furphy* informed his readers that:

> We have a task before us that not only of keeping the name of Australia untarnished but of adding fresh lustre to the name of the youngest nation in the English speaking world.
> Let us grave that name so deeply and clearly in the annals of the future that the highest compliment that can be paid to any man shall be—"He is a true Australian".

The officer commanding the reinforcements on the *Shropshire* voiced similar sentiments rather more epigrammatically in his message in *Dragropes*:

> You have travelled 13,000 miles.
> Have you seen a country as good as Australia?
> Then remember you are an Australian,
> Remember you are Field Artillery,
> Remember Gallipoli.
> Think of these three and you will do your job.

The memory of Gallipoli was frequently used to provide a gauge by which the reinforcements could measure their metamorphosis into soldiers. The promise was held out that they would 'stand in the reflected glory of those who had gone before'. They had to 'strive to the uttermost' to maintain the standard of the initial volunteers. The message was not lost on the recruits as this last verse of 'Skiters' indicates:

> But in spite of all our skitin'
>   There's a fact we don't forget:-
> We must prove ourselves at fightin'
>   We ain't dinkum Anzacs yet.

Osteralia, the souvenir magazine of the *Osterly* in 1917, included a photograph of all the original Anzacs on board who were returning to Europe after recovering in Australia. Their presence, the photograph, and the constant reminder of the Anzac achievement in this and other troopship publications exerted a none too subtle moral pressure on the reinforcements who were left in no doubt what the role model of an Australian soldier should be.

From 1916 onwards exhortations based on the debt to the Anzacs and the Australian commitment were generally more in evidence than those stressing the 'ties of blood' and

The Beltana Bugle

SOUVENIR OF THE VOYAGE

Somewhere at Sea.   July, 1917.

the imperial cause. In 1917, the editor of *Sea-Spray* said of the reinforcements, of which he was one, that 'we had nothing in common save our King, our kinship with the Anzacs and our Resolve'. By 1917 many troopship journals carried items which echoed the sentiments expressed in Lieutenant W.M. Fleming's poem 'Australians All' in *The Euripidean* which in four verses with chorus reflected on Australia's role without a single reference to Britain, motherland or empire. The chorus alone indicates the increasing national self-consciousness of the later war years:

> So come what may,
> By night or day,
>   And let what will befall.
> We all shall be,
> By land and sea,
>   Australians all.

For most Australian soldiers military service only really began in earnest when they sailed for overseas, and yet this first major experience has been almost totally neglected by historians. The weeks spent on a troopship on the Indian Ocean route to Egypt, or the Cape of Good Hope and Panama routes to England, gave the recently enlisted recruits an opportunity to adjust to service life. The length of the voyage reinforced the geographical isolation of Australia from the European conflict and enhanced the sense of adventure felt by many volunteers. The papers and magazines produced on the outward-bound troopships provide us with the opportunity to reconstruct that experience and explore the pleasures and frustrations of the voyage. Indeed, the inward-looking nature of these publications is an indication of the deep impression made by the experience.

The efficient running of a troopship depended upon the observance of strict routines. While most men adjusted to this totally regulated existence it was always resented and regularly featured in the ship's paper or magazine. Physical jerks, training lectures, full-dress meal and church parades and serpentine marches all came in for their share of ridicule as in the poem which complained of 'Boat drill, throat drill, physical exercise / Many hundreds of soldier boys, every sort and size / Stew drill, spew drill . . .' A typical daily routine was printed in the *Souvenir Aeneasthetic*:

6 a.m.	Reveille, turn out and stow hammocks.
6.30 a.m.	Ration.
7 a.m.	Sick parade by orderly Corporal.
8 a.m.	Breakfast.
8.30 a.m.	Fatigue.
9 a.m.	Guard fall in.
10 a.m.	Assembly General Parade, Inspection of Troop Deck.
10.30 a.m.	Orderly Room bedding for airing to be brought on deck.
11 a.m.	Troops allowed below.
Noon	Dinner draw and sit for dinner.
1 p.m.	Sweepers parade and sweep upper decks.
2 p.m.	Troops allowed below.
4.30 p.m.	Sick parade.

5 p.m.	Tea.
5.30 p.m.	Sweepers parade and sweep upper decks.
6 p.m.	Draw hammocks.
6.30 p.m.	Troops allowed below.
7.30 p.m.	Sweepers parade and sweep upper decks.
8 p.m.	First Post
8.30 p.m.	Last Post.
9 p.m.	Lights out, retire, stop smoking, no noise.
9.15 p.m.	Rounds.
11 p.m.	Lights out in saloon.

Notwithstanding all the routine busyness of life on board, many contributors to the papers and magazines commented on the monumental boredom which overtook them:

> There's nought to do all day but sleep and eat,
> And be latrine fatigue by way of change,
> If 'twas not for the fact there's little meat,
> Like lazy dogs we'd get the blinkin mange . . .

A piece in *The Ascanian* looked forward to submarine attack drills to break the monotony, suggesting that they were more diverting when half of the men were on deck, for there then ensued 'a push of war on the companion-ways and much profanity fills the air'.

Entertainment on a troopship had to be self-generated and it always reflected the enthusiasms and talents of those on board. Army chaplains were generally to the fore in endeavouring to organise amusements, but few ships had a proper program of diversions. The troops on the *Aeneas* in 1916 were exceptionally fortunate to have some good musicians on board and also some men with theatrical experience. Between them they arranged several musical events, staged excerpts from opera and Shakespeare, and produced a specially written burlesque, all on a stage rigged up on the forward hatch of the well-deck. Most troopships boasted a band of sorts, but apart from these musical interludes entertainment on many vessels was limited. Lectures by anyone willing to give them, bible classes, tournaments of card and board games, boxing competitions and deck games virtually exhausted the possibilities in most vessels. As a regular diversion, which promised some amusement with its gossip and scurrilous comment, the troopship paper was obviously important.

No troopship journal would have been complete without its complement of seasickness jokes and rhymes and complaints about the food. The first week of any voyage in the Bight or the Indian Ocean must have been hideously unpleasant as a thousand or more men suffered the rigours of seasickness. The sheer number of items which made reference to seasickness, even in serious pieces, is an indication of how many were affected. After a while, however, it was possible to laugh at the experience:

> A very sick soldier leaned over the side of the ship and the inevitable 'Job's Comforter' approaching said—"I say old man you must have a very weak stomach!"
>
> "Weak be blowed", came the disgusted retort, "I can 'eave as far as you can".

> They were parting with their dinners,
> They were wasting Irish stew,
> They were lying in confusion left and right,
> They were pouring all their troubles in to the ocean blue,
>   As the *Makarini* plugged it through the Bight . . .

The diet on a troopship was plain, limited in variety but generally satisfactory. Gunner H.S. Gullett who sailed on the *Osterly* noted that the men got three meat meals a day, two hot and one cold, with a generous bread and jam supper in the evening. He also noted, however, the occasion when the entire ship's company watched the sailor's burial given to the brawn. Driver Millard witnessed the same event:

> They buried it grimly at eventide,
>   Paddy the service chanting,
> 'Neath the watchful Skipper's rueful eye,
>   And the engines softly panting.
> A determined crowd surged round the brawn,
>   With gestures fierce to confound it;
> But it lay like a sinner, repentant at last,
>   With an aroma strange around it.
> So they lowered it quickly over the side,
>   'Mid an atmosphere rank and vicious,
> While Paddy expressed, in a phrase well dressed,
>   His deep concern for the fishes.

There is good reason to suspect that there was a strong element of ritual in the complaints about the food, such as one finds in any school, college or comparable institution. One delicacy, however, assumed mythic proportions and qualities in the troopship press—ship's pudding or duff. It was suggested that portions might be carried in the knapsack to be used in a variety of ways, to build bombproof dugouts, sole boots, fortify Belgium or fire at the enemy:

> Say lad, was that a cricket ball
>   You were bouncing on troop-deck E?
> "Nay, 'twas but some of the pudding, sir,
>   They gave us in No. 3".
>
> "Why is yon gunner upside-down?
>   Explain the thing to me."
> "He's eaten some E deck pudding sir,
>   It's the law of gravity" . . .

Troopship newspapers in particular had another important function beyond entertainment. They provided an outlet for the expression of those minor grievances and irritations which always occur in any closed community—in effect they were a useful safety-valve. In the columns of a ship's paper an individual could be warned about his irritating or anti-social conduct or even punished by this most public remonstrance. When an anonymous correspondent asked if the song 'I wonder who's kissing her now?' grated on other people's nerves, it is easy to imagine sharing a messdeck with someone who sang or whistled the same tune day after day. Through the paper the protest could be registered without personal affront. The unpleasantness of sharing confined quarters with men who did not wash frequently enough prompted regular editorials and correspondence urging better personal hygiene. In one case it was suggested that offenders should be forcibly ducked to persuade them to bathe more often. The announcement that a certain soldier was at last going to have a bath was clearly a public rebuke to an individual, while the complaint that the troops' washing facilities were inadequate, though the officers had bathrooms, was a warning to those in command.

The 'We Want To Know' and 'Who Said' sections, which featured in almost every ship's paper were usually filled with a mixture of gossip, disguised as wild rumour, and more direct criticism. An officer who obviously wore a nightshirt was alleged to wear a nightdress in the hope of getting first place in the lifeboat in the event of a submarine attack. Officers and men had their idiosyncratic behaviour commented on in a rough, good-humoured manner. Direct reprimand was also possible. Usually the victim's identity was thinly veiled behind a description of his appearance or behaviour, although criticism of named individuals was not unknown. 'Capt. MacDonald', declared a complainant in *The Innocents Abroad*, 'is unique among A.I.F. officers on the *Port Nicholson*. He tries to be regimental.' Officers who adopted airs, abused their privileges, or were martinets could expect exposure to public comment and probably ridicule. Whether this risk was consciously appreciated is impossible to gauge, but it is certain that any officer reading a ship's paper would have been struck by the number of 'officer-jokes', most of which hinged on the pretensions of the commissioned rank. The following examples occurred in papers four years apart:

> A sentry, on being approached by a junior Sub., presented arms. The Sub., in a pleased voice said, "My good man, I am not entitled to such compliments." Sentry:- "I know Sir, but anything will do to practice on." And it wasn't reported.

> A young officer at Broady was crossing the parade ground one morning when he encountered a newly arrived recruit who failed to give the necessary salute. "Halt, that man", snarled the officer, "why don't you salute? Do you call yourself a soldier?" "No Sir", came the reply, "not till I've been to France".

Drink and shore leave were always in short supply on a troopship and complaints about the beer ration or incarceration when in port feature in many papers and magazines. In the opinion of the military authorities, desertion, drunkenness and brawling were the probable outcome of shore leave. Consequently, leave was often refused, regularly restricted, and always kept to the absolute minimum. Not surprisingly this was bitterly resented. Men who had spent several weeks cooped up on a ship craved the opportunity to stroll through the streets and markets of Colombo or Cape Town, to see the strange sights and buy souvenirs or fruit for the next leg of the voyage. If the troops were kept confined while the vessel took on stores and coal, subsequent editions of the paper would contain barbed comments such as 'Colombo is a glorious place—so we have READ in books', or 'Died in Table Bay, Capetown, on the 20 inst. Leave R.I.P.' Only a minority of Australians behaved like drunken barbarians but their actions in the early days of the war coloured the attitudes of civil and military authorities alike. When leave was granted and passed off without incident one can detect the surprise and relief in the congratulatory message issued by the O.C. in the paper.

The troopship publications reveal a naïve, unselfconscious racialism among the Australians which was a product of their British heritage, geographical isolation and ignorance. The native people encountered at the various ports of call were all 'coons' or 'niggers' until they became 'Gyppos' or 'Frogs' depending upon the point of disembarkation. The experience of a few hours in port often gave rise to serious comment most of which reflected the writer's sense of white superiority. A correspondent to the *Osterly Keystone* asserted that it was impossible 'to be in Colombo for five minutes without realising how completely the white man dominates this civilisation', and he went on to suggest that the soldiers had seen a practical example of the 'White Man's Burden'. After leave at Cape Town a one-line question in *The Ascanian* asked, 'Is there a man aboard who will argue against a White Australia Policy now?' A piece in the *Port Lincoln Lyre* expressed the view that there was a hierarchy of civilisation which placed the Hottentot and Pygmy peoples just above the ape and gorilla. Occasionally flattering observations on the places visited, and a few appreciative verses on the charms of dusky maidens do not alter the impression that most Australian soldiers viewed all but Anglo-Saxons with amused contempt.

The troopship publications shed a little light on the picture the men of the A.I.F. had of themselves. The souvenir editions in particular were full of tributes to the manly virtues and rugged independence of the citizen soldier. The Australian soldier was portrayed as a man who adjusted badly to the petty discipline required by army life but who came into his own when the real work of fighting began, for it was then that his outstanding characteristics of strength, initiative and endurance were released. It was certainly a self-flattering portrayal, but in helping to reinforce the role-model of the Anzacs as the epitome of the Australian at war, the troopship journals were an important instrument in the conditioning process which turned citizens into soldiers. It was no doubt comforting for the new recruit to learn that he was part of 'a keen eyed, clear brained army of jesting athletes', and that he resented the frustrations of army life because 'the Australian is a hopeless soldier on humdrum routine.' This particular analyst of the Australian military character, writing in *Osteralia* in 1917, went on to suggest that the army leaders could not have it all ways:

> They cannot have the alert aggressive mind of the Australian, which insists upon thinking for itself, and an extraordinary capacity for swift conclusive execution and at the same time have that docile dog-like submission to every petty routine order which is so absolute in the new armies of England. If the new Australian soldier thinks the work in hand of any consequence then he will do it as well as any soldier in the world. If he thinks it of no consequence then he will do it casually despite the worst the dread Army Act can threaten.

The anarchic potential of this flattering self-image was not lost on the writer of a lengthy parable which appeared in *The Log of the Lunatic Ship*. He suggested that because the Australians had always 'done just whatever they pleased they found it hard to do what they were told'. As a result they 'often disobeyed and misbehaved', but this was because they were like children. The regular exhortations to preserve Australia's good name and the reminders of the bad behaviour of earlier drafts indicate that there was a price to be paid for independence of mind. On the same page as the parable mentioned above, a representative of the Y.M.C.A. claimed that the Australian name was in danger of becoming 'a bye-word of disgust and shame'; so much so, that Britain might regret accepting Australian troops 'for men who know nothing of disciplining themselves can never make good soldiers'. Although fears about the potential indiscipline of Australian soldiers feature in the troopship literature, it seems likely that during the voyage most men grudgingly came to accept the constraints of army life.

Troopship papers and magazines always contained a substantial leavening of serious items amongst the gossip, notices and humorous contributions. As might be expected, home and the loved ones left behind were constant preoccupations, though they were expressed in general rather than in specific terms. Home was often represented by an idealisation of the Australian countryside, even though the majority of men in the A.I.F. were recruited from the cities. Sunset and dawning over the bush, the call of the kookaburra, the verandahed homestead, and above all the blossom of the wattle tree were used to summon up memories of home. This verse from a piece in *The Ayrshire Furphy* was most unusual in placing home firmly in the city:

> But for all our fun and laughter we would give a lot to hear
> Just the old familiar rumble of a tram.
> Or the music from the Palais, just beyond St. Kilda Pier
> And we'd freeze Hell for a pot of homemade jam.

For other contributors, home was wherever the loved ones were and many poems connected home with a forlorn mother, a deserted wife or girlfriend, and a fatherless child. Most of these pieces were honestly and openly sentimental in tone and those men who could construct a verse which tugged at the heartstrings probably gave voice to a feeling that was widespread. Sentimentality was a feature of trench and troopship literature throughout the war and its extraordinary persistence suggests that the Anzac and the Digger were altogether more complex beings than the conventional stereotypes would suggest.

All the light-hearted nonsense in the troopship journals could not disguise the fact that the men on board were about to risk their lives. Editorials might tell them that if they fell in battle they would have given their lives 'fighting for the right, for freedom' and that 'none of us can hope for a better death', but such pious notions probably meant little to the ordinary soldier. There were relatively few items in the outward-bound troopship literature which dealt with the horror of war, although there were a surprising number which accepted the inevitability of death on the battlefield. Perhaps these were printed more for the friends and relations in Australia than the men on the troopship, but there was certainly no attempt to obscure the dreadful reality of war. Self-deception would have been impossible after Gallipoli.

By the time the volunteers disembarked in Egypt, France or England they had had an opportunity to adjust to the peculiarities of army life, acquire a sense of identity as Australian soldiers and come to terms with the deadly task before them. The troopship publications which survive are a valuable record of that first stage in the overseas service of the A.I.F.

Shipboard sports and entertainments were devised to deal with the boredom and frustration of weeks at sea in crowded conditions. *The Barambah Souvenir*, June–July 1918. (*Australian War Memorial Printed Records*)

CHAPTER TWO
'A LIFE ON THE OCEAN WAVES'

A RECORD AND A SOUVENIR

The best excuse we can tender for inflicting this, the initial number of the *Kanowna Lament*, upon 1,000 decent law-abiding swaddies is that we feel we would be failing in our duty if we made no attempt to record as unfaithfully as possible some of the doings of the men on aboard. The smallest charge for same would be, we admit, quite out of the question, but the *Lament* will be free to all at 3d. a copy, and dear at that, perhaps. Although up to last night we hadn't sold a single number we are not downhearted...

To all ranks from acting privates to spare colonels, we make a business proposition and it's this:

Contributions will be received and paid for according to merit...

Contributors are requested not to write on three sides of the manuscript, and in no case will poems be received on sanitary paper. Writers are also requested, as a matter of good taste, to refrain from references, veiled or otherwise, to a full pay; and speculations dealing with the speed of the vessel; the fit she threw in the Bight; and the dazzling celerity with which the crew repaired to the boats on Thursday, will be censored with a dull thud and the greatest severity.

Of course, it is thoroughly understood that none of us Grammar School boys will write verse about the cabbage served recently, or the patient vigil in the Canteen queue. Paragraphs of a personal nature will be welcomed, how personal does not matter a Continental... In a few months, when this ship nears our destination, we HOPE to have better printing facilities available... Arrived at our base, we purpose enlarging the *Lament*. Up-to-date camp news, war items, summaries of important happenings in Australia and Great Britain—sporting, general and political—will drift regularly into our columns.

The Kanowna Lament, July 1915

This booklet is intended as a Souvenir of the eventful and, on the whole, happy time we have spent together ... we are confident it will appeal, not only to the members of the Quota, but also to their relatives and friends at home. It is desired that, to those of us who return to Australia, it shall take its place as a real memento; and, in the meantime, that it shall serve to interest and amuse the loved ones we have left behind.

Dragropes: A Souvenir, 1916

Primarily our intention was to produce something that would give the folks at home an idea of what life upon a transport means. It is a life that some 350,000 of our countrymen have already known, yet it has not been written about like the life in the trenches or behind the lines, so comparatively few people realise what a large part it must play in the memories of all Australians who have been on service abroad. By reproducing our daily routine, with its little jokes and small duties, we have endeavoured to convey the atmosphere of transport life to those at home.

Secondly, our intention was to produce a little volume that all on board would value as a memento of this trip. It would be foolish to pretend that our voyage has been uniformly happy. We have had more than our fair share of sickness, disappoinment, and acute physical discomfort. We have seen good comrades buried in lonely seas. We have suffered severely at times from the boredom which is said to be nine-tenths of war. Still, there is a camaraderie that arises between men thrown together in such circumstances as ours, and it is worth trying to preserve.

The Barambah Souvenir, January 1919

WHY WE FIGHT—FOR BRITAIN AND EMPIRE

The Call
The call of Britain stirred his blood
And set his heart afire
It swept across him like a flood
Of unfulfilled desire.

Incomprehensible it seemed
That 'he' should dream of war
But still persistently war screamed
Its summons from afar.

Like silver bells machine guns rang
Unceasing in his ear
In dreams the rifle bullets rang
Upon their wild career.

The strictures of a life time fell
Ambitions ceased to be
His inmost being craved to swell
The ranks of Liberty.

Far on the bosom of the deep
A troopship ploughs her way
Between the decks, where soldiers sleep
Our gallant hero lay.

O God of Wars! if God there be
With power such wars to quell
Guide thou his feet to help to free
The World from such a hell.
The Squeak of the Bally Rats, October 1915

Not many hours will elapse before we reach the Old Land. To some it is no new experience, but to many it marks the most important event since their birth . . . The imaginary line which separates the Northern Hemisphere from the Southern, so divides the Old World from the New . . . In the Old World lies the seat of a War so dreadful in its awful fury, as to make previous wars pale into insignificance. And we are rapidly nearing the seat of our great empire from whence we anticipate, with mingled feelings, that we will cross a narrow strip of sea and join our comrades in the firing line. The glory of war is not spoken of in these times, but never before has the sweetness of true Liberty and Freedom been so emphasised. To the many on board who claim Australia not only as their home, but as their native land, the free unrestrained nature of life in the island Continent has made it difficult for them to fully conceive how any one man, no matter how much power he has wielded, could be so obsessed with ambition as to contemplate and finally plan a war that meant the loss of millions of lives . . . each passing day will add to our appreciation of the bloody waste of lives, and the floods of women's tears, caused by the Kaiser's satanic ambition.
Seang-Bee Sea Breezes: Souvenir, September 1916

The Empire's Call
List to the call that comes today
Sons of the Empire speed away
There is great danger in delay
So do not pause to wonder.
March bravely on to meet the foe
And know ye that your every blow
Will help to lay the tyrant low
And crush the despot under.

Yours is a noble sacrifice
To leave your home, your paradise,
But when such thoughts within you rise
It is but well to wonder
If that dread tyrant held full sway
Your homes would be but mouldering clay
The standing order of the day –
The despots crushed us under.

March on, march on then to the fight
Your cause is just your cause is right
As victory doth gleam in sight
We shall have cause to wonder,
If, turning from the battle long
Both young and old both faint and strong
This be not your triumphant song –
We've crushed the despot under.
The Clan News, March 1915

It is conceivably possible, as Bernhardi and others argue, that the world would be better Prussianised. But we should reasonably suppose that clear-headed men of other communities would be aware of such advantages, more particularly those communities in close contact with Germany.

But the methods of the Prussian overlords have resulted in a complete and bitter hostility on every side. France, Belgium, and Servia prefer destruction. Great Britain and Russia have very little of a material character to gain from the war and very much to lose, and yet these great powers have committed themselves utterly. The biological necessity of war is a debatable question—but undoubtedly it is by war to a considerable extent that communities have secured their existence. But the community is the only means by which ideals may be preserved and developed. Therefore if the community be threatened the individual must fight. Germany has deliberately and methodically assailed all those traditions and ideals which the various Allied communities have evolved: and it now devolved upon every member of those communities to defend to his utmost the traditions of his race.

Port Lincoln Lyre: The Great Imperial Journal, November 1916

We are all part of a great army called together by the common feeling of Right and Justice, for the one purpose of thwarting the deep laid schemes of the Central Powers to foist on the world their system of 'Kultur'. What this system means has been fully exposed by the devilish devices and the methods they have adopted, their disregard for treaties, their flouting of honor, and the murder of helpless women and children. To combat these Powers practically the whole civilised world is now aroused but so cunningly and carefully have the enemy's plans been prepared, that every effort must be made to bring them to their knees.

Shrapnel, May 1917

WHY WE FIGHT—FOR ANZAC AND AUSTRALIA

We are going to the sports
That commenced in Germany
And we've played at guards and sentries
Since the Kaiser called for entries
And we've tramped round camp [*remainder illegible*].
We're the blokes you've picked Austrayler
And, gor-blimey, we won't fail yer.

Now we don't know where we'll race
But we're in the British team
And we've took the job on gladly
Think we'll end up not so badly
And will hold our little end up in old Kitchener's great scheme.
We're the coves you've picked Austrayler
And, strike me, we won't fail yer.

Though we don't know our event
Nor yet who's referee
Still we'll be fair dinkum triers
So just watch the blanky wires
And you'll find there's something doing when we get across the sea.
We're the coots you've picked Austrayler
And, strewth, we will not fail yer.

It's a task that needs some nerve
But there'll be this boshter prize
That every peer and peasant
May, for all time from the present
Live and work in peace and freedom underneath God's own blue skies.
We're the men you've picked Austrayler
And God help us we won't fail yer.

The Expeditionary, November 1914

We are about to do battle, not as crude untrained soldiers, but as comrades of those men who have written for themselves an immemorial name in history as sons of Australia who has already given thousands of her bravest sons in the fulfillment of her duty to the Motherland. We have a reputation to live up to, and it behoves each and every one of us to strive to the uttermost to maintain that standard.

The Makarini Cyclone, September 1915

The Pride of Australia
O'er frowning Gaba Tepe the battle cloud is hung,
Across the cliffs and valleys our Khaki line strung
Clinging with bulldog fierceness the splintering shells among
Climbing death's own ladder steadily rung by rung.

Mid the battery's bursting haze—Mid the rifles flashing hate
See the reinforcements coming before it is too late
New Zealanders and cornstalks, Bananalanders too
Across those shell torn valleys their noblest breed they strew.

With hurricane roar and rush mid the bayonets flashing sheen
With clang of steel on steel—Australia's sons are keen
They cleave through the stricken Turk—Australia knows her work
Though right and left in front and rear the hidden snipers lurk.

At home, Australia's mothers are weeping for their lost
Sweethearts, wives and children dear must help in wars grim cost.
Old England's pride is high—Australia's higher still
And we've sworn by him who rules the world, to help her up the hill.

So Boys of the Southern Cross, when the Empire's at a loss
To find some sturdy lads her hardest work to do,
Go! Give your lives to old England, Australia's pride renew
Australia asks—Australia gives—Australia needs but you.

The Ballarat Lyre, August 1915

Now a word about the future; you and every one have had placed in your keeping the honour of Australia and the maintenance of the reputation gained by your gallant comrades on the battlegrounds of Gallipoli. See to it you do nothing that will do other than add credit to what they have accomplished. To you also has been given the trust and confidence of your womenfolk and your children. They are rightly very proud of you and it is always up to you to remember this and do nothing you would not have them know about.
Lt. Col. H.A. Goddard
The Miltiades Lyre, 1916

Whatever the world destiny of many may be, we in Australia, and those of us who are members of the Australian Imperial Force, are vividly conscious of destiny and duty. That destiny and duty alike for us and all English speaking races, calls upon us to uphold the small nations and to maintain the free and law-abiding rules and ideals of Western Europe, and we feel sure that we, the representatives of Australia, will endeavour to perform our duty as men and cast racial feeling aside, and fight for the cause for which the British Bull-dog took up arms.
Lt. W. W. Stutchbury
Seang-Bee Sea Breezes: Souvenir, September 1916

The Faithful Few
A whisper floated o'er windswept seas,
From the land where our fathers had had their homes.
(No more than a sigh on the restless breeze.)
Searching the shores where the Briton roams
It came to the ears of the Faithful Few.
Who ever alert, had been listening long
"There is need of us", So the swift word flew
And they hastened away with a joyous song.

And we, who had cheered as they passed us by
Went back to our tasks with our hearts at ease
Deaf to the call, vaguely wondering why
They so eagerly sped o'er the tumbling seas.
Nor dreamt of the hell they were battling through
Till we heard the news with a wild dismay
Of the toll of death 'mongst the Faithful Few.

We had dozed at ease through the first alarm
Nor heeded the sigh of the Motherland
But now our brothers had come to harm
And the small still spark into flame was fanned.
Ploughshares and pen were not left to rust
Or be wielded still by our weaker kin
As our eyes grow dim with the fighting lust
And our hearing strains for the battle-din.

We are following swift on the straight-run track, -
That was blazed so clear by the Faithful Few.
To the sound of the shrapnel and rifle-crack, -
For we started late, and there's work to do.
We'll, (some of us) drink in the after years,
To the name of many who have gone before
And thank our stars that we quelled our fears
And played OUR part in the game of War.   F.E.A.
The Ayrshire Furphy, August 1916

The Skiters
We're goin to sock the blighters
If we get 'arf a show,
Of course we're bloomin skiters-
We can do our bit of blow.

But we know our blanky brothers,
Who have gone along before,
Fought as well as most the others,
Though they ain't <u>quite</u> won the war.

But they've kept their little oar in,
Which is what <u>we</u> 'opes to do
And our spirits is a-soaring
As we learns to parley-voo.

Fom our little books we're learning
Bits o' German from 'em too,
And—long lanes <u>must</u> 'ave a turning-
Bill der Kais'—we're after you.

But in spite of all our skitin',
There's a fact we don't forget:-
We must <u>prove</u> ourselves at fightin',
<u>We</u> ain't dinkum Anzacs yet.   *Sgt. C. S. Gilmour*
The Osteralia, February–April 1917

Australians All
Oh! Some were bred beyond the seas,
And some are native born,

But all have had their days of ease
Where blows Australia's balmy breeze
And glows her golden morn.

(Chorus)
So come what may,
By night or day,
And let what will befall,
We all shall be,
On land and sea,
Australians all. . . .   *Lt. W. M. Fleming, A.S.C.*
The Euripidean, 1917

THE FAREWELL

The send off we received at Port Melbourne on 27th May, 1916 will stand out in bold relief in our memories as long as we live. Not a man but had dreaded that inevitable ordeal. We warned our women folk, many of us besought them, not to come to the ship's side and yet they came. From a purely spectacular point of view the scene was that of an animated gala. Through the vista of gaily waving flags and ten thousand multi-coloured, quivering streamers, frail short-lived links soon to break,—inevitably, perhaps, for some of us,—the uninitiated stranger could never have perceived what pent-up emotions the brave demonstration was so effectively obscuring. It was only when our ship commenced slowly to glide from the pier, when most of us saw the receding multitude through very misty eyes, that these emotions gave way. But even then there was no hysteria, and as the vision became more blurred and distant, we thanked God that our women were of such a calibre.
The Ascanian, 1916

With all pride in our enterprise, there were sad hearts enough as we passed on that February morning of brilliant sunshine through the streets of old Sydney, on the way from Moore Park to the quay. No scene associated with the war is more tragic and significant than that; neither could there be anything more typical of our young Australia. The slow throbbing drums ahead, and then the long column in which the soldiers move, not in regular fours, but surrounded by groups of their wives and mothers and sweethearts . . .
The Osteralia, 1917

Farewell
Dear little love, don't fret.
'Tis best that I should go
At Empire's call
To stand or fall.
Whate'er betide, you'll know,
Dear heart, I shan't forget.
So, dear little love, don't fret.

Dear little eyes, don't weep.
It fills my soul with pain
To see you cry
For look, the sky!
A rainbow in the rain!-
And death is only sleep.
So, dear little eyes, don't weep.
J. H. Robertson & R. S. Robinson
The Limber Log, 1917

A LIFE ON THE OCEAN WAVES

Aboard the Trooper
There's lots of fun on a troopship
If you only know where to look,
And the humorous mind can surely find
Sufficient to fill a book.
From the officers' mess to the galley
There's humour on every side,
From the ship's chief cook to the biggest crook
Whoever a "full hand" cried.

Refrain:
Boat drill, throat drill, physical exercise.
Many hundreds of khaki boys, every sort and size,
Stew drill, spew drill, soon the world will find
They'll fight like hell 'mid shot and shell
For the ones they left behind.

When the hammocks are slung at bedtime
And the bugler has blown 'lights out'
When the boys aren't 'doing' their hard earned cash
In the pleasures of 'house about',
Your thinking of home and mother
And you'll certainly smile some more
As you see them all slung to the ceiling
Like hams in a grocer's store.

The Limber Log

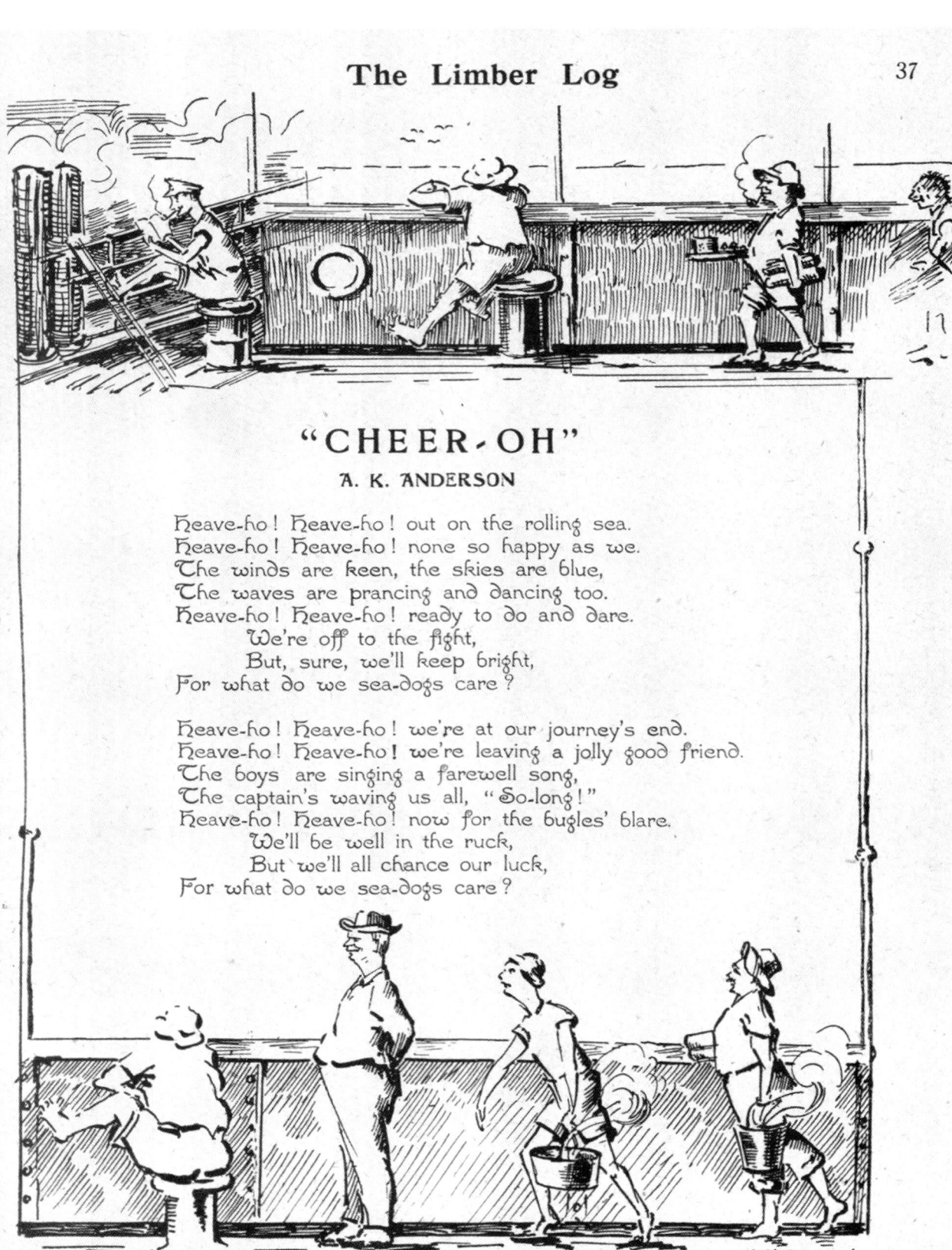

"CHEER-OH"

A. K. ANDERSON

Heave-ho! Heave-ho! out on the rolling sea.
Heave-ho! Heave-ho! none so happy as we.
The winds are keen, the skies are blue,
The waves are prancing and dancing too.
Heave-ho! Heave-ho! ready to do and dare.
    We're off to the fight,
      But, sure, we'll keep bright,
For what do we sea-dogs care?

Heave-ho! Heave-ho! we're at our journey's end.
Heave-ho! Heave-ho! we're leaving a jolly good friend.
The boys are singing a farewell song,
The captain's waving us all, "So-long!"
Heave-ho! Heave-ho! now for the bugles' blare.
    We'll be well in the ruck,
      But we'll all chance our luck,
For what do we sea-dogs care?

The Limber Log was published in Egypt as a souvenir for the reinforcements on board the *Port Sydney* in 1917. (*Australian War Memorial Printed Records*)

And so the ship ploughs onward
And never a growl you hear –
Tho' sometimes when she starts to roll
We're feeling mighty queer.
What care we if the weather's bad,
With storm clouds swiftly scudding,
If the sea is rough and the meat is tough
Why, we still have the Anzac pudding.
The Log of the Lunatic Ship, 1916-1917

There are many ways of making money on a trooper. For instance, one chap did so well out of washing a few handkerchiefs, etc., for his mates, that he subsequently took in a partner, and the business increased so rapidly that they named it the "Chinese laundry". Another increased his capital by running with orders to the canteen at 1d. per time. In a few weeks he was able to put some solid silver into his belt. Gathering bottles from near and at the canteen struck the eye of one young individual as a money-making scheme, and he did so well that he soon met with strong opposition in the shape of about a dozen collectors. They all made money, and several enterprising youths went so far as retailing cases of lemonade at canteen prices and retaining the bottles, thus showing a profit of 5s. per case.

Good business was also done by several privates who purchased lemons and kept them until the tropics were reached, and the drinks made found ready sale at 3d. per small glass. An amateur barber did a roaring trade for about a week with his clippers; but his razor, according to himself, was an issue one, and he could not get a keen edge on it. This was his answer to several he had 'gashed' about the face and neck. Others were able to produce rolls of notes, but how they got them is a matter for conjecture!
Souvenir Aeneasthetic, November 1916

Strike!, Strike! Strike!
The ordinary routine of this ship received a sensational jar just at 1 pip emma on Friday the 30th day of October 1914. This scribe leisurely climbed the stairs after the midday repast, day-dreaming of bygone meals . . . The thoughts of cheese and salad, black coffee, a cigar and liqueurs were quickly put to flight by the sight of dozens of mugs being brandished in the air near the WET CANTEEN. Hurried enquiries elicited the fact that a fierce Beer strike was in progress. The old order had changed and the allowance of 2 p-i-n-t-s per day had been cut in half. "Only 1 pint each day, half now and half tonight" was Jock's reply to the request "Fill 'em up".

A hurried consultation was held and in exactly 35 seconds a general strike was declared. Scouts were posted at every approach and nailed each straggler carrying a vessel capable of holding Beer . . .

The half hour passed slowly but the men stuck to their guns, licked their parched lips and refused to be coaxed by the barman's tempting gestures. The barrel hung its head in sorrow and the slow but persistent drip from the beer tap sounded like lost souls tapping at the gates of paradise, tapping always, but tapping but in vain.

At the appointed time the canteen's doors were closed, the hinges creaking in a ghostly and deserted manner. On Saturday the 31st, a deputation of five interviewed the Major and were received in a courteous and kindly manner. The Major explained that from now on only 1 pint per man was to be allowed. He wished it understood that he would not have any more beer strikes. If the men wanted to complain they should do it in the proper manner. He further stated that he was always ready and willing to listen to any genuine complaints.
The Kan-Karoo Kronickle, November 1914

Life on a Troopship
A soldier's life on a troopship! I reckoned it something to shun.
To me it held terrors more dreadful far than meeting the Turk or Hun.
But Gee! 'Twould be just a picnic, and better than life on our farms
If only they'd cut out the physical jerks and blasted torpedo alarms.
Of course it has its drawbacks too, for your life's one eternal squash,
And the good old fights for early doors are nothing to getting a wash.

They feed us like fighting cocks and there's plenty of fun and sport,
But there's one big fly in the ointment, they close the pubs at each port.
They sell us their canteen ale, but I'd like to tell you here
That I'd give the whole of one week's pay for a pint of good Swan Beer.

Sea Spray, September 1917

The Direct Route
Leaning over the starboard bulwarks of an ocean-bound troopship in the grey morning light of a tempestuous day, might have seen a sergeant's portly figure, in such an attitude as to suggest to the casual passer-by the meditations of a nature enthusiast. A closer observer, noting the sea-green complexion and the general aspect of hopelessness, would have recognised the old-time comedy of the "Return of the Swallows". Suddenly the spruce figure of a mess orderly appeared, and inquired of the sea-sick sergeant: "Will you take your breakfast on deck this morning, sir?" "No", came the prompt rejoinder, "throw it overboard—save time—and trouble".

Berrima Souvenir, January 1917

When the Makarini *Plugged it Through the Bight*

The first day out, for breakfast
We were served with ham and eggs,
And they all rolled up to table with delight,
But they weren't delighted later when they couldn't find their legs,
As the *Makarini* plugged it through the Bight.

Though they didn't feel like dancing,
Yet a few commenced to sing,
To cover up their sad and sorry plight,
And many of them cursed her as a "love child of a thing"
As the *Makarini* plugged it through the Bight.

They were parting with their dinners,
They were wasting Irish Stew,
They were lying in confusion left and right,
They were pouring all their troubles into the ocean blue,
As the *Makarini* plugged it through the Bight.

Some were wishing for Australia,
Some were hoping she would sink,
Some were praying for torpedoes through the night,
Some were howling out for tramcars, some were crying for strong drink,
As the *Makarini* plugged it through the Bight.

The Makarini Cyclone, September 1915

Ship's Pudding
Who has tasted Ship's Pudding? As Begg's whisky advertisement has it, we all did. I have, so I know what I'm talking about. There is nothing in the world like ship's pudding. It is manufactured in the ship laboratories out of the toughest ingredients known to science. It has the toughness and resiliency of india-rubber. Yet it is not rubber. It is heavier than any known metal, including lead. But it is not lead. It is malleable as gold. Still it is not gold. It is not an imitation or substitute for anything. It is just ship's pudding. Served to the troops twice a week it will defy the most perfect set of teeth a man ever possessed. It is rather more palatable than a piece of motor tyre. And if your hearing is good enough you can hear it splash when it hits your stomach. It is recommended by the manufacturers as an excellent method of providing the organs with physical jerks. Its uses are untold. Motors shod with ship's pudding will cover the highest mileage on the roughest and hardest roads. Boots soled with it will outlast three military issues. Men fed on it will in time find that their Little Mary becomes petrified, thus making them immune from shot, shells, bombs, mines, motors, and magazines. Every soldier should carry a piece in his knapsack to aid in the building of shell-proof forts and bomb-proof dugouts. It can also be used for writing treaties on after the war, as it cannot be torn up like the historic "scrap of paper". France and Belgium can be restored and made impregnable against future enemy attacks by using ship's pudding, and the Russian retreat could be definitely checked if the rearguard be enveloped by a wall of this invaluable substance. Emplacement for guns can be made in the wide intervals between the raisins. Amongst all the discoveries that the war has given birth to, the uses that ship's pudding can be put to stand out alone.
        H.J.B. 17th Battn.
        The Euripidean, 1917

It is the small things that count and keep us fit. If every man here were to observe the rule against spitting on deck for instance, we would only be obeying a rule laid down by the doctors to save themselves work. The baths provided are not for the pleasure of a few, but as a necessity for all. Some men we regret to say look upon a bath in the same light as a visit to the dentist, only to be taken in extreme cases.
       The Benalla Sun, 28 November 1916

Transport Life
It's lying loafing in the sun,
And wondering sometimes why you came,
And wishing that the day was done,
And that the beastly war was won,
And knowing others feel the same.

It's drilling for an hour or two,
And getting tired and feeling slack,
And eating greasy spuds and stew,
Or sitting still the mealtime through,
Till your old taste for food comes back.

It's hearing of strange towns and sights,
And smoking till your throat is sore,
And playing cards and watching fights,
And thinking through the long, long nights,
Thoughts that you never thought before.

It's meeting with all sorts of men,
And finding out what mateship means,
And feeling you'll have knowledge when
You find yourself back home again;
That isn't learnt on bowling-greens.

It's dreaming, dreaming night and day
Of things ahead and things behind,
Yet knowing those at home will say
That you are bound the only way;
And they can rest with easy mind. *V. P.*
      The Barambah Souvenir, January 1919

FOREIGN PARTS

Colombo
Just a little hour or two
For to say "Good-day" to you,
Estimate your choicest brew.
Then, alas, to say "Adieu!"

Just a little time to see
Something of the Cingalee,
And, by way of change, to be
Out behind a human "gee".

Time to buy a souvenir –
Elephant, or token queer –
Cable, "We have landed here:
Well, and feeling splendid dear".

Short as it was, bright and gay;
That was our Colombo stay,
Pray to get a longer stay,
Trav'lling in the "civvy" way.

It was a steaming hot day when we pulled in at Colombo. Since as the heat had steadily increased, and our clothing had as steadily decreased, we did not take too kindly to our hot uniforms again. What a picture Colombo was at first sight! There in a maze of green palms, with occasional patches of the vivid colouring of native flowers, nestled the quaint red-roofed houses of Colombo. Away to the right the Bluff frowned its protection, while scattered everywhere over the face of a beautifully calm sea were the graceful fishing 'calamarans' of the natives. Into a few hours leave were crowded all the delights of Colombo—and they were many. Here one saw a group frantically arguing with the natives about money matters, there another group cheerfully attacking a huge bunch of bananas, while passing along in rickshaws were those whose grins—real Australian—rivalled those of their not altogether understanding native steeds. Some rushed around in cars sight-seeing, admiring the beautiful gardens, surveying Buddha in all his glory in the temple, or purchasing numerous novelties. We left Colombo with many impressions, but chiefly of natives who always yelled, of thirst that could never be quenched, and of a coinage that could never be understood. A typically tropical rain came on as the barges steamed slowly back to the boat; but we were all happy, and showed it by lustily singing "Smile, Boys, Smile". What odds if, when getting back on board, someone discovered that he had paid thirty shillings for an article for whose fellow another had paid two shillings! The fun was worth it.

The Limber Log, 1917

The C.O. of Troops to his Men
At the commencement of the last portion of our voyage, I take the opportunity of expressing my feelings of pride and privilege in my command of men who go to serve their King and Empire on Active Service—men who have shown their keen sense of discipline in recreation as well as on duty, as evidenced by the exemplary conduct of all ranks while in Cape Town. Our thanks are due to the residents of that city for the lavish entertainment of the troops, when permission was granted for a route march only. The excellent conduct of all concerned on that occasion was duly noted by the Authorities, and resulted in general leave being granted the next day, which was fully appreciated and not abused. I placed trust in you and your honor, and my confidence was not misplaced. All ranks returned to ship as ordered, without any absences. *G. H. Holland, V.D., Col., O.C. Troops. Cape Town.*

Fears of complete quarantine, and high hopes of leave, kept the troops in alternating hot and cold perspiration at Cape Town till a march to Green Point Recreation Ground was ordered. From then on an even temperature prevailed. A certain amount of anxiety was felt on Friday till leave from 11.30 a.m. till 11 p.m. was granted, but the splendid conduct of the men right through Thursday justified plenty of confidence that Friday would be all right. The arrangements for Thursday were the next best thing to leave, and most enjoyed themselves as much as if the town were theirs. The wise and temperate address of the O.C. not only warned the troops, but set a high standard of conduct and honour before them, and the men rose to it. The A. 60 easily broke the record for Cape Town . . . and we left port without a man missing.

The Aeneasthetic, 2 November 1916

How It Happens
Hullo, Digger! Hullo, Winger!
Cheero! Fill 'em up! Chin chin!
'Ave another! Let 'er bring a
Glass 'er Vermouth and some gin!

Mine's similar! Here's a lookin!
At yer Cobber. Happy days!

DURBAN
Snaps of Nigs.

A Durban "Monopolist."
The Two with Their Hair
Up are His Wives.

"Pals." Native Women in Civies.

"Jim Fish," Ricksha Boy.

Coaling and victualling stops in exotic locations gave most men their first experience of foreigners. 'Snaps of Nigs' at Durban, *Yandoo*, Troopship issue, 1916. (*Australian War Memorial Printed Records*)

Fill 'em up Miss. Don't go rookin'
Heads like us. No, chum, I pays.

'Ere now Aussie, no reneggin',
Dinkum Jack, cut out that tripe,
Or else yer tub'll go a beggin'
An' I'll do me bleedin' stripe!

Keep yer hair on, kid, and drown it!
S'luck! And one ter keep that down.
We'll find a new M.P. and down it,
And with the bits clean up the town.
The Barambah Souvenir, January 1919

A magnificent reception awaits the R.M.S. "Osterly" with Australian 'warriors' on board. All the pubs will be closed during the stay of the vessel, and the local military authorities are providing 4000 military police to take the troops in hand. By special edict it has been decided to allow proprietors of Chewing Gum Factories and Ginger Beer Dispensaries to remain open until 6 p.m. By special indulgence also, the troops will be permitted to smoke two cigarettes per diem whilst ashore and to purchase four post cards.
Osteralia, February–April 1917

A shine tart at the Cape I met,
I lined on when I seen her winkin',
She was no timid violet.

I interjuced meself, you bet,
We had some wine, our glasses clinkin'-
A shine tart at the Cape I met.

You take my tip, she was a pet.-
In less than no time arms were linkin'-
She was no timid violet.

Her bonser eyes, I see 'em yet,
Smilin' there as we sat drinkin'-
A shine tart at the Cape I met.

We had to part, to my regret –
I kissed her and there was no shrinkin'-
She was no timid violet.

Dear little kid—remembered yet,
Every time a beer I'm sinkin'.
A shine tart at the Cape I met,
She was no timid violet. *Pte. Rowley Clark, 19/7*
The Rising Sun, August 1916

Scene at St. Vincent
The natives cluster around our vessel, A70, displaying their worthless wares and their nudity. We, like foolish children, buy their baubles. Primitive men they are, with modern vices I believe; beautifully carved—in fact their limbs (not their faces) would be the envy of the sculptor's model. Their complexion is a dark bronze. They beg for coins, and we gladly toss them our superfluous pennies, in order to see their graceful dives, their quick eye work and wonderful swimming.

Their knowledge reveals enough of good old English to cadge and swear . . .

Potatoes! Our lads are using them as missiles, and making targets of the dark hides of the natives. One coon loses his temper, swears vociferously in splendid and ancient Anglo-Saxon, picks up a bottle and threatens to annihilate the Troopship. The lads continue to pelt and jeer —the result is that the poor coon collects the weapons of offence, consigns them to the bottom of his boat, and departs to hand over the potatoes, no doubt, to his one or many wives.
The Heavic, July–August 1917

In Tropical Seas
Before us lay a hybrid town—half native, half European—appearing clean and white 'neath its protecting hills; and slightly reminiscent of Albany. Of course, we all wanted to go ashore. But alas—nothing doing. We were faced with the prospect of an indefinite stay, with only the bum-boats of the native vendors of fruit to relieve the monotony. The prices they asked for their goods would have made a Melbourne dago blush. Its effect on the atmosphere around the ship was similar. Profanity was rife, but cash was scarce. As a matter of course barter was resorted to; and such exchanges as a loaf of bread for a cocoanut, or a half-gnawed bone for a mango were effected—until someone rang in a sandwich of bread and soft soap. One bite—and then . . . well even an Australian can be shown points in profanity!

This incident closed the usual dealings in foodstuffs. Unbeatable, as usual, the Australian soldier promptly brought forth his kit bag, prepared to sacrifice the lot at bargain prices, and trusting to his luck and initiative to replace the deficiencies before the next kit inspection. The result, however, was disastrous. Watchful M.P.s checked the prodigals and orderly room exacted its toll upon them in due course.

The Book of the Ballarat, 1917

Souvenirs of Trinidad
We've heard the war a calling,
To every British heart,
We heard the war a calling,
When Australians took their part.
When you hear the shore a calling,
When you've been long at sea,
It's a drink, a kiss, a smile or two,
Then fourteen days C.B.

We paid for our loves in Trinidad,
Those ruby lips cost dear,
We paid for our loves in Trinidad,
And paid in fines back here.

There was a big run of Clink Cottage after our visit to Trinidad. By what we hear of the fines it seems to have been a clink of gold.

"Port" of Spain must go to your head by the look of some of the boys who went ashore there.

We wonder what became of the clothes belonging to the man who was brought aboard by the picket, clad only in an identification disc and a coloured policeman's belt.

The Euripidean, 1917

THE REPUTATION OF THE A.I.F.

Is a soldier less a soldier?
We all remember the revulsion of feeling against the previous forces caused by Capt. Bean's remarks concerning our brother Australian soldiers when in Egypt. The verse here produced has been published in Melbourne but will withstand reprinting here because it is a frank reply to somewhat distorted ideas . . . This reply was written by an Australian soldier at Mena Camp.

Ain't yer got no blanky savvy;
Have yer got no better use,
Than to fling back home yer inky
Products of yer pen's abuse?

Do yer think we've all gone dippy,
Since we landed over here;
Is a soldier less a soldier
'Cause he socks a pint of beer?

Do yer take yer whisk' and soda
In a cool and shady spot,
Waited on by little Hebes,
Who the boys don't know as 'ot?

Have yer got no loving mother,
Waiting for yer over 'ome;
Do yer own no smiling sister,
Over there across the foam?

Do yer think they like yer better
For yer tales of drink and shame;
Do yer think they'll praise yer action
In defamin' our fair name?

One swaller makes no summer;
Three shickers not a force.
When the few makes it a welter
Yer condemns the lot, o' course.

Do yer think yer Gawd Almighty,
'Cos yer wears a Captain's stars;
Think us blokes is dirt beneath yer,
Men of low degree and bars?

Say yer cannot be Australian?
Let us say in our defence,
Yer can read it on yer coinage:-
'Honi soit qui mal y pense'.

Cease yer wowseristic whining.
Tell the truth and play the game;
And we only ask fair dinkum:-
"How we kept Australia's name?"

We're not out to fight the Devil,
On a new Salv'army stunt;
To reform the Arab's morals
While we're waiting for the front.

Any diversion helped to boost spirits and break the monotony. *Yandoo*, Troopship issue, 1916. (*Australian War Memorial Printed Records*)

Let me tell yer Mr. Critic,
Try and face things with a smile.
Don't be finding all the [*illegible*];
Studying them blokes all the while.

Then write home nice and proper,
'Bout the boys that's all true blue,
And they'll love you better. Mister,
That is my advice to you.

The Euripides Ensign, June 1915

Remember, also, that when you go to France you go to a country where every fit man is an experienced, seasoned soldier whose courage and efficiency... has earned the admiration of every fighting man. See that you show respect for him and his deeds. You will find him a gallant gentleman eager to welcome you as a comrade. It's up to you to do all you can to deserve his trust. Remember this when you meet his loved ones in their homes or in the streets. Be punctilious in your respect and courtesy to them. Let them learn that the Australian soldier is at all times a chivalrous gentleman. Above all things no 'skite' about ourselves. Never a word about what you do or have done before anyone outside your regiment. You will find that you get all the praise due without asking for it.

The Miltiades Lyre, 1916

The man at home is not the man at war. He is for the most part selfish, careless of the finer points and higher ideals of life, too busy to think and too sensitive to speak of them. But the man at war begins to think, and what is more, realises that the higher things are the real things of life.

If you have lost your faith in men—in the churches, in the mart, in the workshop and the business house—the companionship of these men in the A.I.F. will restore it. We were no lambs. There was little piety. But there was the rough, solid, splendid heart of a man in each of the Billjims on board.

Fed-Up
Oh, if I had another chance
A 'civie' I would be;
No more the blessed Army,
No more I'd cross the sea.
I'd walk along the public street.
The heroes I would cheer,
And murmur, "Oh, you blanky fools!"
Then go and have a beer.   *Jock*

The Cold-Footers Confession
Me go and leave the trots?
Me go among the shots?
Me chuck up beer and pool?
Me be a bally fool?
   Not me!

Me do my little bit?
Me show Australian grit?
Me go and be a man?
No! I'm an also-ran;
   That's me!   *W. H. Davies*

Recruit Unit
We've enlisted in the Army, and we're goin' to the war;
We've been inoculated, and they say we'll get some more;
There's no need us a-tellin' you our arms are very sore –
   As we go fightin' for Australia.

We're not a conscript army: we are straight out volunteers;
From city life and from the bush—the sort Australia rears;
And when we get to Berlin we will drink his lager beers –
   As we go fightin' for Australia.

We heard the Anzacs calling and our answer to their cry
Is that we're daily training and we'll be there bye and bye,
To uphold the name of Anzac we will have a real good try
   As we go fightin' for Australia.   *J.H.G., The Book of the Ballarat*, 1917

By comparison with the European Armies engaged in the war, the young Australian is supreme in his physique, his intelligence and his shrewd sense of humour. Returning to Australia after a few years abroad, you swiftly decide that there is more intelligence to the square mile in the thinly populated Commonwealth than in any ten square miles of the crowded older countries. Add that high intelligence to a manhood which for its big average weight is without rival in the activity and ease of its movements, and grace it with that real sense of humour which revels in the small comedies of life, and you have an Army which apart from the justice of its cause and the greatness of its fighting qualities, is a ceaseless joy to every man embraced by it. These grand young men of ours make up a keen eyed, clear brained army of jesting athletes.
Gnr. H. S. Gullett, A.F.A., Accredited Official Correspondent

The young Australian soldier makes one condition. If you want him to work you must keep him keenly interested. At humdrum tasks of no importance, or, what amounts to the same thing, of no importance to his mind, he is a shirker and malingerer without equal in the world. No man can work more rapidly and convincingly: none can avoid work more scientifically and good-humouredly. Put the men in an artillery camp on the guns in the blazing heat of an Australian December day, and they double and hustle gaily all day . . . Put the same men on foot drill and they are the most troublesome fellows to be found in the whole war . . . You can pick the new men half a mile away by their excellent bearing, but those who have been in camps for a couple of months are bored by the 'footslogging', and they slouch along like a lot of sundowners. And no schoolgirls' party ever equalled men for talking.
'*Recruit*'
Osteralia, February–April 1917

Keeping Fit by a Hospital Surgeon
The young man who keeps straight is, it is true, devoid of one of life's experiences, but he has his reward. He can say to himself that he has not contributed to any woman's ruin. He is absolutely healthy and wholesome. He is untainted with disease, and when he marries, he will neither infect his wife nor beget tainted children.
Shropshire Tatler, 1917

Play the Game—For Honour and For Her
. . .
Somewhere a woman watches—thrilled with pride;
Shrined in her heart you share a place with none.
She toils, she waits, she prays, till side by side,
You stand together when the battle's done.
O, keep for her dear sake a stainless name;
Bring back to her a manhood free from shame!
The Boonah Buzzer: Souvenir, December 1918

HOME AND LOVED ONES

Leave the Panels Down
The little grey home had a lonely look,
There wasn't a soul around,
But we saw as we crossed the shallow brook
That the slip rails lay on the ground.
We rode on up to the kitchen door,
For the stock might take the track;
But the woman said with a weary smile,
"My boys are absent many a mile,
And we'll leave the panels down awhile
To wait till the lads come back".

And over our southern sunny land
The same great thought holds true,
From the timbered hills to the parching sand
And the wide green stretches too.
All of the boys who've done their bit,
Though many a pal we'll lack
Whether they come from bush or town,
Will know they'll find the panels down
To the hearts they left . . . and love will crown
The day that the lads get back.
The Miltiades Lyre, 1916

Memories
The golden light of dawning
The murmur of the breeze
The first faint flush of morning
Thro' the forest trees,
The magpie singing on the hill
The bellbird o'er the range,
The jackass laughing by the rill
Make memories sweet and strange.

And lights of summer evenings,
The moon and stars above –

When man with maid is drifting
Whispering low his love,
And music o'er the ocean steals
As lights go gliding by
Soft chimes across the waters peal.
Then fade away and die.
     The Weakly Effort, January 1917

Wattle Blossom
Golden flower of our land,
Planted there by Nature's hand
By soft breezes gently fanned,
 In our home Australia.
As the song-birds trill and sing,
Welcoming the coming spring.
Wattles forth their blossom bring,
 Nature's own regalia.
Oftimes have I sought a tree –
Brought a sprig along with me,
Always thinking, dear, of thee,
 Waiting in the gloaming;
And when days of peace descend,
Happy be the hours we'll spend,
Gathering blossom without end,
 O'er the hills a'roaming. *Jock*
     The Book of the Ballarat, 1917

Mother's Letter
You may write a thousand letters to the maiden you adore,
And declare in every letter that you love her more and more;
You may praise her grace and beauty in a thousand glowing lines,
And compare her eyes of azure with the brightest star that shines.
If you had the pen of Byron you would use it every day
In composing written worship to your sweetheart far away.
But the letter far more welcome to an older sweeter breast
Is the letter to your mother from the boy she loves the best.

Youthful blood is fierce and flaming, and when writing to your love
You will rave about your passion, swearing by the stars above,
Vowing by the moon's white splendour that the girlie you adore
Is the one you'll ever cherish as no maid was loved before.
You will pen full many a promise on those pages white and dumb
That you never can live up to in the married years to come.
But a much more precious letter, bringing more and deeper bliss,
Is the letter to your mother from the boy she cannot kiss.

She will read it very often when the lights are soft and low,
Sitting in the same old corner where she held you years ago;
And regardless of its diction or its spelling or its style,
And although its composition would provoke a critic's smile,
In her old and trembling fingers it becomes a work of art,
Stained by tears of joy and sadness as she hugs it to her heart.
Yes, the letter of all letters, look wherever you may roam,
Is the letter to your mother from her boy away from home.
     Pte. G.R. No 3143, 7/38 Batt.
     The Book of the Ballarat, 1917

Homesick
We were seated together, my mate Bill and I:
We were talking of old times, of days long gone by;
Talking of harvesting and shearing time too,
But when talking of home, love, my thoughts flew to you.

When the kiddies are older they'll know what it meant,
How sad was the parting when I soldiering went.
But I sure couldn't help it, the blood in each vein
Would cause me to do it and enlist once again.

But soon I'll return, dear, for God up above
Will sustain me and guide me to those whom I love.
And when peace comes my darling, and earth is at rest,
I will stay home contented with those I love best.   *Jock*
                                      The Book of the Ballarat, 1917

The Girl at Home
Just a sprig of golden wattle
From a girl I left at home
Brings my laughing, sunny country
Gleaming right across the foam.

All her letters closely written,
How I read them through and through!
And her photo, though its dusty,
Seems to say, "I do love you".

At dusk she comes in vivid visions,
And her hand I fondly hold,
Whilst the wattles 'neath their shadows
Our fond murmurings enfold.

'Tis dreary work, this waiting;
For I want you blue-eyed girl.
May it not be so much longer
Till we see the war-flag furl!

May our golden southern wattle
In your dear eyes ever shine,
Till I land in God's own country.
Which holds you, girl of mine.
                              Billjim at Sea, 1918

A Sunset Reverie
There's a sheen of gold on the skyline, a tinge of gold on the sea,
With a wreathing cloud of grey smoke drifting away to lee;
There's a land to the eastward yonder, there are thoughts that wander wide,
From the hearts of the lads in khaki, afar on the far-flung tide.

Visions of smiling valleys, of corn fields rich and deep,
Swelling with golden harvest, brighten their hours of sleep;
All that they have to cheer them in the lonely days to come,
Linking their thoughts to kindred, binding their hearts to home.

'Twas theirs to be proud of home-land, and of their best they gave,
Counting as nothing the valleys, the hills where the wattles wave,

Giving their love of kindred, of mother, wife, and friend –
Sons of a glorious empire, ready to fight to the end . . .

There's a sheen of gold on the skyline, a tinge of gold on the sea,
With a wreathing cloud of grey smoke, drifting away to lee,
There's a land to the eastward yonder, a love that wanders far,
From the hearts of the lads in khaki to a land where the old folks are.

Sea Spray, 1917

IF I SHOULD DIE

The Plea
Lord, when the evening closes, and I stand
With eager fearful hands towards heaven's far shore,
Bring me no gift of roses, as the sand
Runs out, to run again for me no more.

But give me one clear hour at close of day,
And whisper as the darkening shadows fall
The name of friends I lost along the way,
The faithful friends I can no more recall.

And while their names upon my lips are set,
Oh, speed the silent tides that I must stem,
That 'ere again I slumber or forget,
I may begin my eager quest of them.

The Berrima Souvenir, January 1917

If They Only Know How To Die
Life's a thing we hang on to
Though the path may be drear and dark;
Fate points a steering finger
The course which we embark.
Some find a peaceful valley
Sheltered from world-swept storms,
Just following nature's dictates,
Not touched by creeds or forms.
Some find the eddying whirlpool
Of vice and its glittering flare
Which leaves them, worn and tired,
Stranded they know not where.
Oft with a bitter mem'ry
Of things which are left undone,
To follow the gaudy bauble,
Which is flung aside when won.
Some show no respect for women,
Luring them from their height
Of purity—to the funeral
Of what is woman's right.
Some lead a false existence,
Striving against their fate;
Trying to do their duty,
But doing it all too late.
Some find their souls in battle
Answering their country's cry,
Their past may be forgiven
If they only know how to die.

C. Chester, 10/54th Battn.

In Memoriam
Peace comes again with placid eyes,
The world is sweetened with her breath,
And lyric songs like incense rise,
For we are sick of hate and death.
O! women weeping in the night,
Be comforted, and proudly tread
Among the children of the light!
Your boys are with the sacred dead:
Peace bides with them, and quiet joy,
For they have won a laurelled crown
That iron shards shall not destroy,
Nor the grave hide, nor waters drown.

Vance Palmer
The Barambah Souvenir, January 1919

REFLECTIONS

Nearly every troopship voyage produces a Souvenir publication, designed for the purpose of depicting the general life on board from day to day. Reading a number of these, one has before him pictures of hundreds of Australian volunteers, light-hearted and happy as the proverbial sandboys, without a care in the world, enjoying every day of a life on the ocean wave, under the paternal care and guidance of officers, who spend sleepless nights devising means of entertainment for those under them. There were obvious reasons why, during the last four years, these pictures should . . . have been given to the public, but now, with the end of the war at hand, there are just as strong reasons why this camouflage should be dropped and a true picture painted.

The *Barambah* is a German interned cargo ship, converted into a troopship, with the crudest possible appointments both for officers and men. On the ship for eleven weeks were approximately 1,000 men all told. The troops' sleeping accommodation was between decks, a number, however, sleeping on deck in favourable weather. The conditions of sleep were such that the atmosphere was thick and the odour of human body and breath vile. The boat was not in port long enough to be cleaned, and when she left Melbourne she was filthy. The iron decks were boarded over, with spaces between and underneath the planking. Under the planking refuse collected, at times the smell being awful. On one occasion, near the cooks' and butchers' shops, the space under the planking was filled with putrid matter, the smell being vile. The troops' wash-houses were poor, and frequently there was no water. For the first nine days out the salt water showers were out of repair, it apparently being nobody's business to attend to them. About the food generally there was not much to complain of, though in the hot weather the way it was dished up left much to be desired, even by common privates. Of deck space there was but little, and the troops had practically no exercise, the physical jerks being carried out under difficulties and reduced to a minimum. For entertainment we had four concerts on the hot, stuffy troopdeck, about one-fifth of the boys being able to see or hear. Of the band one cannot speak too highly. It was a boon indeed without which we would have had a miserable time. At Fremantle we were not allowed ashore, though it was our last port in Australia. We had been eight days aboard, and many very sick, going through first sea experiences. This was probably because of trouble given by troops on previous ships, but why we should be penalised because of others is known only to the powers that be.

Perhaps that which tended most towards the discomfort of troops was the attitude of officers towards them. In magazine stories we read of the care taken of the men by loved officers, of the comradeship and esprit de corps existing between them, and their readiness to stand up for their men. The experience one gains going through Broadmeadows Camp and the voyage just completed, leads one to think it is only in fiction such things exist, and Australia needs to reserve her jeers directed to the alleged military caste of other armies. Indeed experience leads one to believe that already in Australia's young military system there has grown up a caste altogether inconsistent with our democratic ideas and political constitution. Our army is a citizens' army, and if it is to continue such, this thing called military caste must be stamped on with both feet. What is the position? The troops on this ship were men drawn from all classes, of all social and intellectual grades. With an appreciation of their responsibilities as citizens, they enlisted. The moment they entered Broadmeadows Camp they were no longer citizens, or even men. They were not only mere numbers, but our officers appeared to take a special delight in impressing the fact upon them. This is entirely against the spirit of a citizen army. It seems to be forgotten we are not professional soldiers, and when the war ends we return to citizenship. There was little or no comradeship, in fact, when off parades the officers lived on little isles of isolation. Even the sergeants, or some of them, believed it against 'military etiquette' to take part in the sports with privates, and in one case two sergeants were reprimanded for skylarking in front of privates. On the voyage little or nothing was done to interest the troops or help them pass the time.

Appeals to officers were too often neglected, and on one occasion, at least, a complaint about food was met with a threat of punishment. In fact, any man complaining was looked upon as a trouble-maker. As for the sergeants, they were, with few exceptions, too boyish and tactless to deal with men.

This is no way a complaint against discipline, as it might appear to those in charge of us. Discipline does not come into the question.

A loud voice and stern look does not count for strength, as seems to be the prevailing idea; it is usually a substitute. Our leaders may have plenty of military knowledge, but with a few exceptions they know little of men. The troops had a kindly word for some of them; there were others without a friend. Our trip over was anything but a pleasant one. The ship, of course, did not lend itself to a pleasant time, but it might have been made less unpleasant by just a little effort on the part of some of those over us. These ironic reflections may help to tone the general good humour of this Souvenir. *A Digger*
The Barambah Souvenir, January 1919

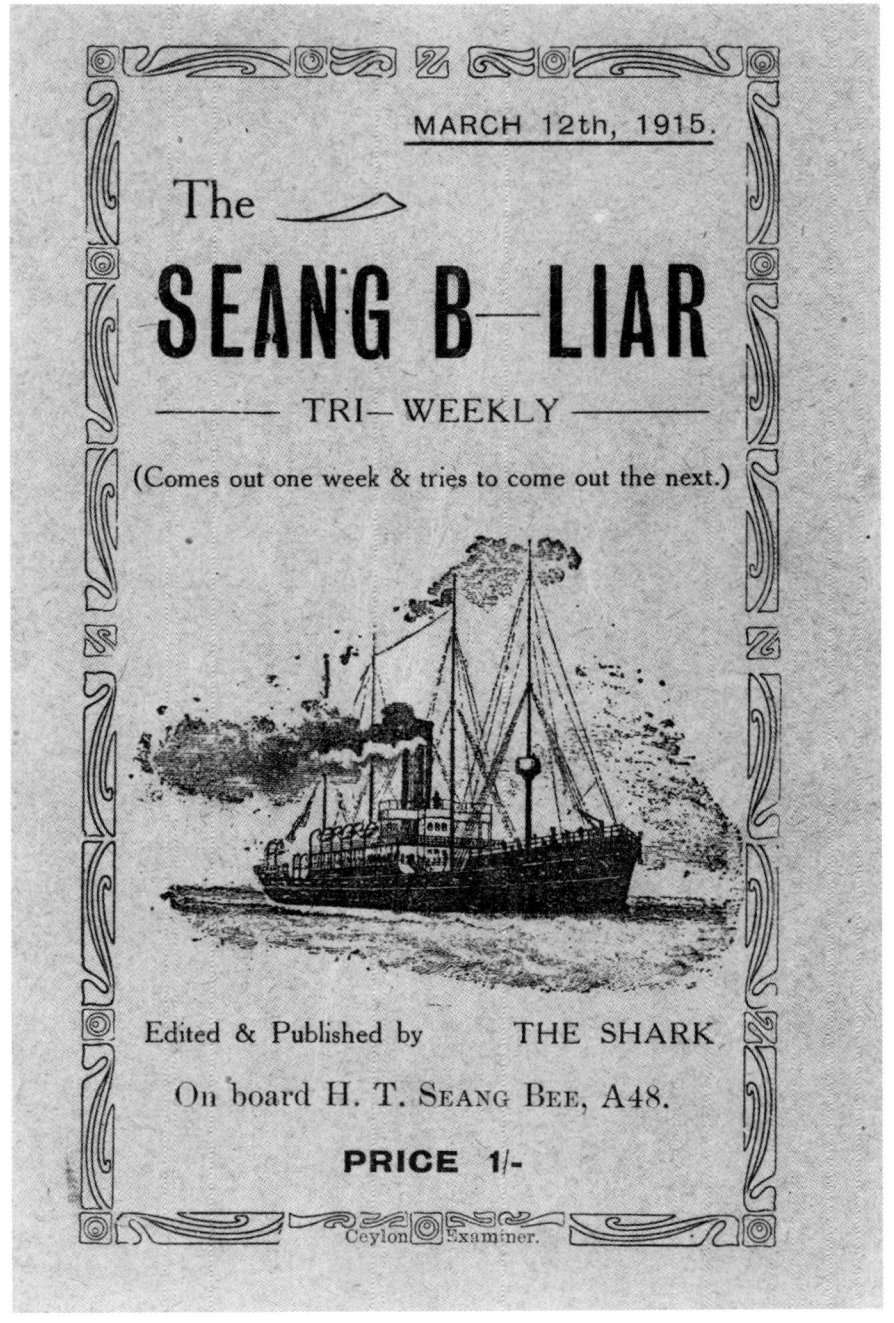

(Australian War Memorial Printed Records)

Infantrymen and Light Horsemen in the trenches at Gallipoli. The soldier smoking a pipe and the soldier with a periscope were father and son. (*Australian War Memorial, Neg. no. C00667*)

CHAPTER THREE

GALLIPOLI, EGYPT AND PALESTINE

The men in the first convoy had left Australia confidently expecting that they would be flung into the struggle against the German armies in France and Flanders. While they were crossing the Indian Ocean the decision was taken to disembark the A.I.F. in Egypt to defend that country and the strategically important Suez Canal against an anticipated attack by Turkey. Thus it was that Australian forces were conveniently to hand when the political and military planners in Whitehall devised their ill-conceived and ill-fated scheme to deliver a swift, pre-emptive blow at the heart of the Turkish Empire. The plan was doomed, however, from the moment British warships failed to seize control of the narrow waters of the Dardanelles. When armed landings were made at several places on the Gallipoli peninsula, the soldiers faced not only the difficulties presented by geography, in the form of steep, deeply gullied hillsides, but also well-entrenched Turkish forces commanding the high ground. The role of the Australian and New Zealand soldiers in this particular battle is too well known to need restating here. What is less often recalled is the fact that the Gallipoli misadventure was an unsuccessful episode in the larger Middle East campaign against Turkey. As a result the strategy was developed of making Egypt secure and then confronting the Turkish armies in the desert wastes of Sinai and the hills of Palestine. From mid 1916 the allies pushed the Turks back, slowly at first and then with astonishing rapidity. In this war of movement, Australian mounted troops played a central role, enjoying triumphs which contrasted sweetly with the gall of Gallipoli. This is the context for the examination of trench newspapers and unit magazines in this chapter.

Although it is highly probable that the custom of the troopship journal was carried over into the training camps of Egypt, the most determined searching has failed to locate any titles which can be dated to the period before the Gallipoli invasion. This is unfortunate since these were months of great frustration for those men who had hoped to go into action immediately and it is likely that the newsheet would have reflected their irritation and anxiety. The drunken roistering, disobedience and ill-discipline characteristic of many Australian soldiers at this time attracted much adverse comment and led directly to the intensification of training in the hope that physical exhaustion would curb excess. While this seems to have worked to some extent the impression remains that Australian troops were ill-suited to the routines of camp life. The embarkation for Gallipoli, therefore, with its promise of action, came as a welcome relief.

Among the myriad dangers and difficulties the Australians faced at Gallipoli, the shortage of reading matter and the lack of hard news were a constant irritation. Newspapers sent from Australia were generally retained at the base hospitals and those from England were several weeks old before they arrived at the front. Stories of soldiers being reduced to reading labels on tins of jam are part of the folklore of Gallipoli, but they are equally an indication of the genuine scarcity of both news and anything to read. It is not surprising, therefore, that in due course trench newspapers appeared. Nine titles are known to have circulated in Australian ranks, but given the particularly ephemeral nature of these

News was in short supply at Gallipoli. Men of the 1st Battalion read *The Peninsular Press* in 'Rest Gully'.
(*Australian War Memorial, Neg. no. C01923*)

Australian soldiers were famous for their ingenuity. Soldiers at Gallipoli pounding hard army biscuits with a shell case and sifting the meal through mosquito netting in order to make porridge.
(*Australian War Memorial, Neg. no. A00849*)

documents and the extraordinary circumstances in which they were produced, it is possible more titles existed.

The *Peninsular Press* and *Local News* were distinctly official publications originating from G.H.Q. The former first appeared on 10 May, barely two weeks after the landing, and was specifically designed to overcome the chronic shortage of news and forestall the proliferation of rumours. It was very well received and C.E.W. Bean noted how men crowded around to read it when it was posted in their unit or on the beach. With only a few gaps the paper was issued daily from 10 May to 31 July, thereafter it appeared twice weekly until its final post-evacuation number on 3 January 1916. The *Peninsular Press* was usually a single-sided, foolscap sheet of two well-printed columns containing a selection of news items. Although many topics featured in the ninety-five issues, the bulk of the content focused on the progress of the war, on diplomatic activity, and on rebutting enemy communiqués which misrepresented events. As befitted its purpose as an official news-sheet, the tone of the paper was always congratulatory and dismissive of the enemy. It was good propaganda writing. The usual smattering of atrocity stories found a place in its columns as did extracts from speeches by Churchill and Kitchener. It must have been reassuring for the Australians to learn that the latter thought the news from Gallipoli was 'thoroughly satisfactory'.

It is arguable that the *Peninsular Press* should be excluded from any review of Australian trench newspapers. Not only was its provenance decidedly official, and British to boot, but it contained much which must have reinforced the Australians' sense of isolation, even if they appreciated the war news and enthusiastic reports of their exploits. There was hardly any worthwhile Australian news, whereas English sporting events and some racing results were reported as was Asquith's attack of 'gastro-intestinal catarrh' and the death of Keir Hardie. It is impossible to imagine what Australian soldiers made of the extracts from the London *Daily Mail* which gushingly recorded the war work of the boys of Eton College who cycled off every day in their overalls to take their place 'side by side with the other workers without any distinction'. If the *Peninsular Press* was intended to make British soldiers feel they were not forgotten, by giving them a link with home and the world beyond the battleground, it very probably had the reverse effect on the Australians.

As avid readers of the *Peninsular Press,* the Australian troops were susceptible to any influence it may have exerted. From early July 1915 a most significant change is noticeable in the paper. There was a marked reduction in comment on the Peninsular campaign, in sharp contrast to the frequency of references in earlier issues, and it ceased to be an almost daily bulletin. In its twice-weekly form the information flow diminished and the earlier refrain of an immediate victory disappeared. The change in tone was so pronounced that perhaps it points to a decision by G.H.Q. that the soldiers had to be encouraged to accept the stalemate. Issue 81 reproduced a leading article from *The Times*, entitled 'Heroism at Gallipoli', which pointed out the virtual impossibility of the task. How much the *Peninsular Press* influenced the Australians at Gallipoli can only be guessed at, but it seems likely that most would have regarded it as the official account of events. This was certainly the view of one soldier who sent a copy home to his father with the instruction 'Keep this as a memento of the Dardanelles. This is our field newspaper'.

Peninsular Press provoked an almost immediate response in the form of *The Dardanelles Driveller* which, as the name suggests, was a pastiche on the former. The first and possibly the only issue appeared on 17 May, and, even if the paper's provenance is uncertain, the Anzacs would have recognised much that was familiar in its columns. The humorous verse, ridiculous advertisements, laboured puns, and gently anti-authoritarian tone were all features of the troopship publications and of Australian trench papers throughout the war. It seems possible that the editor of *The Dardanelles Driveller* drew on these examples and it is certain that he realised the official news-sheet, with its bulletins of world news, offered little amusement to the men in the trenches.

Unofficial trench newspapers were an important factor in creating that sense of community among ordinary soldiers which is always the foundation of unit loyalty and good morale. They published material with which their readers could easily identify. The communality of experience and attitude in their pages reinforced a sense of solidarity in the face of shared danger and privation. *The Dardanelles Driveller* would have drawn a grim chuckle from the men who read it, especially the description of 'Y' Beach:

> "Y" Beach, the Scottish Borderer cried
> While panting up the steep hillside,
>   "Y" Beach!
> To call this thing a beach is stiff,
> It's nothing but a b----- cliff.
>   Why Beach?

Jokes at the expense of officers who considered themselves superior beings, or the staff officers whose active service was largely confined to manoeuvres at headquarters, also strengthened the bonds among the other ranks.

Genuinely Australian trench papers began in early June. Although it is uncertain which was the first such publication, nor when exactly it was issued, the honour probably belongs to *Snipers Shots*. On 8 June Bean saw a copy which was circulating in the 6th Battalion. It was a humorous topical paper, and although no copy seems to have survived, it was probably very like *The Dinkum Oil* which it directly inspired. The only possible rival to *Snipers Shots* as the first Australian paper at Gallipoli was the *Anzac Argus*. The surviving copy is dated 13 June, but the text contains a reference to a previous issue and a note that the paper was 'Published nearly every day'.

The *Anzac Argus* was a handwritten news-sheet and the copy in the Australian War Memorial, consisting of seven pages, was written on the reverse of forms used for messages and signals. Carbon paper was used to make several copies which were presumably posted at convenient points. It contained only news items which suggests that *Peninsular Press* was either felt to be insufficient or, perhaps, was unevenly distributed. Of particular interest is the evidence that 'by courtesy of General Birdwood' the *Anzac Argus* intended to keep its readers informed of their own situation by a 'daily communiqué'. This might sustain the conclusion that there was a demand among the Australians for their own source of news about their own arena and that this was understood by those in command. It also seems possible that the paper was produced in a way which pronounced its front-line authenticity and, perhaps, gave it a credibility the official organ lacked.

More in keeping with the tone and character of the earlier troopship journals was *The Bran Mash*. Produced in the 4th Light Horse Regiment, the first and probably the only copy was issued on 15 June. Handwritten in indelible pencil on the blank sides of sheets headed 'First Australian Division', it contained a humorous editorial, a few jokes, some verse, and a comment on a recent rumour. The use of only one side of the paper and the presence of pin holes in the only surviving copy indicate that it was probably posted on a noticeboard. The editorial reflected and reinforced the Anzac tendency to make light of difficulties. While noting the shortage of both paper and ink and observing that an enemy shell might provide a necessary enlargement of premises, the editor called for contributions of verses, skits, and news items. The joke about the troop leader who 'gave the order to fall-in, and even his dug-out obeyed', was probably apocryphal but it was the sort of incident that all the readers would have recognised. Perhaps the encouragement to find humour in discomfort and the public acknowledgement of private fears and grievances made things easier to bear.

First Aid Post, the 'Official Organ of the 2nd Field Ambulance', came out on 16 June and at weekly intervals thereafter until 11 August. This run of nine issues probably represents the full life of this title, but given the circumstances its regularity and durability was remarkable. Printed on one side of an octavo sheet, the little paper consisted chiefly of funny snippets and unit gossip with occasional notices of injury, recovery, and posting. Like so many unit publications much of the humour in *First Aid Post* focused on the actions and idiosyncracies of named or nicknamed individuals; nearly fifty men are identifiable in its columns. Although some of the content is incomprehensible at this distance in time, it is obvious that the men of the unit would have had no such difficulty and it seems reasonable to suggest that this coded humour, which derived its meaning from prior knowledge, helped to bind the 2nd Field Ambulance together.

A note in the third issue suggested that the paper had 'been received with open arms' probably because of its intention to 'promote good feeling and a little humour amongst one another'. The editor relied heavily on one of the most familiar components of trench and troopship publications, the short notice. The following examples convey the general tenor of such material.

> Lost–A sense of security. Finder will be rewarded by returning same to Pte. Afriat.
> Wanted–A man with a wooden leg to break up biscuits. Apply, Hospital.
> Personal–Notice how the cap sits on his head? Surely it has not swelled since it got mentioned.
> Advertisement–Miss STEPHANIE TURNER
> Clairvoyant and Spiritualist
> Shrapnel Green
> Marvellous Predictions The Future Foretold
> Your end predicted within 48 hours
> Call At Once
> Joy! Sadness! Madness!

Of all the trench newspapers circulating among the Australians at Gallipoli, *The Dinkum Oil* is the best known. The reason for this is that Bean played a part in its founding and recorded that fact in his diary, later mentioning the paper in a footnote in the official history. According to Bean, Gallipoli in early June was full of rumours and Major Blamey, the Intelligence officer of the First Division, approached him with the suggestion that he produce a 'Furphies Gazette' which would so exaggerate the rumours and spy mania 'as to laugh them out of court'. Bean noted Blamey's request on 7 June and the next day recorded that he had seen a copy of *Snipers Shots* put together by Sergeant Noonan in the 6th Battalion; he thought the humorous topicality of the paper was 'very good indeed' and he sought Noonan's help with the new venture. In the event it was Bean who helped Noonan. The two met on the afternoon of 11 June and prepared the first issue of *The*

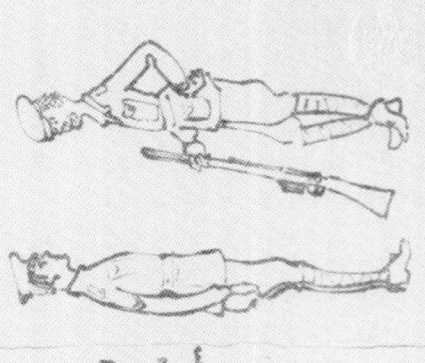

The *Dinkum Oil*, the most famous of the Gallipoli papers, was designed to provoke a chuckle even in the direst circumstances. (Australian War Memorial Printed Records)

Dinkum Oil at Noonan's dictation. Bean acknowledged that the former Victorian journalist had a 'remarkable wit' and that his own role was merely 'to hold the pen and write clearly'. This was important, however, for the handwritten paper was duplicated and Bean's tiny, but well-formed, handwriting allowed maximum use of each single-sheet issue.

The name of the paper was chosen to emphasise the nonsense of its contents; in contemporary parlance 'dinkum oil' meant reliable information. Each issue consisted chiefly of outrageous, totally unbelievable 'furphies' which appeared under the banner heading 'WAR NEWS'. The rest of the sheet was filled with comic advertisements and notices, one or more cartoons, and a few lines from a serial story which was notable for the absence of any connection between the episodes. The eight issues which circulated in less than a month contained no leavening of serious items nor anything related to a particular unit. The humour of *The Dinkum Oil* was whimsical and frivolous; it relied on the readers' recognition of absurdity and incongruity in familiar situations. It is easy to imagine weary soldiers grinning at the nonsensical statements which were represented as facts:

- There is a great amount of grumbling amongst the Turkish troops since they received the order that they were not to use cognac in their coffee for supper.
- A man had a narrow escape from a sniper yesterday. He was walking past a gap in the trench when a stray bullet flicked a piece off each of his ears without doing further damage.

Noonan did not emphasise the peculiarities of individuals but rather found amusement in the ridiculous and dangerous circumstances surrounding the Anzacs. The daily difficulties of living and fighting on Gallipoli were acknowledged in the notices and advertisements:

- To Let—Nice dugout on the skyline. Owner leaving for field hospital.
- Wanted—Section commander requires pair of good field glasses to find his men when there is shrapnel about.
- Notices—The electric elevator will not be working up the gullies for a while. Some cook stole the current to make a pudding.

It is doubtful if any trench newspapers were compiled and produced under greater danger and difficulty than those at Gallipoli. The effort which went into them is a clue to their value for those men who were facing death and disease so far from home. The Gallipoli trench papers are a tiny fragment of the total volume of this material but even in their brevity they enlarge our knowledge and understanding of the Anzacs.

Following the evacuation of Gallipoli, the Australian forces returned to Egypt where the mounted regiments remained when the infantry was transferred to the Western Front. The disappointment and humiliation of the peninsula was never forgotten, but was soon balanced by ever larger successes which, in terms of prisoners taken and territory gained, were unequalled in any other theatre of war. In August 1916 the Turkish advance towards the Suez Canal was halted at the battle of Romani, some twenty miles east of the Canal. This made Egypt secure and preserved the vital sea link between Europe and the East. From this moment on, the Turkish army was pushed steadily backwards. Although much bitter fighting had yet to take place at Rafa, Gaza, and beyond, the story of the Imperial forces became one of inexorable progress northward. By the end of 1916, Sinai had been occupied and the following year saw the conquest of southern Palestine culminating in the capture of Jerusalem in December. During the early months of 1918 General Allenby consolidated his position and built up his forces until he was ready to release his master plan for the encirclement of the Turkish army. The patient progress of the previous years was instantly replaced by the exuberant rout of the Turks which ended with the capture of Damascus at the end of September and the armistice with Turkey in October.

The men in the Australian Mounted Division, and those Australians who served with the Imperial Camel Corps, were evidently unwilling to relinquish the custom of a field newspaper or magazine. Twelve titles originating in the Middle East have survived, references exist to two more and there were almost certainly others that have passed unrecorded. The months between the occupation of Romani in April 1916 and the battle for that oasis saw a flurry of shortlived publications. At Tel-el-Kebir, the Divisional Base Depot published a single issue of *The Kookaburra*, Lieutenant Oliver Hogue of the 2nd Light Horse Brigade edited *The Mirage* which had two typescript issues, and at Serapium Trooper Boyd Orr produced six numbers of *The Desert Dustbin*. The latter was printed in Cairo and the availability of commercial printing houses in the city enabled editors to produce, if they so wished, magazines which were thoroughly professional in printing, layout, and design and made possible the reproduction of photographs and line-drawings.

The most sophisticated publications were *The Cacolet*, the journal of the Australian Camel Field Ambulance, and *The Kia Ora Coo-ee*, an official magazine for the Australian and New Zealand forces. These were printed at the Nile Mission Press and the Sphinx Press respectively. The latter magazine was the most successful of all such publications. Not only did it have a long and regular publishing history, with ten monthly issues between March and December 1918, but it also sold more widely than any other journal and had a standard of presentation which was unrivalled. At the other extreme was the *Musallabah Mirror*, of which, unfortunately, no copy survives. This handwritten effort originated in May 1918 from the Orderly Room of the 1st Battalion, Imperial Camel Corps. Although the editor, tongue firmly in cheek, claimed 'the largest circulation in the Jordan Valley' it seems obvious that the eight small pages were read by very few since only one copy of each of its two recorded issues was produced. The *Kia Ora Coo-ee* and the *Musallabah Mirror*, in their different ways, are both testimony to the enthusiasm of Australian troops for their field publications.

The Kia Ora Coo-ee was the most noteworthy service magazine produced during the war. As the title with its mixture of New Zealand and Australian expressions suggests, it was intended for all antipodean troops. Unlike most field publications it was not restricted to, or limited by, a provenance in a particular unit or regiment. Its purpose was to 'gather and dispense all interesting information concerning the different units in Egypt, Palestine, Salonica and Mesopotamia'; it was a magazine for all the Anzacs in the Middle East. Other service journals were usually either shortlived or irregular because the demands of the war interrupted the activity of editors and contributors; for example, nine months elapsed between the third and fourth issues of *The Cacolet*. *The Kia Ora Coo-ee*, however, was free

"COMRADES"

The cover for the first issue was drawn by David Barker of *Anzac Book* fame. (Author)

(Australian War Memorial Printed Records)

from such constraints and limitations. It drew on a wide pool of talent and its official status ensured its regular appearance. It also had an editorial staff with considerable journalistic experience. The editor, Sergeant Charles Barrett, had worked on the *Melbourne Herald* before the war and Trooper M.E. Lyons had been a sub-editor on *The Christchurch Sun*. These advantages, together with the security of a permanent base in Cairo and access to a good printing house, enabled the editors to produce a magazine which looked good, was well supported by contributors and readers, attracted some advertising revenue, and made a comfortable profit for service funds.

The popularity of these journals is demonstrated by their remarkable sales figures. The first issue of *Barrak*, the magazine of the Imperial Camel Corps, sold over three thousand copies and the second over four thousand. The Corps had around 2500 native English speakers so that sales must have extended beyond the ranks of the cameliers or, perhaps, many copies were sent home. The editor recognised this probability when he offered a dedication to those sending a copy to Australia:

> Shelterless under a Turkish sun
> We yet contrive to have some fun –
> Witness the doughty deeds we've done,
> This magazine, what ho!
> Produced on a foeman's conquered soil
> See the result of our sweatsome toil
> Though the pen may melt and the ink may boil
> Are we downhearted? No!

The Kia Ora Coo-ee maintained an average of 13,000 copies for ten months and the editor believed that 'probably nine published copies out of ten have been posted overseas'. The committee organising this magazine made arrangements for it to be sent directly overseas and soldiers could pay for it by a deduction from their pay-book. The popularity of these magazines as souvenirs probably had something to do with the conviction of the men in the Middle East that they were a largely forgotten army, ignored by the press which tended to concentrate on the war in Europe. The fact they were also a successful army doubtless contributed to their readiness to share their experiences with the folks at home.

Few aspects of service life went unremarked in the Middle Eastern field publications. Every journal had its quota of comment on the eternal discomforts of the desert, the heat, the dust, and the flies. A correspondent to *The Kookaburra* reflected on the capacity of sand to insinuate itself into 'the eyes, ears, nostrils and mouth' until it occupied 'every crevice of the body'; he also claimed that sand tainted the food at every meal. Flies were such a nuisance that one member of the Imperial Camel Corps, writing in *Barrak*, was provoked to pen a poem of several verses dedicated to 'The Foe' which ended with the lines:

> Oh, he's wonderful and curious,
> He's savage and he's furious,
> He's filthy and injurious -
> You might even say 'manurious'-
> Is that ogre grim, the FLY!

The irritation of training exercises, fatigue parties, kit inspection and stable duty in the horse and camel lines, was all duly and fully chronicled. Although most field papers contained expressions of frustration and even mild discontent, as for example over delays in the issue of pay or the trivial offences for which a soldier could be 'crimed', their tone, overall, was invariably humorous and optimistic. In 'The Pilgrimage', Hogue, the editor of *The Mirage*, writing as 'Trooper Bluegum', probably captured the sentiment of most Australians in Egypt:

> It aint no use a swearing,
> It aint no good to fret;
> There's little gained by grousing,
> Or getting all upset.
> This wilderness is rotten,
> All flies, and dust, and tears,
> But the Israelites, they stuck it,
> For years and years and years.
>
> The Willie-Willies choke yer,
> The dust-storms get yer down:
> The red sun robs yer beauty
> And burns yer black and brown.
> The drought is something shocking,
> The thirst our squadron fears,
> Can only be abolished,
> By beers and beers and beers.
>
> But war wont last for ever:
> This scrap'll soon be done.
> An' we'll have done our little bit,
> A strafing of the Hun.
> An' when we get back home again.
> An' meet our little dears;
> All thought of Egypt will be drowned
> In cheers and cheers and cheers.

Humour, in verse, prose, short paragraph and notice was the central, unifying element in all field publications. The humorous items covered every imaginable topic and tell us a great deal about what soldiers found amusing. The discomforts and dangers of service life were almost invariably dealt with in a way which stressed the idiotic and farcical aspects of the war. For example, the gruesome tale of 'Lost-A-Leg' in *The Kia Ora Coo-ee* tells how repatriation was achieved at the expense of that limb, pieces of which were left at different locations in the Middle East as a result of a wound and subsequent infection. The permanent hostility between the troops and the army cooks inspired many items and the out-manoeuvring of dim-witted authority was evidently something which most Anzacs relished. The magazines and papers, with their many accounts of a superior outwitted, a triumph over petty authority, or an advantage cunningly taken, offer endorsement to the popular belief that the Australian soldiers' contempt for authority went far beyond a mere reluctance to salute.

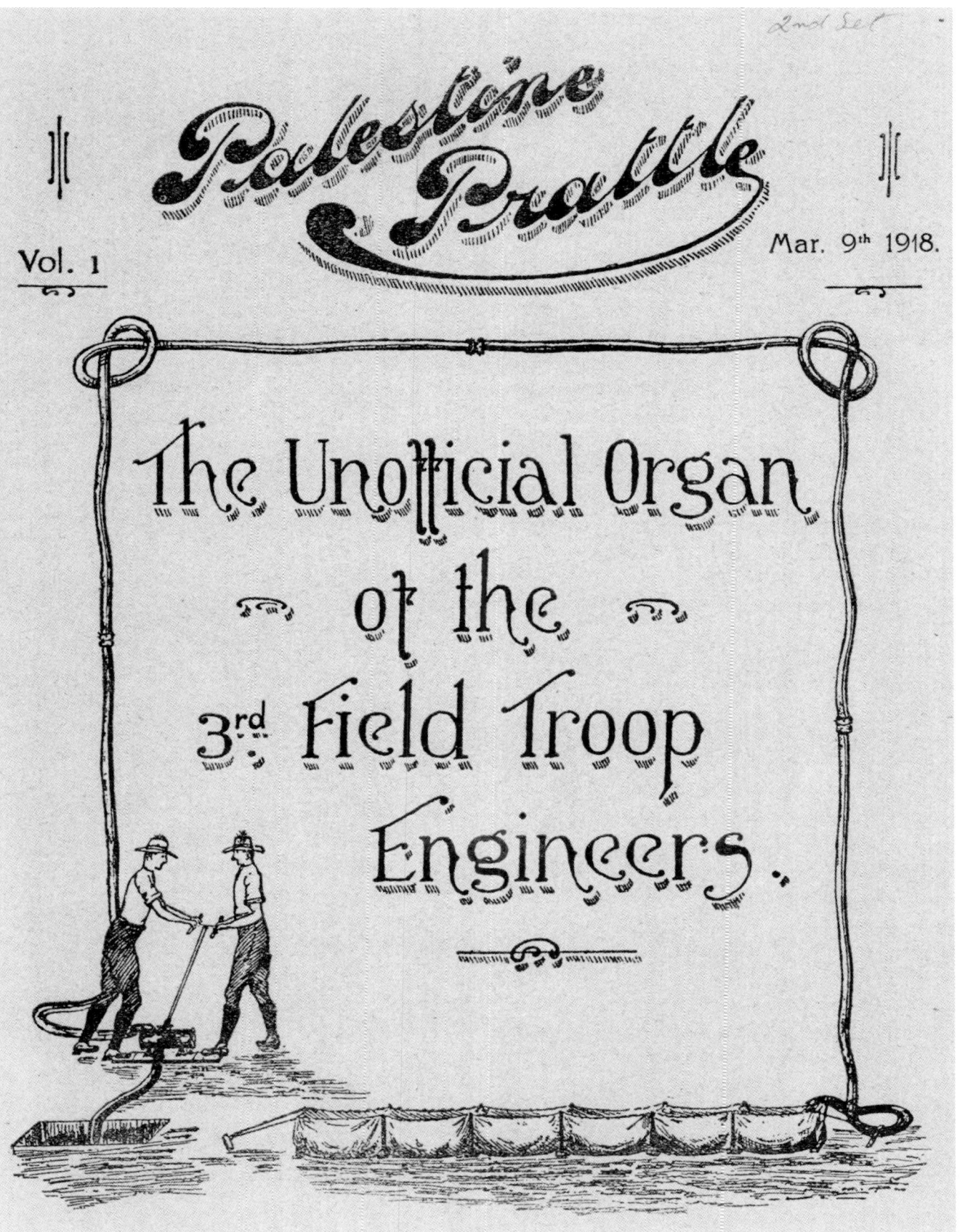

(Australian War Memorial Printed Records)

Cairo had many attractions for the soldier on leave, not all of which were included in this cartoon.
Kia Ora Coo-ee, April 1918. (Author)

The tedium of camp life was relieved by the diverse entertainments offered especially in Cairo and Alexandria. There could be few more dramatic contrasts imaginable than between the spartan life of an army camp on the edge of the desert and the inducements to hedonism offered in the streets of the major Egyptian cities. Geoffrey Norton, one of the New Zealand editors of *The Anzac Records Gazette*, was unique in publicly acknowledging the moral peril facing the troops: '. . . this Egypt, with its Oriental frankness, where invitations to be drenched with sooty showers of vice are so frequently pressed upon us, will leave its imprint'.

The Anzac Records Gazette, which appeared in late 1915 and early 1916, was much less of a souvenir magazine than many later publications which might explain Norton's readiness to comment, so very primly, on one of Cairo's major attractions for the soldier with a leave pass. In later journals a veil is drawn over the brothel visiting which, together with heavy drinking, was a routine part of a visit to Cairo or Alexandria for many soldiers:

>Give me a place in a wet canteen,
>With a two-up school beside it,
>When things are slack in the "in-between",
>And the hump's too poor to ride it,
>And a trip to town where the girls are chic,
>And the P-M's not a Nero,
>And a "broke" return, with a head—well—thick,
>Then call me a Camelero.

As the above verse indicates, occasional, oblique, coy references can be found which hint at the pleasures of the flesh, but in general this aspect of service life in Egypt is not well recorded in the field publications.

There was much less self-consciousness about drink and drunkenness, even in the publications which were to be sent home as souvenirs. Innumerable items included references to the longing for drink and the consequences of heavy drinking. Almost every tale, in verse or prose, that depicted Australian troops returning from a desert operation mentioned their heroic thirst. A contributor to *The Kookaburra* claimed:

> since my advent into Egypt I have seen some drinking, and amongst our boys too. Here they drink and drink again. I suppose it is due to the heat or fresh supplies for perspiration. However the drinking goes on and not only the men, but others with bars on their arms as well as with their arms on a bar.

The Light Horsemen who read *The Desert Dustbin* in June 1916 were reminded of an earlier commanding officer's advice, 'Get drunk if you must, but shut up about it'. The outrageous or comical behaviour of drunks returning to camp always provided good copy, and even though names were rarely mentioned the reports usually contained sufficient clues to the culprit's identity. The editors of the various publications clearly did not feel constrained to moderate comment on this particular topic; perhaps heavy drinking was seen as relatively familiar behaviour which was all the more easily forgiven in the dust and heat of desert service.

The Australian soldier at Gallipoli was an 'Anzac', in Egypt and Palestine he became a 'Billjim'. The character, who features very prominently in the short stories, anecdotes, verse and factual reports was apparently both saint and sinner. In his least attractive guise the 'Billjim' was a boozing, unscrupulous bully whose greatest delight was duping and terrorising 'Gyppos' and making officers seem foolish. T.V. Brennan, editor of *The Cacolet* in 1918, noted how the very frequent repetition of this stereotype was making it a reality 'at the base, in details, or elsewhere'. He implied that many men felt obliged to adopt the self-image which 'well-intentioned historians' had allocated to the 'Billjim'. Brennan was anxious to stress the heroic qualities of tenacity, endurance, and determination which the 'Billjims' displayed in the desert of Sinai and the hills of Palestine, and also their generally impeccable behaviour towards the civilian population in general and women in particular. *The Cacolet* of June 1918 was very much a souvenir edition and it is possible that Brennan was endeavouring to reconstruct the image of 'Billjim' for the Australian public. The editors of *The Kia Ora Coo-ee* had a similar purpose in mind when they admitted that some items in the first series had been intended for the troops and were 'not quite suitable for Home readers of all classes'. What is particularly interesting about Brennan's article, however, is his clear belief in the power of field publications to modify behaviour. This may, perhaps, have satisfied Australian readers as an explanation for the persistence of 'Billjim', but it was a misrepresentation of both the purpose and the power of the soldiers' magazines.

The value of field publications lay in the bonding they encouraged and the sense of a shared destiny they developed. This could not be achieved by journals which consistently described a personage the majority of men failed to recognise. Brennan may not have liked the image of 'Billjim' in the soldiers' papers, but the regularity with which it appeared and the consistency of characterisation suggests that it was fairly close to the truth. It was, furthermore, an image which evolved from a great many written contributions. Brennan was concerned that the image of 'Billjim' was a misrepresentation, whereas, in fact, it was a partial representation. The unsavoury conduct associated with 'Billjim' was the behaviour of a soldier on leave in Cairo or Alexandria after months of demanding, dangerous activity which stretched resilience to the limit. It was the same behaviour displayed by the troops during their stay in Egypt before Gallipoli and in the months of garrison duty after the evacuation. The 'Billjim' was neither saint nor sinner. He was a remarkably effective fighting soldier, perhaps the best in General Allenby's armoury, capable of prolonged activity in difficult circumstances, generally uncomplaining and determined to enjoy himself when lucky enough to earn a respite from active duty. In the event, Brennan need not have worried overmuch about the image of 'Billjim'. The Australian soldiers in the Middle East were largely forgotten and, as a result, 'Billjim' failed to enter the language and consciousness of Australians in the manner of 'Anzac' and 'Digger'.

The Australians and New Zealanders serving in the Middle East were predominantly troops from the mounted divisions, and their concern for, and dependence upon, the animals which provided their mobility was constantly recorded in the field magazines. Horses were written about in a serious or sentimental vein and mules usually attracted a grudging admiration. Camels, however, seemed to merit only scorn even though the desert raids of the Camel Corps and the work of the Camel Field Ambulance were essential to the successful conquest of Sinai and southern Palestine. Many of the Australians in the Imperial Camel Corps had transferred from the Light Horse and the poor camel was always unfavourably compared with the trooper's usual mount.

Careful attention to the welfare of their horses underpinned the success of Australian mounted troops and showed through in their sentimental writing. Horses at water, Palestine, 1918. (*Australian War Memorial, Neg. no. B01507*)

The scene of some desperate fighting in the summer heat of 1918, the hills of Palestine tested men and animals to the limit. A Light Horse camp in the Jordan valley. (*Australian War Memorial, Neg. no. B00236*)

War Correspondent: "And could you inform me what happened hereabouts?"
Bill: "Aiwa! This is where Julius Cæsar was copped running a two-up school."

The War Correspondent with a striking resemblance to the Official Historian C.E.W. Bean has his leg pulled.
Kia Ora Coo-oee, December 1918. (*Author*)

You splaw-footed cow,
You humpty backed freak!
Listen here now,
You lop-sided streak!!!

With ticks on your hide,
As thick as the sand
And there to abide,
Till picked off by hand.

My back-bone is bent,
My pains are all hidden.
The Lord never meant
You to be ridden.

Splutter, spit at me,
And blow out your bags,
But let me go free,
And back to the nags.

The prejudice in favour of the horse was a recognition that the Walers used in the desert performed most remarkably. A fully equipped trooper carrying rations for his horse and himself might weigh anything between seventeen and twenty stone (119kg to 140kg), and yet on the dash to Damascus the horses covered not less than forty miles a day for ten days on end with limited food and rest. Prose and verse comment on the horses grew more appreciative and unashamedly sentimental as the campaign developed. In 1916, during the defensive phase, the horse was often seen as a nuisance requiring constant grooming and care, but by 1918 the truly amazing stamina and durability of the Walers was acknowledged. Not surprisingly perhaps, the items about horses in *The Kia Ora Coo-ee* in 1918 often paid tribute to the trooper's reliance on his mount and the sentimental attachment this created was the stimulus to some poignant writing.

A great many soldiers who served in the Middle East succumbed to bouts of dysentery, malaria, and other fevers; at least as many were hospitalised by these complaints as by war wounds. As a result, sickness, treatment and life in a military hospital were themes which featured quite prominently in the soldiers' magazines. The horrors of anti-malarial injections and the rigours of hospital diets were easy to laugh at, and anyone who had worn hospital 'blues' would have recognised the 'Sister-With-The-Bedmaking-Mania' and the 'Night-Sister-Who-Must-See-That-␣You're-Asleep' described by 'Tralas' in *The Kia Ora Coo-ee*.

Because the first task of the field magazines was to entertain, their principal content invariably consisted of humorous verse and prose covering the whole spectrum of life in the desert. Conspicuous by its virtual absence was material which dwelt on the causes of the war or which sought to bolster morale by jingoistic appeals to patriotism and imperial loyalty. While these themes were evidently considered appropriate to the troopship journals they met with little encouragement from the editors of field publications. In his 'Advice to Correspondents' section, the editor of *The Mirage* told a contributor that his poem 'Pro Patria Salutamus' was 'too sentimental' for the journal. So rare were protestations of attachment to Britain's cause that it seems likely that the field magazines were a barometer of sentiment which reflected a profound disillusion with the British high command after the disaster of Gallipoli. As the desert campaign proceeded with ever-increasing success, the later journals began to include articles which recorded the active service and war history of particular units. *The Palestine Prattle*, issued in March 1918, had as its first article a piece on 'The Birth and Life of the Third Troop, A.E.', and the second series of *The Kia Ora Coo-ee*, from July to December of the same year, had accounts of the Cameliers, Signallers, Flying Corps, Field Ambulance and other units. This development almost certainly reflects the realisation that many soldiers valued their magazines as souvenirs and sent them home to their loved ones.

Some of the publications which appeared in the later stages of the war contained articles which drew attention to the historical, archaeological, and Biblical significance of the land over which the troops were fighting. Charles Barrett was the editor of *The Cacolet* and *The Kia Ora Coo-ee* and he included a leavening of educational material in both. Whether this was primarily directed at the men in the field or at the readership in Australia is uncertain, but both magazines contained regular nature notes on the flora and fauna of Egypt and Palestine written by Barrett himself, and articles on the history and culture of the region by a variety of authors. Most notable among the latter were the pieces written by Mary McConaghy for *The Kia Ora Coo-ee* about the people of Palestine among whom she had worked as a missionary before the war. Her articles were unusual in their genuine affection for the people of the region, whereas most soldiers saw the Arab as a villainous cross between a beggar and a thief and referred to him in contemptuous and derogatory terms.

The trawl-net of mobilisation drew a cross-section of Australian society into the A.I.F., including a number of artists, journalists, authors, and men of some literary skill. In the Middle East, where circumstances favoured the production of field magazines, some of them emerged to give shape and direction to those publications. Oliver Hogue, 'Trooper Bluegum', was an enthusiastic contributor first to *The Mirage*, his own shortlived paper, then to *Barrak* and finally to *The Kia Ora Coo-ee*. Hogue, who had enlisted as a trooper in the 6th Light Horse and had spent five months on Gallipoli, was already building a literary reputation out of his wartime exploits. In 1916 he found a commercial publisher for his *Love Letters of an Anzac* and in the following year for *Trooper Bluegum at the Dardanelles*. After the evacuation he served in Sinai and Palestine, but still found time to write for the field journals and also produce a collection of verse published in 1918 as *Homesick Anzac* and sold to aid the Australian Red Cross. Hogue's two years with the Imperial Camel Corps provided the material for *The Cameliers* which he published soon after the war ended. Prolific and presumably popular though Hogue may have been, his verse and jingling ballads do not strike the modern reader as especially noteworthy, although his simple colloquial style was well suited to his subjects.

Charles Barrett, a journalist in Melbourne before the war, deployed his experience and talent in no fewer than three service magazines. He was a member of the Camel Brigade Field Ambulance and had organised *The Stretcher* for that unit before it left Australia in 1917. On arrival in Egypt it was revived as *The Cacolet*, a name derived from the basket-like stretchers the camels carried, again under his editorship. After three issues of that magazine, Barrett was transferred in 1918 to a full-time position with *The Kia Ora Coo-ee*, first as co-editor with 'Frank Reid', and then as sole editor. Barrett wrote a great deal for each of these journals, but his contributions were always essentially serious and informative. He had written two books about the Australian bush before the war and in both *The Cacaolet* and *The Kia Ora Coo-ee* his best articles dealt with the flora and fauna of the region. After the war he returned to his position as literary critic with the *Melbourne Herald*. He wrote nothing more about the war, although he published several volumes of literary criticism and many other books about Australia's landscape and history.

One of the most energetic contributors to *The Kia Ora Coo-ee* was Alexander Vindex Vennard. Using the nom de plume 'Frank Reid', Vennard had published material in *The Bulletin* before the war and had tried his hand at many forms of commercial writing. He had served at Gallipoli and in Sinai and Palestine before succumbing to malaria at Gaza in 1917. During this period he wrote several pieces for the *Egyptian Mail* and for the Camel Corps magazine. While convalescing at Moascar, Vennard conceived the idea of a general antipodean magazine in conversation with David Barker, whose illustrations had appeared in *The Anzac Book*. Their joint proposal took shape as *The Kia Ora Coo-ee* and Vennard was first editor, then co-editor with Barrett, and after four issues field editor. In that last role he scoured Palestine for copy, solicited contributions wherever he went, wrote pieces as 'Frank Reid' and 'Bill Bowyang', and supplied many unacknowleged items. After the war, his only publications were a book for children, a collection of bush recitations, and an account of his wartime experiences in *The Fighting Cameliers*.

Edwin Gerard was another who was able to combine his peacetime occupation with his military duty. A journalist, Gerard had some of his early war verse accepted by *The Bulletin*. In 1918 a collection of his poems was published as *The Road to Palestine and Other Verses* and a revised and expanded version, *Australian Light Horse Ballads and Rhymes*, appeared the following year. 'Gerardy' was a prolific contributor to *The Kia Ora Coo-ee*; in addition to the verse printed under his pen-name, he also wrote topical items under a variety of aliases. He was the only writer who attempted epic ballads with any degree of success; his skill lay in his ability to convey the narrative of an event with a 'firm clear imagery and swift rhythmical movement' well-suited to his tales of the mounted troops.

The Kia Ora Coo-ee also drew several contributions from A.B. ('Banjo') Paterson. While he was serving in Egypt as an officer in the Remount Service, Paterson wrote three poems and three short stories for the magazine. 'The Army Mules' is without doubt the most noteworthy of these pieces and it must be reckoned among his finest ballads; it has that simplicity and mastery of phrase and rhythm which is a feature of his best, mature work. The humour and irony in the ballad never dominates the eloquent tribute to the men of the Remount Service who broke and conditioned thousands of horses and mules at the Moascar and Heliopolis depots, men who risked their necks many times daily to prepare the animals on which the war in the Middle East depended. Paterson's willingness to write for this particular magazine is a measure of its literary standard and professionalism but it must be stressed that in this, as in all the field publications, the overwhelming majority of contributions were from men of no literary reputation or pretensions.

The 'Answers to Correspondents' and 'Candid Comments' columns where editors reviewed the contributions they received were a feature of most magazines. Through them the editors passed on advice, criticism, and encouragement. They are interesting for the light they shed on the problems of producing a magazine which would maintain some sort of literary standard, avoid excessive sentimentality or obscenity, and pass the censor. The Australian enthusiasm for versifying meant that all editors were regularly swamped with doggerel epics. The editors of *The Kia Ora Coo-ee* advised 'Harry Quail' to make the twenty verses of 'A Soldier's Life' into a book which could be usefully thrown at the enemy. These few lines may be indicative of much that was received and never published:

> I was always known as a slogger,
> The best in our town called Wagga;
> And when the war came
> I prats in my frame,
> And they gave me a new khaki clobber.
>
> The boys all gave me three cheers
> (I can hear them still in me ears).
> In me uniform so bright,
> I said, "I'm going to fight",
> And swallowed all their free beers. . . .

Regrettably, only the few stanzas printed in the 'Answers' columns as a warning to others have survived from what was undoubtedly a large body of material.

The large amount of verse published in all the service magazines suggests that poems and ballads with simple, regular rhythms were well appreciated by the troops. The enthusiasm for this verse form was, perhaps, a reflection of the literary taste of the countrymen who made up the bulk of the mounted divisions. The editor of *The Kia Ora Coo-ee* noted in October 1918 that for every piece of prose submitted there were at least two poems. Many soldiers who had grown up in the bush would have felt comfortable with the ballad style made popular by *The Bulletin*; many who tried to write lyrical verse only succeeded in producing doggerel, but many others showed that they could master the genre reasonably well. The published verse was generally lyrical and simple, it played directly on the emotion and experience of the reader. Although often unsophisticated, it is an important facet of Australian war literature for it has an immediacy, derived from the author's engagement with events, which is missing in most of the post-war reflections. Objectivity and detachment are noticeably absent from this material, as are introspective and intellectual qualities; humorous and sentimental, the verse in the soldiers' magazines was designed to raise a smile or a sigh from a weary trooper.

The editors of *The Kia Ora Coo-ee* were also fortunate to have the artistic talents of David Barker, Otho Hewett, G.W. Lambert and others to illustrate the magazine. Most field journals contained a few drawings or cartoons, but these were often very amateur compared with the rest of the production. Barker was the most active artist providing covers, marginal illustrations and many cartoons based on notes sent in by the troops. Some of his best illustrations, the 'Light Horseman' and 'Hospital Blues', later found a place in *The Palestine Book*, so that with his work on *The Anzac Book* he contributed to the two most famous compilations of the war. Hewett's ability had been noted by General Antill while he was at Gallipoli. Antill secured his transfer to the Anzac Divisional Headquarters as a panoramic artist and he continued in this capacity for the rest of the war, sketching every battlefield until the end of the Palestine campaign for the official war record. G.W. Lambert, the noted artist, was in the Middle East to make some preliminary sketches for the commemorative paintings commissioned by various Australian governments and while he was in Egypt the editors persuaded him to draw a fine cover for the June issue.

The war, and particularly the Gallipoli misadventure, helped to shape the Australians' image of themselves as the independent, resourceful and hardy inheritors of the pioneer tradition. The inappropriateness of this identity for most of the A.I.F., who came from urban and suburban backgrounds has often been stressed. For the men of the Light Horse, however, it was altogether more valid. It is not surprising that the Middle East field publications display all the legendary virtues and values of the bushman. H.S. Gullett in his volume of the official history of the war drew a portrait of the Light Horseman which, in the absence of other evidence, seemed to be an exaggerated lionisation of the Australian countryman. The significance of the soldiers' magazines is that they reveal a self-image which adds substance to the picture Gullett created.

The fighting over, there were opportunities for fun. Light Horsemen snowballing in the mountains of Lebanon.
(Australian War Memorial, Neg. no. B00840)

G.W. Lambert, the noted artist, was in Egypt to make sketches for paintings commissioned by Australian governments when he was persuaded to provide a cover. (*Author*)

CHAPTER FOUR
'WE'RE OFF TO THE SAND AND THE SIN TRA-LA'

GALLIPOLI

The Shortest Path to a Triumphant Peace
Mr. Churchill on the Dardanelles Campaign

The following is an extract from Mr. Winston Churchill's great speech to his constituents at Dundee on June 5th:-

"I have two things to say to you about the Dardanelles. First you must expect losses by land and sea; but the fleet you are employing there is your surplus fleet, after all other needs have been provided for. . . . military operations will also be costly, but those who suppose that Lord Kitchener (loud cheers) has embarked upon them without narrowly and carefully considering their requirements in relation to all other needs and in relation to the paramount need of our Army in France and Flanders–such people are mistaken and, not only mistaken, they are presumptuous. My second point is this. In looking at our losses squarely and soberly, you must not forget, at the same time, the prize for which we are contending. The Army of Sir Ian Hamilton, the Fleet of Admiral de Robeck, are separated only by a few miles from a victory such as this war has not yet seen. . . . The struggle will be heavy, the risks numerous, the losses cruel; but victory when it comes will make amends for all. . . . Through the narrows of the Dardanelles and across the ridges of the Gallipoli Peninsula lie some of the shortest paths to a triumphant peace."
Peninsular Press, 18 June 1915

The Heroes of Australasia
IMPRESSIVE SERVICE AT ST. PAUL'S
THE PRIMATE'S ADDRESS
The Archbishop of Canterbury, who took for his text St. John xv. 13, "Greater love hath no man than this, that a man lay down his life for his friends", said in the course of his sermon:-

We are met here tonight for a definite and a very sacred purpose. Here at the centre and hub of the Empire's life we desire to thank God together for the splendid devotion of our brothers from Australia and New Zealand and who in the cause whereunto we, as a people, have set our hand regarded not their lives unto the death. . . . They were manly sons of the greatest Empire in the world. They were brave and buoyant with plenty of the faults and failures which go so often with high spirit They need, as we shall need, forgiveness and cleansing and new opportunity, and they are in their Father's keeping and He knows and cares. . . . The feat of arms which was achieved on the rocky beach and the scrub-grown cliffs of the Gallipoli Peninsula in the grey dawn of St. Mark's Day, April 25, was a feat we are assured has never been outshone, has scarcely ever been rivalled in military annals. . . . And who did it? It was not the product of the long discipline of some veteran corps of soldiers. It was mainly the achievement of men from the sheep-stations in the Australian bush or from the fields and townships of New Zealand, who a few short months ago had no dream of warfare as they went about their ordinary work. But the call rang out and the response was ready, and the result is before us all. . . .

The service was simple, but with the simplicity of grandeur. It was the expression of deep and common feeling. The brave men whom it commemorated had come from far off to die, far off from both home and from this central point of the Empire for whose idea and purpose they have given their lives; and last night St. Paul's Cathedral seemed to speak with the single voice of the Empire in love and honour of its heroic children.
Peninsular Press, n.d., 1915

ANZAC! ANZAC!! ANZAC!!!
THE GREAT STICKFAST!

Liman von Sanders writes:-
"Its glutinous powers exceeded all my expectations."
Enver Pasha writes:-
"The bottle you sent me suffices all my needs. I do *not* want any more. I find a little goes a long way."

NO ARMY SHOULD BE WITHOUT IT

Try it To-day.
ANZAC!   ANZAC!

The Dardanelles Driveller, 17 May 1915

The Troopers' Lament
(Note. Where dashes are encountered in the following verses readers may substitute such words as 'blooming', 'bally', etc. or any suitable adjective of two syllables according to taste. Author)
I come from good old Weup-Weup, and me monicker's Gus Headers,
An' I joined the 4th Light - - 'orse at Broad - - meadows.
I brings along me old prad, and shoves the claim in 'ot,
But th' - - vet 'e crools me pitch, an' 'arf was all I got.
I gathers in th' - - cash and gets off on the spree,
An' the C.O. ups and passes me a week's C - - B.
CORSTRUTH!!
Then off we goes to Egypt, and in the - - sand,
I does a fortnights doublin' with a rifle in me 'and.
An' then we took our - - prads an' stuffed them well with tibbin
(Which sorter calms them down a lot and stops their - - jibbin).
An' round about the Pyramids, the desert an' the Sphinx,
We does a five month stunt amongst the flies and - - stinks,
But when we all gets pretty 'ot and fit to take the track,
They hikes me off me 'orse an' makes me 'ump a - - pack.
CRISE!!
Next thing I finds meself a dodgin' shrapnel in the trenches
Where a bloke can 'ardly turn around for periscopes an' stenches.
'Owever, its all in th' game a soldier's got to play,
An' I'd rather be out here than - - Egypt any day.
But let me feel just once more me old prad shy an' reef,
An' you can have me biscuit and me tin of bully beef.
MY - - OATH!!

The Bran Mash, June 1915

Stretcher-bearers descending 'Bridges' Road', Gallipoli, having recovered men buried by a shell. One carries a towel, probably intending to bathe at the beach before returning to duty. (*Australian War Memorial, Neg. no. C01761*)

Fighting at Gallipoli was conducted at close quarters. Men of the 18th Battalion at Steele's Post, December 1915; the front trench was about ten metres from the crest. (*Australian War memorial, Neg no. A00769*)

Ode to Tenedos
O Tenedos, thy peaceful island green
A stirring passage in the fight has seen;
Eight generals and half-a-hundred men
First packed their kit, and then unpacked again.
The Dardanelles Driveller, 17 May 1915

NOTABLE DEED
A very brave deed has been brought under our notice. 'Dad' Crawley, while regulating traffic at the 'Wine Café', was struck by shrapnel in the leg. Although the bullet was 'imbedded in the flesh', he bravely stuck at his post (by the bung hole). Such deeds as these are the ones that make the Empire famous. We are pleased to hear he has been recommended for the W.S.M. (Wine Swillers Medal).
First Aid Post, 16 June 1915

THINGS WE WANT TO KNOW

Why does Pte. Armstrong go 'acidy' when he receives the paper called *Joyful News*?
Why Scotty Robertson speaks with his mouth full?
Has 'Muldoon' got a 'little girl' at home?
Why 'Feather' turns snaky when the orderly 'Sergeant' tells him to do the washing?
Why Somerton does a 'growl and grunts' when Sergt. Eddie calls him?
Why Scotty Ewen never asks a Turk to play him at 'draughts'?

During the last week a fine 'latrine' was excavated by our pioneer squad on the beach in close proximity to our corps. It was fitted with every comfort and overlooked the sea. On the opening day it was patronised by everybody whether they required or not; in fact it was like a park seat. Great was the consternation on the second morning to find that someone had pinched the seat. The crowd gave vent to their feelings in true Australian fashion on making the discovery. It was well watched during the night as several were heard to say that "they had slept on it".

(Sung to the tune of 'Cock Robin')
Who 'pinched' the seat?
I, said Dick Howard,
For I am no Coward;
I pinched the seat.

Who helped him take it?
I, said 'Dad Cawley'.
In the morning early
I helped him take it.

Chorus -   And the boys of the corps
           Fell a sighing and a sobbing
           When they saw what had been done
           By Dick Howard robbing.

First Aid Post, 4 August 1915

'Abdul Mohammed' of artillery fame
Has earned this corps' respect;
His shooting is good in all but aim.
From a Turk, what would you expect?

At trawlers and cutters he is always at sea,
Though his range very often is grand;
But on shore his shrapnel will always do me.
As for cheek—well, he beats the band.

Who gives us all a sleepless night
With his blooming infernal skite,
Brings us joy which turns to fright?
Why, don't you know?—'The Furphyite'.

If we could catch the Furphyite,
The mob would end his silly skite;
His death would be so expedite
That peace would reign and all be quiet.

First Aid Post, 11 August 1915

War News

Australian rush to surrender.
(Cable from Gumtree Gully)
A German aeroplane passed over Anzac yesterday & distributed a lot of leaflets advising the Australian troops 'not to hesitate any longer but come in and surrender'. [This is the first bit of true news *The Dinkum Oil* has published and we thoroughly expect it will be the last.] We have received the following urgent cables from our correspondents:-

Quinns Post. 2 a.m. Scramble of Australians out of trenches to get into Turkish lines is so great that parapets completely broken down. Scene reminded on-lookers of memorable rush on canteen in 1902.

Quinns Post. 2.5 a.m. Dreadful mistake has occurred. Turks did not realise that Australians were coming to surrender and accordingly made a tactical adjustment of their firing lines and our men found trenches empty. Thousands of Australians are now wandering about disconsolately looking for some Turk to surrender to.

Later. Found one German officer asleep in trench. After having finished remaining beer bottle for him the Australians awakened him and nearly smothered him with kisses.

Melbourne. 11 a.m. All recruiting has been stopped.

Sydney. 3 a.m. The State Parliament has passed a vote a thanks to the Germans for the great compliment they have paid our people.

Courteneys Post. 11 p.m. The German proclamation to Australians states; 'Come in and surrender your honour is safe'. The men on this post are immensely relieved. The Australians have been looking about for somebody to entrust their honour to, & Germans are exactly the people they would choose. Germans are good judges of Australian honour.

The Dinkum Oil, 26 June 1915

Situations Vacant

Wanted—man with active imagination to supply furphies to the Beach, where the supply is running short. Average day's supply needed is about 160 lies.

Full private requires fatigue party to carry a pair of boots which has recently been issued to him.

Non Com wants active man to shoo flies while he has 40 winks in the Afternoon.

Serial Story
Chapter VII

"Love me and the world is yours", cooed Sir Jasper into Muriel's shell-like ear. But Muriel was an old soldier and knew better. Still she was a woman. "Oh this is so sudden", she murmured through her clenched teeth. "Give me time". N.B. She wanted to give Reginald, who was doing mess orderly in the trenches, the time to send another field service postcard. Then she (to be continued) . . .

The Dinkum Oil, 2 July 1915

ADVICE TO CORRESPONDENTS

Since gratitude is defined as a lovely sense of favours to come, we desire to express our gratitude to those literary Light Horsemen, who intend to send along articles for publication in subsequent issues. The more the merrier. *The Mirage* can only be a reflex of the ideals and ideas of the Details if the men of the Regiments come forward and give expression to their longings.

Moascar Camp near Cairo. (*Author*)

We don't want any inarticulate Shakespears or mute inglorious Miltons. They might afford inspiration for an elegy but they won't provide copy for *The Mirage*.

The Mirage, June 1916

Space alone has prevented us using more of the contributions so kindly sent in—space and the law of self-preservation.

Heaven and the activities of the energetic 'Jacko' alone know when the next number will appear, so contributors should send in their masterpieces as soon as possible, thereby assuring themselves a place in the sun—or the Summer Number...

The amount of verse—and worse—in this issue we can only attribute to the Spring weather we are having...

Barrak, July 1917

This paper invites soldiers... to contribute... any items of interest of which they may be possessed. Said items may be either true or invented, and as humorous as possible. We have no time for sentimental gush, but there's a hearty welcome at this office for copy with a laugh in every line...

The Kia Ora Coo-ee, March 1918

Poets are born in the Desert; many a man who never wrote a couplet before he donned khaki, is now chasing rhymes o'nights by the dim light of a candle in his bivvy.... A strong current of sentiment flows through much of this soldier verse; but much of it is humorous. Many aspiring young bards are careless of technique... But the fact remains, that hundreds of Anzacs are beating out rhymes in spare time, and many of them never gave poetry a thought before they became soldiers.

The Kia Ora Coo-ee, October 1918

EGYPT: CAMP AND CAIRO

"How does I like Egypt?" barked back a Tel-el-Kebirian of about nine months residency, "How does I like Egypt?" repeated he from the land of the evergreen gum, in answer to the question asked by a big red haired barbarian of the same land. "Blime the more I see of the cussed sand, heated up by old Sol the more I pities Moses and the Israelites". "But" answered Ginger, "the nights are bosker". "Oh yes" answered the weary one taking the pipe from his mouth, "Just as well there's something bosker about it or a cove 'ud go balmy; you reads of the romance and mystery of Egypt in these 'ere stories and novels. about the Finx and the Pyramids, and how they longs to get back to 'em, and the droring powers Egypt has for 'em. Strike me, they can have it for my part; wonder how they'd get on spending the summer in a bell tent in the middle of the Delta".

The Kookaburra, July 1916

On the end of the plain where the desert sands glare,
Our tents are aflap in the dust smothered air,
And the distant mirage spreads in shimmering streams,
That we never may reach like a river of dreams.
And the arch of the sky where the desert hawks wheel,
Is as hard and as blue as the polish of steel.
But in spite of the dust and the desert immense,
We made it a home when we put up our tents....

The Mirage, No. 2, June 1916

I wonder if in days to come,
When strife shall cease and guns be dumb,
And they pay me all my money,
I shall shed a tear as I wave my hand
To the fading shores of the Promised Land,
The land of milk and honey?

Shall I regret the M and V,
The sand for dinner, the sand for tea,
The ration of frozen bunny;
And all the hundred and one fatigues,
When I sit me down a thousand leagues
From the land of milk and honey?... W.C.M.

Barrak, November 1917

Weather Notices
Abbasia–Mostly hot–in places 'very dry'.
Heliopolis–'Beermeter' rising. Cloudy and uncertain.
Luna Park–'Barmy', Thursdays and Sundays.
Cairo–Red hot everywhere.

Condensed milk was a great luxury. This carefully staged photograph shows why Australian troops appeared rough and unmilitary to British eyes. (*Author*)

This happy-looking fatigues detail appears to have posed for this photograph. (*Author*)

Gezireh–Hotter.
Ezbekieh–Too hot.

The Lake of Palms
Its waters are so bitter that if only a few drops pass the lips one thirsts for an hour, but it is pleasant to plunge into the lake, blue and sparkling in the sunshine, to swim amid sleepy little fishes, and watch the ripples die along the shore. . . . The way from camp to the lake passes across hot, shifting sands on to a hard, white road beside the sweet water canal. Good marching for half a mile; then over London Bridge into clinging sand again, and down a dusty by-way, walled on one side, and on the other cool green plots of maize and water melons. . . . The dressing place is on the southern shore, in a grove of palms whose branches sway in the wind like green ostrich plumes. Australians are happy here, for gumtrees grow amid the palms and on the hot air floats the fragrance of the Australian Bush.

Always when we went swimming, natives flocked to the lake side, vendors of fruit and other wares carried in baskets and wicker crates. The palm grove and the beach became a market. Hot and thirsty, we were tempted to buy at fancy prices, and lightened our money belts. It was worthwhile being fleeced just to study the cunning and cupidity of the children of Egypt, who love piastres as King Midas loved gold. . . . After the swim it was pleasant to rest on the sand and watch the passing show, camels and donkeys and natives, toiling along the beach. Coal black Nubians, veiled women, hook-nosed Copts, young Arabs and bearded patriarchs went by, clad in robes of glowing colour, purple, orange, crimson, and blue: figures from the Arabian Nights, an Oriental Pageant on the shores of the Lake of Palms. '*Ibis*'
The Cacolet, September 1917

Ode to Polish
Cobbers of Australia, blokes and coves and coots,
Get a b---- y move on, rub your b---- y boots.
Polish up your bandolier, give your spurs a shine,
That's the way to drive the Turks out of Palestine.

Hup, yer crimson crawlers, where's your Brasso tin?
Polish for the ruddy Turk, go and rub it in.
You'll never get to Turkey where the Harems are,

If your stirrups are not like a gory star.

Then make a victory of it, spit and shine and rub;
You can't develop water looking like a grub.
Heave yer lumping carcasses, drop your b---- y sloth.
That's the way to win the war—MY COLONIAL OATH !!
Palestine Prattle, March 1918

A highly successful concert was given on the thirty-first of April last at the Town Hall, El Sha'uth, by the Brigade Field Troop, assisted by such local talent as was available and out of jail.
 . . . We must mention Lieut. B. Rooke's monologue 'Belah by Bomblight', so vividly rendered that one could almost see the white figures of the pajama-clad staff tripping lightly over the tent-ropes on their swift course to the dugouts, and hear the rush of gallant Anzacs dashing to save the beer in the shattered canteen.
 . . . Other items which claimed popular support were:- 'I'm afraid to go home in the dark', Lieut. Rowan; 'Why do they call me Archibald?', Sergt. A. Jayem; 'Far, far away', Concerted item, A.A. Guncrew . . . and 'I may be among the missing, Mother, but never among the slain', Lieut. O'Bee.
The proceedings terminated in the usual way, but fortunately no one was injured in the rush and the supply did not run out.
Barrak, July 1917

It's a long time to wait till Friday
It's a long way to go.
It's a long while to wait till Friday
When we all get our 'dough'.
Good-bye, Camp de Caesar,
Farewell Picture show
It's a long long while to wait till pay-day
So we must go slow.
The Anzac Records Gazette, November 1915

Sunburned troopers take a dip in the Sweet Water Canal. (*Author*)

The men of the A.I.F. were tourists as well as soldiers. Members of B Squadron 8th ALH on top of a pyramid. (*Australian War Memorial, Neg. no. H03071*)

Why did I come a soldiering?
For love of fun they say,
But how can you get fun, boys,
On the glorious 'bob' a day.

It would not be so bad boys,
If only the 'Heads' would pay,
So that we could get it regular,
That glorious 'bob' a day.

The Kookaburra, July 1916

Cameliers Lament
When we lob in from the Desert with a thirst that's worth a crown,
Heavy laden with piastres, and the mood to paint the town,
Having left our smelful camels somewhere East of El Arish,
Then the world is full of sunshine, and we've just one little wish,
For feathers and leggings and spurs,
Feathers and leggings and spurs.

On the desert we're 'Camels'; we're rough, rude and coarse men,
But when up on leave, we're once more 'Light Horsemen'
With feathers and leggings and spurs.

We mooch up to the Kit Store, Abbasia, like a thief,
Like a sneaking, crawling Gyppi who has pinched some bully beef.
Shorts and puttees are discarded and we don our breeks again,
We fling away our Jamboks and we swish a little cane.
Oh feathers and leggings and spurs,
Feathers and leggings and spurs.

Out east with the 'Hooshters' we're rough, rude and coarse men,
But round about Cairo we're 'Pukha Light Horsemen',
With feathers and leggings and spurs,
Feathers and leggings and spurs.

Our boots are brightly polished, like the old-time Kiwi Lancers,
We join the gentle Soiree and we mingle with the dancers,
Till a maiden gently 'sniffing' knocks us all into a lump,
By disdainfully exclaiming, 'Camels do give me the hump'.
Tho' plumed and booted and spurred,
Plumed and booted and spurred.

Once you join Camels you're smelful and coarse men:
Goodbye to the swank of the Kiwi light Horsemen,
All plumed and booted and spurred.   *'Trooper Bluegum'*.

Barrak, September 1917

A Night in Cairo
Leave pass in my pocket and cane tucked under my arm, I strode jauntily from the lines to spend my maiden night in Cairo....

"Donkey, Corporal? Very good". I paid two piastres, jogged away to the tram track and into a maelstrom of Arab bootblacks. "Me very good boy, no fader no modder". A babel of cries arose. A cunning imp collared one foot and I let him make mirrors out of my boots; charge one piastre. Then Ali touched my belt, scowled at the buckle and protested against 'an officer' displaying dim brass in Cairo. I yielded like a lamb, and Ali mouthed another coin.

Three minutes later I was aboard the Heliopolis tram, on the way to Cairo. A cheap ride at seven milliemes. Alighting in Opera Square, I stood for a while bewildered. Then came the cane seller, the donkey boy, the vendor of lemon squash, all the motley crew that pluck the tourist pigeon. Hassan, an Arab boy, came to the rescue, and for a few piastres, accepted office as guide and friend.

Piloted to the Anzac Hostel, I mopped my brow, and ate ice cream in an atmosphere of khaki. Good O, the Anzac!–but it was 19.00 by my watch and I hadn't seen all of Cairo yet: so I flicked the ash from a piastre cigar, stepped into a gharry, and cried to the driver, "Esbekia Gardens". "Yes Sir. Ten piastres, gibbit money", was the suave response. "Pay when I get there" quoth I; but that gharry man was obdurate and would not start his horse until he got his fare.... Tea at the Y.M.C.A., then out to the bustling streets again. I dived into the Mouski, where guides battened upon me and importunate shopkeepers clutched at my arm. They were the spiders and I was the fly. I was caught in a silken web, but escaped at the cost of 100 piastres, with a parcel for Helen at home.... A gharry drive to the Nile, where it flows beneath the lion-guarded bridge, I went down a flight of steps to the river side and was instantly beseiged by boatmen. "I am the man, Sir, I show you everything". The old refrain. The tide or feloos was ebbing fast, but after all, twelve piastres is not much for a trip on the old River Nile; besides the moonlight was thrown in baksheesh.

It sharpened one's appetite, that felucca voyage. I dined at the St. James' where my one little stripe was dimmed by many stars. Gharry to Camp–shower, sleep, and the end of my night in Cairo.

'Lance Corporal'
The Cacolet, September 1917

Nobody, except those who were sick, broke, or orderly officer, ever dined in Mess. The flood tide poured into Cairo about 6 o'clock; the ebb set in between eleven and twelve, being usually terminated by one blithe spirit who stepped quietly from his gharri into morning parade at 0600.

A.P.Ms. were unknown in those days and a semblance of order was maintained by piquets–'a certain liveliness' pervading the thoroughfares which is now lacking.

For instance, on engaging a gharri it was considered a graceful act to offer the senior officer present the ribbons, the protests of the 'arbuggi' seldom receiving the attention to which they were entitled. Challenges from rival gharries never fell on deaf ears, and provided quite a lot of excitement for the local pedestrians.

Barrak, November 1917

"Gibbit baksheesh", cried the voice of one on the wilderness of wharf when we landed. This was our greeting from Egypt and be like, it will be our farewell. We were scarcely ashore when the siege on our money belts began, and it has not yet been raised. The demands for baksheesh were incessant.... Money is not the only object of those who cry for baksheesh. The begging Arab seeks your belt and your shirt, your hat and your pipe–in fact nothing is immune from the curse of baksheesh. With smile and salaam, a Gyppo hails you, calls you his "cobber", and wins his "baksheesh".... It is in vain to cry, "mafeesh feloos"; the beggar knows better, and his importunity ceases not till you curse, or fling a piastre.... In city, town and village, wherever you travel, you are asked for "baksheesh". Boot-black, Pyramids' guide, gharry driver, all the soldier tourists' friendly foes, demand "baksheesh". At first it is flattering, the droned assurance, "Australia verree good, plenty monee", but the gilt wears off, and your heart becomes hard as the wail of a mosque.

Baksheesh! In the name of the Prophet who coined the vile word. Baksheesh! It dogs one's ears from

Suez to Cairo, and out into the Desert beyond; it sounds like a knell in our dreams, and when we awaken we hear the moan for baksheesh.

The Cacolet, September 1917

Contentment
This is alright. Let us be satisfied,
Nor fret our hearts with longing after leave –
To Cairo or,
Dirty old Port Said;
To kiss old Daphne's lips.
Or see our Eve.
This is alright!

This is alright–old bully beef and biscuits.
Cairo can keep her macaroons, rat–
Ifias, and little pink ice cakes–I'd jis–
Or rarver have our canteen beer–and that–
This is alright!

This is alright—too many red-tabs –
I find in Cairo –
And military poleased,
So that I feel I look a dreadful fright,
The only tab-less—only hair ungreased.
This is alright.   *'Soft and Hard'*
14th Company Magazine, June 1918

CAMELS AND CAMELIERS

"You'll learn to love him", I was told, when introduced to my camel. I confess, I was dubious. At any rate, 'Abdul' showed no affection for me. I stroked his head and purred "good old fellow", whereat 'Abdul' opened his long, loose lips, unmasking an alarming dental battery, and growled like a hungry lion. His eyes looked wicked, too, and when he swung his ugly head towards me, I skipped away politely,—not afraid, certainly not, but I am a stickler for etiquette, and when a camel snarls, it is correct form to remain at a respectful distance.

"Barrak him", cried a Sergeant . . . "Barrak him, can't you!" was snapped at me again. Then the Sergeant softened and showed how the deed should be done. 'Tis thus. First you catch your camel; then, standing below the jaws, pull downward and make a noise like a sick hyena coughing. This means, for the camel, "down on your knees"; and, if so disposed, down the camel goes, front legs first. If you desire your dromedary to rise, you make another queer noise, "tschick, tschick, tschick", rapidly, and he reverses the 'down' process, bringing the hind legs up first.

Well, I barraked my camel, and, with assistance, put riding halter and saddle on him. Of course, he remonstrated, and I kept the tail of an eye on his head all the time. More than once, he tried to test his teeth in my flesh, but failed. I was feeling pretty good on the job, when something happened which caused all my confidence to ooze away. 'Abdul' shot from his mouth a blood-stained skin bubble, big as a toy balloon. It was fearsome, but the Sergeant explained, and I steadied up some.

Mounting was a maelstrom. Following directions, I kept the head-chain tight placed my right hand on the rear pommel of the saddle and my left foot on 'Abdul's' neck. Then I tried to swing lightly and quickly into the saddle, but somehow I failed to get there. 'Abdul' arose, like a wave of the sea, and I did a catherinewheel stunt . . .

I was not beaten, however, and at length persuaded 'Abdul' that I was to be his rider. In the saddle, legs crossed on the apron, I seemed to be very near the sky. But it was all serene till 'Abdul' got into his stride. Things hummed then. I bumped and swayed and tossed till my bones ached. There was worse to come. 'Abdul' reckoned I was too much of a burden, and, lacking manners, he showed his opinion plainly. He bucked worse than a maknoon mule, and when I dismounted in a manner contrary to Army regulations, he surveyed me with a reflective eye.

I didn't learn to love 'Abdul' that morning. Time has passed, however, and my camel and I are now on good terms. Still, 'Abdul' is a wilful beast, and if I didn't humour him occasionally it would be "Goodnight nurse" for one of us, and that one wouldn't be 'Abdul'. . . .   *'Apron'*

The Cacolet, September 1917

(Australian War Memorial Printed Records)

On Trek
Lucky my girl can't see me now, as I take my place in the line,
With three days' whiskers on my face, and a thirst that's quite divine:
With all my goods around me, like a second-hand broker's shop,
A lazy lump of a brute beneath, and a lazier man on top.
No, we ain't been into the battle, on the blooming Gaza front
But carrying out a specimen of a typical Camel stunt:
Busting up rails at Auja–and 'twas worth the loss of sleep
To see those railway arches come down in a tangled heap.
Marching all night and sleeping (if you're lucky) during the day:
A long trek over the sandhills–with a guide to show you the way –
And longer still if he doesn't–till you've lost all feel in your back
And an hour's halt for a bite of food in a damn cold bivouac.
All you need is a sandstorm, to keep your eyelids shut,
A camel that either falls behind, or falls in a blasted rut,
A pack that won't stay packed at all, and a saddle that rubs you sore –
And then you can boast in your letters that you're glad you joined the Corps.
                                                                        '*Cpl. Cuss*'

Daily Routine
Extracted from First Battalion Orders by the aid of a corkscrew–found locally.
0500–Inspection of camel bladders.
0600–Bubbling drill.
0630–Route march—speed limit, 26 miles per hour.
0700–BREKKAH
0900–Hump polishing—tooth picking—breath classing.
0930–Barraking by numbers—Language drill for N.C.Os.
1000–Roaring, Grunting and Growling parade.
1200–Tibben Tiffen.
1500–Tick drill by the clock—ticks smaller than a twenty piastre piece exempt
      from incineration.
1600–Rutting exercise, tails unslung, - cow camels optional.
1630–Gas drill with 'Leonard' pattern helmets. Camels with 40 H.P. breath
      exempt.
1645–Dhurra sifting and grain counting.
NOTICE–The practice of misappropriating 'Dressing, Mange, Overproof' in
lieu of 'Oil, Hair, All Ranks, for the use of' must cease.

Demolitions
Where the Turco-Gypie frontier swings down South towards Akaba,
Where there ain't no Ten Commandments, and there ain't no motor car,
Where the Camel Column straggles like a league-long desert snake,
There's a weeping Beduin Maiden, and she cries: "For Allah's sake
Don't come back to Abiad,
Oh the shocking time we had,

Although generally detested, the camels brought a note of romance into the desert war. Australians of the Imperial Camel Corps Brigade. (*Australian War Memorial, Neg. no. B01627*)

The Lighthorsemen had a dismissive attitude to camels. *Kia Ora Coo-ee*, March 1918. (*Author*)

The Camels are coming, they are, they are.

When your wild-eyed Camel sodjers smashed our railway awful bad.
On the road down Abiad,
Poor old Enver Pasha's mad,
And at dawn he swears like thunder from Asluj to Abiad".

'Er petticoat—she 'ad none, and 'er dress was chocolat' tint,
We never knew 'er proper: she was just a Beduin bint,
But she missed 'er baa baa lambie when the Anzacs hurried by,
And all the long night marches we could hear her plaintive cry:
"Don't come back to Abiad,
For the Turks are ragin' mad,
And tho' my lamb tastes better than the bully beef you've had,
Don't come back to Abiad,
Now you've gone I'm mighty glad,
For you rather wrecked El-Auja when you trekked down Abiad".

Ship me somewhere West of Suez, where a bloke can get a sleep;
Where there ain't no blank Fray Bentos, and yer needn't pinch a sheep;
For my camel's getting dopey and I cannot keep awake;
My bleary eyes are closing, and I pray "For Heaven's sake,
Don't go back to Abiad,
For I need a snooze so bad;
Men are falling off their camels with a bump that sends them mad;
On the road to Abiad.
Oh my humpy, grumpy prad,
You have brought me scathless sleeping, from the Wadi Abiad".

'Trooper Bluegum'
Barrak, July 1917

Ambulance Work in the Desert
Cacolets are used for carrying patients on Camels. They are of two kinds. The 'sitting-up' Cacolet consists mainly of two chairs, slung one on each side of the Camel. The 'lying-down' Cacolet takes the form of two stretchers, resembling lounge chairs. These devices do not give patients a smooth ride, and are used only when no other method of conveyance is available. All the medical and other equipment of the Ambulance is carried on baggage camels, instead of in transport wagons.   *Lieut. Col. G.D. Croll*
The Cacolet, September 1917

Some Camel Corps fellows invented a new game during the big stunt, when tobacco was as scarce as generosity is among Quartermasters. I call it a game, but it was played mighty seriously. Six chaps sat in a circle and one produced a cigarette, took a couple of draws, and passed it onto his neighbour. And so it went round the circle till only a tiny butt remained. These butts were carefully preserved, and from them other cigarettes were made. Not a shred of tobacco was wasted. I joined a smoking circle myself and it was Good O.   *'Cedric'*
The Kia Ora Coo-ee, May 1918

THE KOOKABURRA

DINKUM OIL EDITION

FIRST DIVISIONAL BASE DEPOT

TEL-EL-KEBIR.

26. 7. 16

(Australian War Memorial Printed Records)

Call Me A Camelero
Give me a sea of raw, red, rum,
And a ship of the desert to sail it,
And a trek, if you will, to Kingdom come,
With a flag right there to nail it –
In an old felt hat, with a five days pack,
And a pass any side of zero,
O'er a mud-swamped plain, or a mountain track,
Then call me a Camelero.

Give me a badge of the 'Rising Sun'
And a place in the sun to win it,
And a full band'lier and a handy gun,
And a fight for the fun that's in it,
And a cobber true, when there's cobbers few,
Whether 'Tourist', 'Dinkum', or 'Cheero',
And a boss in a push, who'll pull things through –
Then call me a Camelero.

Give me a place in a wet canteen,
With a two-up school beside it,
When things are slack in the 'in-between',
And the hump's too poor to ride it,
And a trip to town where the girls are chic,
And the P-M's not a Nero.
And a 'broke' return, with a head—well—thick,
Then call me a Camelero.

But,-
When the war is o'er and done,
And we're all bound for Australia,
You can take back your prad and your handy gun
And a new bloke then I'll hail you –
With a Light Horse plume and a pair of spurs,
A dinkum returning hero;
Though then if you value your lives, good sirs,
Don't call me a Camelero.   'NANNEBR'
                        The Cacolet, June 1918

HORSES AND HORSEMEN

The Song of the Stable
Groom, - groom, - groom, - groom, - as long as yer able,
That, - that, - that, - that's the song of the stable.
Flies, - flies, - flies, -flies, - torment yer all the time,
But–to–stop–for–one moment is a crime.
Rake, - rake, - rake, - rake, - manure off the sand,
That's–what–we–do–for months, - it is simply grand.
Shove, - shove, - shove, - shove, - the stuff up into bags,
Do–yer–wonder–that every moment drags?
Lift, - lift, - lift, - lift, - the bags into a cart,
Yes, - yes, - yes, - yes, - enough to break yer 'eart.
Smooth, - smooth, - smooth, -smooth, - the sand out with great pain,
Jist–for—yer moke–to mess it up again:
Feed, - feed, -feed, - feed, - they always want to eat,
You–must–feed–up–though you are dead beat!
Thus, - thus, -thus, -thus, - yer go on through the war,
Yes, - by gad, - it's–enough to make yer roar.
Days–weeks–months–years–we'll always do the same,
Spend–our–lives–at–it–an' die at the game. . . .   *Felix*
                           The Desert Dustbin, 14 June 1916

... The 3rd L.H.F.A. came back to camp
At Heliopolis, and there rejoined
Their mates, who through the Summer's heat had watched
With care over the horses, and had sent as well
A party to Matruh. For several weeks
The corps was rested–reinforced, reformed,
And brought once more back to its old time strength.
The Light Horse, too, were strengthened and reformed,
For every man a horse, - the Bushman's pride,
And mounted thereupon in full array
They moved unmatched–Australia's finest sons.
   Once mounted and equipped it was not long
Ere all were sent from Cairo to defend
The silvery Canal, which, mile on mile,
Runs through the land from Suez to Port Said.
Inland, along its length, the Light Horse pitched
Their camps, and from that time to this, they watch
With vigilance unmatched, both night and day
The World's famed waterway, - the East's strong Gate,
And Britain's pride–freedom of trade at sea!
   The 3rd L.H.F.A. encamped at first
Among the trees, close by the water's edge.
And here they watched the great ships passing bye
Stately and slow, on passage to and fro.
But soon they left this sheltered spot and moved
Further afield, pitching once more their tents
Upon the desert sand–eastward–in hostile land.
Here many weary weeks were slowly passed
Midst flies, and sand and heat; - and many sick
Were rested, fed and tended with skilled care.
Trips too, there were, (Called by the Light Horse 'stunts'),
Against the Turkish foe, at places named
Jif-Jaffa and Muksheebe ...   *Felix, The Desert Dustbin*, 28 June 1916

The Army Mules
For if you go where the Depots are as the dawn is breaking grey,
By the waning light of the morning star as the dust cloud clears away,
You'll see a vision among the dust like a man and a mule combined–
It's the kind of thing you must take on trust for its outlines aren't defined,
A thing that whirls like a spinning top and props like a three legged stool,
And you find it's a long-legged Queensland boy convincing an Army mule.
And the rider sticks to the hybrid's hide like paper sticks to a wall,
For a 'magnoon' Waler is next to ride with every chance of a fall,
It's a rough-house game and a thankless game, and it isn't a game for a fool,
For an army's fate and a nation's fame may turn on an army mule. ...
                                                         A.B. Paterson
                                        The Kia Ora Coo-ee, March 1918

Troopers Overell and Stewart of the Remount Unit dressed for work. (*Author*)

Many of the remounts sent to Egypt were half-broken station horses. (*Author*)

Pal O'Mine
I chose you not for symmetry of form, beauty or well bred looks (you had none of these), but for the brand you bore, KY under bar KY, sure in the knowledge that you would carry me well, you desert-bred son of a desert-bred dam. Light you made of the endless miles of loose sand and the whaleback dunes of Sinai, for there are wide areas of 'sand' country in that north west corner of New South Wales whence you came. But what of the shade and perfume of golden-blossomed mulga, the silver-leaved boree and pungent-scented Gnelia? What of the tree-fringed lakes, blue as the summer sky, that came into view when you raced to the top of some pine-capped sandhill, and stood at gaze, your mane and tail flowing in the wind? Was it in search of these that, with ears pricked, you eagerly topped those dunes of Sinai? And was it of regret, that sigh which vibrated your velvet nostrils when you saw only the burning sand? I believe so.

Were the journey never so long, and the food and water never so short, you would still carry me 'on the bib'; distance, drought and days between drinks were your heritage. On lonely patrol or nerve-trying night screen you were company and ears and eyes to me–aye, and shield to me too. . . .

To the sound of grimmer plaudits than were wont to greet your forefathers, your last race was run, and the goal was reached, Pal O'Mine. Your exile was worth the while for that glorious charge on Beersheba. With foam-flecked lips and ears laid flat, you strained to be in the van; and just when it seemed that your patron saint, or mine, was working overtime–'plunk', and with a sob, you pitched and went 'West'. Mercifully swift was the end, for which I commend some Turk's soul to Allah.

Your spirit is surely in that Happy Hunting Ground of Honest Horses, where drought, heat, and 'regulation scale for light mobile' are unknown. When I, too, go 'West', my spirit shall go on pilgrimage to the Mecca of Loyal Friends; it will cross over the hills of the mountain-bred, and the treeless haunt of the Plain-bred to a scrub-fringed sandhill whose base is aflame with Desert Pea blossom, there to call to your spirit, Pal O'Mine. *H. Spence*
The Kia Ora Coo-ee, May 1918

Light Horse Anthem
(Written on a scrap of paper picked up on the Jerusalem–Jordan Road.)
We are the mobile forces,
The Desert Mounted Corps;
We roam around the country
In search of Turkish gore,
In every kind of weather,
In heat or dust or damp;
But every time we settle down
They shift the blooming camp!

We dig the winding trenches,
As well as groom the horse,
Mid Jordan's heat and dust-clouds
And Auja's swampy course.
Yet when we go to Bethl'hem
To easy up the strain,
Somebody gives the order,
And off we go again!

Sometimes we ask for transport,
To shift some extra kit;
The answer is, "You're mobile",
Or "You should not have it".
Yet when we form a small dump
Way down along the line,
Some irate 'red-tab' fellow
Kicks up a blinkin' shine!

And so we keep on moving
As days and weeks roll by;
The records of our movements
The Turkish Staff defy.
And when we get to Berlin
The Kaiser he will say:
"Hoch! Hoch! Mein Gott! They Cannot
At last have found the way!"   *'Bitten'*
The Kia Ora Coo-ee, October 1918

The Light Horseman
Tall, brown, broad-shouldered, deep-chested, clean-shaven, with a slouching gait like that of a sleepy tiger, and calculating eyes: there is the Light Horseman as I know him. Easy going mostly, he is full of surprises when aroused. On leave the Light Horseman is smartly dressed; but even in Cairo he

has a wonderful love for his trusty hat, which never looks new, and is never by any chance turned up at the side.... His round consists of motor trips to the Pyramids, Heliopolis, Helouan and San Giovani Café on the banks of the Nile. Apart from these three trips, and possibly one to the Barrage, the Light Horseman sticks chiefly to Cairo. He listens to the band in Esbekieh Gardens, buys new clothes, visits the picture shows and the few inferior vaudevilles Cairo contains. He invariably visits the Pay-Master to try and squeeze another pound from his book, and then returns stone-broke, to the field.

Back with his horse, with singlet on and leggings off, and the brown hide of him beaded with moisture, you see him at his best. His chief duty is to keep his horse fit and well under trying conditions. Between an original horse and an original man there is a bond that even death cannot break.... The daily patrols that leave in the cold grey dawn to probe the enemy's lines are part of the Light Horseman's life. With his belt and bandolier crammed full, his coat on his saddle, his nosebag, quartpot and waterbucket tied, mostly in his own fashion, to his horse, he sallies forth to joust with 'Jacko's' outposts.... When orders are out for the big fight, you see him and his mates clustered around the feed dump. To cram nosebag and sandbag with more feed than they will hold is then his chief aim in life. After his horse's requirements are drawn he sees to his own. He visits the nearest canteen and fills his own wallets to overflowing; then, smothered in dust and perspiration, he drains his waterbottle and refills it, stands to his horse, and is ready for the long night ride that is usually the prelude to a hard fight next day. Slow and wearisome this night ride always is; many halts, much dust, mounting and dismounting from the overladen old horse, until the most equable of tempers is upset.... Just before dawn there is usually a long halt.... It is here that the Light Horseman gives his gear a final overhaul. There is no excitement about these preparations. The short, sharp ride under artillery fire, the rapid dismount for action, the handing over of his horse, and the steady advance under ever increasing fire changes that careless gait into a livesome, athletic swing, that takes him over the ground much quicker than other troops.... It is only when the led horses come up, and the long night ride back to the bivouac area commences, that he realises the loss of some of his mates. The horses with empty saddles that he has to lead tell the tale.

'*Surcingle*'
The Kia Ora Coo-ee, June 1918

A FORGOTTEN ARMY

The Return of the First Division
Though it was as far back as 1917 that an agitation was first raised in Australia for the return hither on furlough of the surviving members of the First Division of Anzacs, our politicians were too busy winning the war to attend to this trifling matter until 1939, when the war was just as nearly over as such a war could ever be. And when Senator Pearce, Junr., son of the great Minister of Defence, was convinced that the veterans of the A.I.F. would be granted their first leave from the front, in order to see their relations once again, the excitement in Australia was intense....

When the Minister for Defence announced that the survivors of the famous First Division were on their way home, all Australia was thrilled. The Veterans' Reception Committee was besieged by eager mothers who dimly remembered having sent sons to the war about 1914, and by women who wanted to see for certain whether they had really married Original Anzacs before their departure. As most of these women had since married other men, and had forgotten or mislaid their original husband's name, or death notice, they were naturally somewhat worried....

However, it was felt by Australia that no honour too great could be bestowed upon these Saviours of the Empire, already almost mythical to the generations growing up. On the day fixed for the arrival of the transport, politicians delivered patriotic speeches to all the school-children; enthusiastic flappers importuned eligible uncles to buy buttons; live stock and old hats were auctioned in Martin Place; kewpies were loyally raffled in the Winter Gardens of the Hotel Australia; and the aged Prime Minister, Sir William Hughes, Kt., delivered his 10,378[th] speech on winning the war. Beyond these fervent expressions of hero-worship it was rightly felt that even Australian patriotism could not go....

Amid tumultuous cheering the surviving members

Nearing the End.

Many soldiers believed the war would go on forever. *Kia Ora Coo-ee*, March 1918. (*Author*)

of the First L.H. Regiment disembarked, and greeted once more his native land. There was only one of him.

He was a very nice old man; he was physically complete, but looked a little run down, and had to be assisted down the gangway. As he listened to the noble oration poured forth upon him by the Earl of Holman, his eyes wandered curiously about, like a lost child seeking its whereabouts . . . "I say, boss, is this here place really Australia? We blokes sometimes used to speak of Australia–in between battles–but I never found any bloke as could rightly get the hang of it".

The Earl graciously answered him that this really was Australia, and that he was actually in the presence of the Lieut.-Governor–the permanent Lieut.-Governor of New South Wales. . . . "But your comrades, the other glorious heroes, where are they?" the Earl anxiously asked. If necessary he was willing, nay eager, to reel off his oration again. "They're coming in the other transports, I expect?"

"No", sighed the old man. "There ain't no more. It's this way. We've fought in every battle that ever took place these last score years, and . . ." "I know!" The Earl smiled his famous reassuring smile. "Those immortal battles, Lone Pine, Suvla Bay, Romani, Rafa, Beersheba, Gaza . . ."

The tottering old man in the frayed khaki vaguely shook his head, "I don't remember them scraps", he muttered. "We won so many battles. Those must have been some of the first we won. I don't know. I lost count . . . No I can't say as how I've heard of them before; but I'll take your word for it boss".

"But where are your heroic comrades?"

"Well, boss, you'll find a good few of them dotted all over Palestine. They never relieved us; nobody down here seemed to think we was worth relieving. So we dwindled down and down. Every battle we won we came out of with fewer mates. If you go on dodging bullets long enough, you'll dodge too slow once".

"All killed?" the Earl sighed.

"Not Much!" said the old man. "There's a bigger mob in Egyptian hospitals, and a much bigger mob married in Cairo and Palestine. And you ain't likely to see any of them out here. Their wives won't let 'em!"

"But surely the transport was full before she left Egypt?" the Lieut.-Governor asked.

"Yes, boss, but the night before we left the blokes got telling about this here Australia of yours; and, from what we heard of it, it didn't seem the sort of country a decent bloke would go to. One chap told us that it was inhabited by anti-conscriptionists. Well, it didn't look good to us, to go into exile among a mob of antis. So they cleared back to Palestine".

"But you?"

"Oh, I was too slow; they caught me" . . . The Anzac's lips trembled pathetically. "I don't like this here place. There's too much speechifying about it. I miss the sand storms and the rain. It ain't natural" . . . "Don't keep me here, boss!" he implored. "Send me back to the firing line!" He blubbered, "I w-want to go-o-o home!"

The Kia Ora Coo-ee, March 1918

To Mr. Macpherson
(Mr. Macpherson states that there are still some officers serving at home who have not yet seen service overseas, but that steps are being taken to replace them by officers from France who need rest. The War Office is considering the question of getting rid of some of the unfit officers, that officers with prolonged service overseas to their credit, or convalescent from wounds or sickness, may be employed at home.

Times, London)

Say, what about a billet in your office, Mister Mac?
For coves who carry bigger loads than Sam Brownes on their back;

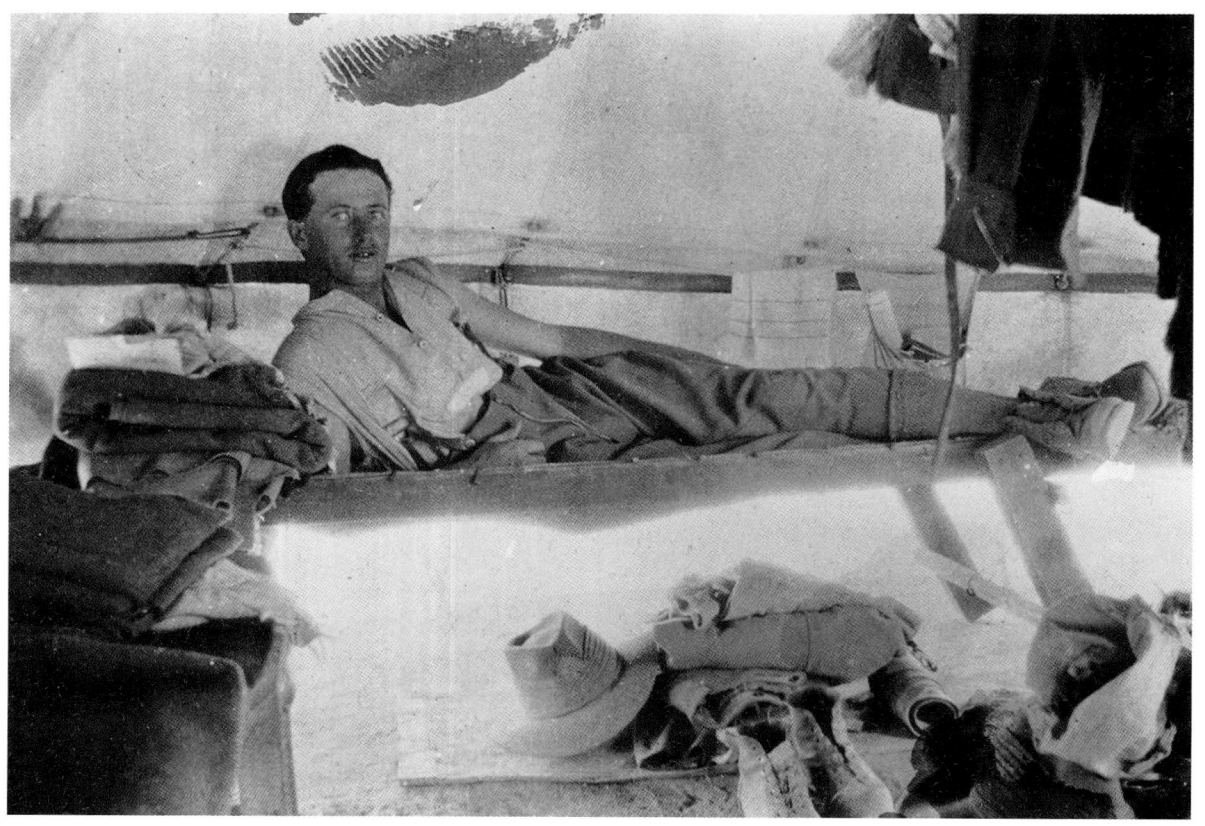

Trooper Overell at ease and out of the heat. (*Author*)

Gambling reached epidemic proportions in both Egypt and France. *Kia Ora Coo-ee*, April 1918. (*Author*)

A LUCKY SHOT.
Yer.......... lucky yer stopped that stray one. I 'ad a full 'and against yer three kings.

For battered blokes who've plugged along and battled through the brunt,
And never 'ad old Buckley's chance for this 'ere 'oming stunt.
Australia don't seem keen to give 'er 'fourteen' men a chance;
'Er politicians only yap 'er motto to advance;
They dilly-dally with their job of dishing out a pack
To those who'd reinforce us—give us 'opes of going back.
So what about a billet in yer office, Mister Mac?

We've melted down to skin and bone, we've dimmed each shining eye.
Got crows-feet in the corners squinting over Sinai.
Our shoulder blades are cutting through our loaded bandoliers;
We've gained a blood-shot, beefy look with 'bully' all these years.
We're weary, slowly withering—a parched up, perished 'eap;
We're sinking, slowly slithering away for want of sleep.
Our legs seem lined with leather through the friction on the 'ack,
We've only bones to sit on where the legs fix in the back.
So what about a cushion in yer office, Mister Mac?

We've journeyed through Jerusalem to far-off Jericho.
Where mothers, when we worried 'em as kids, wished we would go.
We've seen no milk and 'oney that sky pilots preach about,
Bar 'Ideal' milk on issue and the bees are never out!
We 'aven't 'eard a buzzer, not a 'wahad' bally bee!
But 'ope to catch some cockles in the Sea of Galilee.
Our stomach-skin is sagging but we reef in all the slack!
A belt wrapped twice around it warms the marrow in the back.
We'd like to 'ave a luncheon in yer office Mister Mac!

We've seen no roaring lions, which gave Sampson such a stunt,
But when we search for smaller game we 'aven't far to 'unt!
We've cursed the stabbing skeeters raiding un-protected flanks,
A weary band of Billjims on the Jordan's muddy banks;
Where the stench of war arises in the cause of Victory,
By an 'oly river running to a Dead and bitter Sea.
It ain't the bullets 'umming or our old opponent Jack
That turns our thinking 'omewards on a far-off Southern track;
It's just an easy armchair in yer office, Mister Mac.

We've barked and bent our skinny shins on Judah's stony rocks,
And wept compassion's bitter tears on ribs of bony crocks.
We've drunk from Jordan's waters, with sad colicky results,
And prayed for something stronger for us frolicky adults.
We're fed up seeing dusky bints and toothless Arab hags,
And picture maids of fairer tints in smoke of issue fags.
We'd like to see some 'Blighty' girls when time is running slack,
And spin 'em yarns of Palestine—they've 'eard about Anzac.
We'd like to tell yer typist in yer office, Mister Mac!

Kit inspection, Moascar Camp. Trooper Arthur Overell, 2nd Remount Unit. (*Author*)

We've sympathy for Moses who 'ad one last longing look
At Israel's cussed selection—there's no wonder 'e took crook!
We've seen the slums of Jaffa, and the flies and dust of Ludd,
And washed our dirty faces in the Jordan's muddy flood.
If this is that great Promised Land, once offered to the Jew,
We'd sooner live in Lapland, or Siberia would do.
So if you've any officers who 'aven't done their whack,
Just punt 'em out to Palestine—they've *surely* earned the sack;
And let us pitch our bivvies in yer office, Mister Mac.   'KOOLAWARRA'
The Kia Ora Coo-ee, June 1918

ANZACALITIES

An Australian soldier in a well known hospital in Egypt developed a habit of picking up every bit of paper he could find. A Medical Board decided he was harmless and might be better for a trip to Australia. On the trip to Australia he still continued the practice and on arrival there he was again boarded and the Board decided he was too eccentric for active service. On receiving his discharge he looked at it closely and remarked with a dry smile. "Thanks! That is the piece of paper I have been looking for".
The Anzac Records Gazette, November 1915

At a certain camp in Egypt the Officer of the Day was visiting the Guard at night, and the Guard was a little slow in turning out.
   The following conversation took place:-
   Orderly Officer:- "Come on now, shake a leg; am I to be kept standing here all night?"
   Voice from the Tent:- "No Sir, call around again in the morning".
   Subsequently . . . (What the Officer said did not pass the Censor.)   'NMN'
The Anzac Records Gazette, December 1915

The Regimental Hymn
(No Mess Programme is complete without this)
Only one more marching order,
Only one more Church Parade,
Only one more Kit Inspection,
And of that we're not afraid.

When we get our 'Civvy' clothes on,
Oh! How happy we shall be,
When this blanky war is over,
No more soldiering for me.   '*Amen*'
The Kookaburra, July 1916

Joe
No "Please explain" disturbs our rest
Or Indents vex our slumbers,
Nor frantic comments when sacks are shy,
To "Double up by numbers".

The Irish nation's taken charge
And calmed our hungry passions;
No more the starving soldiers cry;
"We want our blanky rations".

With saddles, dhurra bags and tanks
Concealed around his 'bivvy',

Officer: "What were you before the War, Jones?"
Jones: "'Appy, Sir."

Ask a silly question. *Kia Ora Coo-ee*, December 1918. (*Author*)

When shortages are in the air,
Joe declares a 'divvy'.

With bakshee rations waxing fat
From neighbouring units stolen
Joe sits at ease and counts the spoil
Brought home by 'Knock-out Nolan'.

On milkwhite charger proudly set,
A pitifully decayed 'oss,
He ambled off across the plain
To spar a round with D.A.D.O.S.

Grim Desmond sits and rules the roost,
Lets off a few mild snorters,
To keep at bay, till Joe returns,
The hungry Company Quarters.

The Company Commanders cry:
"We've done with anxious toilin'",
And sinking on their septic knees,
Ask blessings on Joe Moylan.   *R.W.C.*
Barrak, July 1917

Young mutton
Number umpteen has a little lamb
Whose bingy will not shrink;
Although red tape is his only food
Cold tea is not his drink.

"Sergeant Major" is his plaintiff cry,
Night and day unceasing:
The poor S.M. charges back and forth,
Horrid swears releasing . . .

But soon we are going to lose him,
Salt onion tears are shed:
Now he is booked for Australia;
Sergeant Major—go to bed.   *'Spud'*
Barrak, September 1917

Proverbs of a Private
Take heed of the Sergeant, and Obey his Commands, lest thou eatest of the fruit of thy ways, and thy cap be 'snatched' from thee.

But heed not the 'old sweat' nor his kind, for their ways are Crooked . . .

Fear thou the A.P.M., and his myrmidons that thy days may be long in the land on leave.

When thou journeyest to the Rest Camp afar, look not too much upon the biera, or thou shalt surely be returned to thy unit . . .

When thou wouldest tarry a-while with the sick and lame, guard thy speech with the physician, lest thou be 'rumbled', for he is a man of profound understanding . . .

Be of humble countenance and simple mind when on rations fatigue, that thou mayest twist the A.S.C. and lift the 'baksheesh'.

Verily I say unto all men: who shall understand a Quarterbloke and his indents? And who shall be wise concerning his reserve rations? . . .

He that, rising early in the morning, greeteth his friends with a loud voice, it shall be counted a curse unto him. Therefore shall an Orderly Sergeant abandon all hopes of forgiveness.

Display not thy talents promiscuously, lest they make of thee an 'acting Tipperary unpaid', to become the slave of all men.

Take not the Army seriously, my son, for 'tis but a gamble and a joke. Therefore, keep smiling, keep thine head (down), keep the eleventh commandment (Thou shalt not be found out), and thou shalt be accounted wise in the wiles of men, and in due time return to the land of thy fathers.   *R.F.R.*
Barrak, February 1918

Last night, I held a little hand,
So dainty and so neat –
Methought my heart would burst with joy,
So wildly did it beat!
No other hand, into my heart,
Could greater solace bring,
The hand imprisoned in mine was
Four Aces . . . and . . . a King.   *'Nimrod'*
14th Company Magazine, June 1918

While we waited for the billy to boil, Billy Cronin told me all about it. It was just before the Gaza stunt, on April 19th, and one of the Billjims, who had a forty horse-power whisky thirst, was sent back to the L.H. dump at Rafa for a spell. He carried a note from his C.O. to the Sergeant in Charge, which contained the following words, 'See that . . .

gets no whisky'. For two days Billjim longed in vain for the forbidden juice, but on the evening of the third day a truck containing 40 cases of 'O be joyful' was shunted on to the siding, and two gaunt camels proceeded to take it case by case to the Canteens. When darkness fell twelve cases still remained, and these were carefully counted and stacked just outside the R.T.O.'s door, and a sentry put on guard. At 7.30 p.m. the Billjim with the whisky thirst walked briskly into the R.T.O.'s office, saluted, and said, "Excuse me, Sir, but when does the next train leave for Kantara?" "In half-an-hour", replied the Officer. Billjim thanked him, and retired. When he reached the sentry and the twelve cases of whisky just outside the door, he bent down, seized a case and called out, "From here, Sir?" "Yes", came the reply from the R.T.O. inside the tent. At the inquiry next day, a bewildered sentry stated that he heard the R.T.O. tell an Australian to take a case of whisky. The R.T.O. told him he was a liar. Just about the same time a bleary-eyed Billjim was seated on a half empty whisky case somewhere in the sandhills, and was passing more spirit through his neck than any other forty troopers in Palestine.
'Getis'

Who said we couldn't get smokes sneaked into the Clink? I was doing the twenty-eight days for telling a certain sergeant that he had no father. The Clink was a wire netting enclosure somewhere on the Canal. My cobber heard that I was without smokes, and immediately got to work. He approached the Clink from the rear, yarded up half-a-dozen of those beetles that old Pharaoh's missus used to call sacred scarabs, squatted himself outside the wire, and pretended to be reading a book. After a while, he digs a straight line under the wire, fastens a smoke to one of the beetles, and puts him in the furrow. The insect marches straight ahead, and I got the cigarette. Others followed, and when one of the scarabs showed signs of going on strike, another one was detailed to the job. *'Booligal Bob'*
The Kia Ora Coo-ee, April 1918

ENGINES OF WAR

Two Rings Are Right
There's something humming in the Air,
And eyes upturned and all astare,
And walads scooting here and there
    And everywhere.

And hasty shufflings through the night,
And vague alarms and grave affright—
When peals, in accents of delight,
    "Two rings are right!"

There's something humming o'er the dump,
And lens aquiz and hearts athump,
And Archie hid behind his 'hump'
    Feels such a chump.

For something soaring at a height,
With bombs and fearsome things bedight,
Till—what relief!—she heaves in sight
    And "rings are right".

There's humming o'er the gas parade
And sage discursions promptly stayed,
And gas precautions thence delayed
    While others made;

And 'Woodsy', ceasing to recite,
Breathes for "Gas cover!"—"Nurse good night!"
And 'shows a leg' when—glad respite!—
    "Two rings are right".

There's humming down the Wadi sides,
And Bill, as up aloft he rides,
Grave fears, though shiv'ring in his strides,
    In song he hides.

While 'G', the fearless 'Furphyite',
Decides to hurriedly alight,
Till someone laughs and cries "Sit tight,
    Two rings are right!"

There's humming on the evening air,
The morn, the noon—and everywhere,
Where danger is and 'de'il may care',
    There's humming there.

And though oftimes 'tis in disquiet,
We view o'erhead each pilot wight,
We trust while wings are wings in flight
   Right will be right.   T.V.B.

To A Ford Car
Beyond repair! My humble fearless car,
You had but lived one year, one gallant year
Of uncomplaining service, constant strain,
That would have killed all other cars but you,
And now you're left behind.
It was no question
Of an oily plug or broken axle;
The very heart of you was cracked across;
A rasping shock, a wheeze, and sudden stop,
That was your end.
We left you in a wilderness of rock
Near Akaba, a pioneer of cars,
A wonder craft. A thing for Bedawe
To marvel at. Your bones will start surprise
From every traveller on the ancient way
That Moses chose. Then may no idle touch
Disturb you there! May honoured rest be yours,
My old Ford car!

Real life began for you near Bir el Abd.
You loved to cruise about the Bardawil –
That dread Serbonian bog which long ago
Did swallow part of many a fleeing host,
And more than once reached out to swallow you.
You searched its scattered isles, and daily prowled
About its shores for Arab spy or Turk;
Explored a ruined church at Flusiat;
And oft-times picniced by the cool blue sea
At Zaranik. Around Masaid you sniffed
The woods for game,–but carried home your gun
   disconsolate.

Then when the Column moved you tried to lead –
Failed; and broke your eager heart to follow.
Along that six mile sandy strip of shore
We pushed—and hauled you. 'Twas the only time
You humbled both your willing self and us;
For while the guns were banging at Magdhaba
A mule team towed you in to El Arish.

Happier days were stored for you at Rafa.

The sand you loathed was past. There were flowers,
Orchards and crops. And then there came a day
When over fields where youngsters, negligent
Of bursting shell and hurrying troops, kept watch
O'er browsing flocks, you sped with eager load,
Unheeding when machine guns found your range,
But raced along to use the gun you bore.
Fleet sturdy car! You found yourself that day;
And when, as darkness fell, you turned about
And toiled unwearied through the long sad night,
Carrying wounded back to Sheikh Zowaied;
Our hearts were prouder in some strange new way,
Because you were so strong and swift and sure.

The months that followed were the months of quest,
And honoured days. Men smiled to see you pass,
And cried "Good luck!", and "Bring us home a
   lance".
Your hunting days are over, now, my Ford—
The eager chase of frantic Jackos,
The sweet clear music of your laughing gun,
The easy dodge of shell-bursts. Do you dream,
Down there, of those glad days—and laugh?
   Perchance
Some moonlight night a spirit form will come
And gently mend that heap of rusted bones.
We'll journey back across Kossaima's heights
To old familiar places round Shellal
And Gaza, Ali Muntar's eastern slopes—
And Atawineh, where you met the Turk
And held him, Mendur where the Camels lay
And fought those ridges in their own fierce way—
And then we'll saunter home to Abasan.

You wonder for your friends of long ago?
The cars that roamed the Bardawil with you?
That envied you those bursts of speed, that sweet,
Clean throbbing of a motor thoroughbred?
But one survived to see Jerusalem,
And he still lives, an unmatched veteran
Of the older build. The other four saw death
In cold dismemberment. For them, the shops,
The careless grasp of men who knew them not;
For you, a worthier end, my old Ford car—
For you, the great red hills of glistening rock,
The peace of work well done, the playful gaze
Of lizards, the wheeling flight of eagles,

'My Pipe', Kia Ora Coo-ee, November 1918. (Author)

The deep blue, comprehending sky,—
And silence. *Number Seven Light Car Patrol*
The Cacolet, June 1918

A FOREIGN FIELD

A Mountain Fight
The shadows fall on the lonely dead,
Where the murderous guns held spree,
And spattered the stones of Moab red,
In the sight of the blue Dead Sea.
The hills are mute in the aftermath
Of a long and bitter fray,
And the shattering voice of battle-wrath
Has died with the fatal day.

The moon rolled over the naked range,
On the night we ambled forth.
Fair was the tranquil vale, and strange
All trails that led to the north.
The Jordan wound like a monster snake
Away to the left below;
And flickering faint in our dusty wake
Were the lights of Jericho.

We followed the trail up scars and seams
On a flood-worn broken floor;
The sky looked down, as a night-sky gleams
Through a roofless corridor.
We climbed where the crags weave sombre shades
On the ledges lone and high;
Where the rocks are sharp as bayonet blades
Held sheer at the limpid sky.

Our guns moved close in the trailing rear,
And many a curse was thrown
At the brazen hills we purchased dear
With blood and muscle and bone.
We stumbled on till the dawn awoke,
And cradled the moon to rest;
Till a golden bar of sunlight broke
On a tapering mountain crest.

The light of an amber sun was blent
With the mists of morning then,
And the hoofs of the surging regiment
Rang clear in a wid'ning glen;
But sudden and sharp, on either flank,
The rattle of rifles told
How fate had played us a murder prank
In the heart of Dead Man's Hold.

As a shaft leaps forth from an archer's bow,
Through a withering rain of lead,
We sprang from the shock of a sudden blow,
And raced for the rocks ahead.
The foeman hurried us on as hard
As a blast of autumn wind;
And the guns with the straggling afterguard
Kept rumbling on behind.

We turned at last where a mountain wall
Arose in our broken course—
No more would a speechless horseman fall,
Hard hit, from his startled horse.
We left the saddle and screened the guns,
And our rifle bolts replied
To the soulless Turks and the master Huns
Who approached on either side.

They swarmed like ants, till the vale seemed black
With a seething human flood,
That the shrapnel failed in holding back
With its toll of life and blood
They tumbled over the men that fell
From the frantic, foremost line,
And gave us a taste of earthly hell,
In the hills of Palestine.

The mass bore down, as a greedy tide
Sweeps over an ocean beach,
While the bombardiers toiled side by side
At the hot, recoiling breech.
But the saving shells gave out too soon,
And the batt'ry ceased to rave,
As many a man was seen to swoon,
And sprawl on his stony grave.

We sought the saddle and bounded then,
Like a team of startled stags;
We left behind us the crowded glen
And clambered among the crags.
But ere the Turk, in his hasty greed,

'My Bivvy', *Kia Ora Coo-ee*, December 1918. (Author)

Was able to hold us all,
We gave him a taste of hell indeed,
From the leaning mountain wall.

We hung to the high ground all that day;
And all through the night we kept
The cowering foe from the guns away,
While never a horseman slept.
When the anxious hours began to drag,
And the fight seemed left to chance,
They set their guns on the Red Cross flag,
And shattered our ambulance.

A fresh dawn broke on a day of dread,
Our bandoliers were light;
We hadn't enough of rifle lead
To commence another fight.
But the beat of hoofs rang sharp and clear
Ere the noon-sun crowned the day,
And we knew relief was forging near—
That the Turk had crept away.

They found us perched on the mountain wall
Where the twisted dead were strown;
The perishing wounded ceased to call,
And the dying ceased to groan.
We staggered away like listless ghosts
To the heart of Dead Man's Hold,
While the fresh relief took up their posts,
And the guns began to scold.

The shadows fall on the lonely dead,
Where the murderous guns held spree,
And spattered the hills of Moab red,
In sight of the blue Dead Sea.
And memory robs my eyes of sleep,
For half my comrades sprawl
Where half of my heart lies buried deep.
In the stones of a mountain wall. *'Gerardy'*
The Kia Ora Coo-ee, June 1918

Amman—Easter '18
There's a church bell rings down the Hawkesbury,
When the night hush hovers near,
And an old boat swings on the Hawkesbury,
'Longside an old worn pier.
There's an old wife dreams o'er the Hawkesbury,
By the pier and the swaying spar
While prayer-ships swim out o'er the Hawkesbury,
To seas and strange lands afar.

There's an old bloke down by the Jordan-side,
And an old bloke aweary there,
For a mate gone over the Jordan-side,
And a 'bivvy-sheet' to spare,
For a task that films all the Jordan-side,
In a huskiness of tears,
And a tale, far-flung from the Jordan-side
To the Hawkesbury's listening ears.

There's a new-made grave on the Amman Ridge,
Where no limelight's staked a claim,
Though some brave blood crimsoned the Amman Ridge,
With the 'red' that knows the game –
But the Hawkesbury to the Amman Ridge
Is a forlorn cry and wide,
And the Bedouin prowls o'er the Amman Ridge
With the dead that the mountains hide.

There's a church bell rings down the Hawkesbury
When the night hush hovers near,
And an old boat swings on the Hawkesbury
'Longside an old worn pier
And an old wife dreams o'er the Hawkesbury,
Through the pier and the swaying spar,
While a shadow flits down the Hawkesbury,
For a soul gone o'er the bar. *'Brentomnan'*
The Cacolet, June 1918

The smiles and jollity which marked the issue of steel helmets to these men of the 6th Brigade newly arrived in Flanders from Egypt in 1916 would soon disappear in the mud of the Somme. (*Australian War Memorial, Neg. no. EZ00003*)

Quiet villages not far from the front contrasted with the horror of the trenches. Men of the 12th Battalion resting at Naours on their way to the Somme, July 1916. (*Australian War Memorial, Neg. no. EZ00163*)

CHAPTER FIVE

THE WESTERN FRONT

For the men of the A.I.F., the Great War had two very different faces. The soldiers who remained in Egypt after the Gallipoli evacuation became part of a campaign that was built around mounted troops. In Sinai and Palestine the combatants feinted and parried over vast tracts of desert and mountain; skirmishes were common, pitched battles rare, and the Allied force enjoyed almost continual success against an enemy in retreat. Movement and territorial conquest characterised the campaign which became, in the popular imagination, a romantic venture, a latter-day crusade, with sweeping charges and moonlit patrols in the silent desert. But the men who were sent to the Western Front, and the tens of thousands who joined them there, were consigned to the desperate immobility of trench warfare. Most of those who served in the A.I.F. saw no obvious gains from their enormous sacrifice in the numbing war of attrition fought out in the mud of Flanders and Picardy. It is often asserted that Australia 'came of age' at Gallipoli, that it was a critical moment in the birth of the nation, but that is a shallow judgement born of a cultural and imperial cringe. It was on the Western Front that Australian soldiers began to forge a distinctive national identity as a military force, and it was there that the previously automatic and instinctive reverence for all things British and European began to evaporate.

The troops from Egypt landed at Marseilles in March 1916 and moved northwards through France to a position behind the 'nursery' front near Armentieres on the border with Belgium. By July over 90,000 Australians were in Flanders with as many more at the bases in England where most of the reinforcements were landed. Between 1916 and the armistice there flowed from Australia a stream of volunteers who were casually squandered by inept commanders pursuing strategically short-sighted goals. This book is not a military history, however, and readers seeking a detailed account of the remarkable feats of the A.I.F. must look to the many studies which deal with the topic more thoroughly and more sympathetically. But a brief outline is needed, if only to establish the context in which the Australian soldiers on the Western Front produced their trench newspapers and magazines.

Among the British and Imperial forces, Australia had the highest ratio of battle casualties to troops in the field. In battle after battle, A.I.F. losses were staggering. After a short period of training and acclimatisation, the men of the Fifth Division were sent into action south of Armentieres on 19 July in what is usually known as the battle of Fromelles. Intended as a diversionary screen for an attack further south on the Somme, the engagement was badly mismanaged. It was also subsequently misreported as stretcher-bearer Edward Penny recorded in his diary.

> The charge took place at about 6 p.m., and a horrible slaughter occurred. Our losses were estimated at 8,400 of which 1,300 were killed. The 8th Brigade entered the German trenches, No Man's Land being about 90-100 yards wide in front of them. They took about 120 prisoners, but it is doubtful if we could call it a success as the Germans forced us back again. This was a terrible affair, but the papers call it a small successful *raid* on German trenches. I was carrying wounded all night and most of

the next day, but there were hundreds left when we were relieved. Dead were lying in heaps blown to pieces.

After Fromelles the Fifth Division was out of action for months. A few days later, on 23 July, the First Division began an assault on the village of Pozieres which General Sir Douglas Haig believed was the key to achieving the much awaited 'break-through'. This phase in the prolonged battle of the Somme eventually drew in the Second and Fourth Divisions also and was arguably the most costly period of the war in terms of Australian losses. Captain Reginald Gill of the Second Division, which went into action on 26 July, described the slaughter in a shockingly matter-of-fact way:

> In one charge we lost 19 officers (14 killed and 5 wounded) and 670 men in about one hour, personally I was knocked down three times by the blast of shells and once buried and yet came out untouched, talk about luck or providence, our battalion came out with 67 rifles only.

In twelve days of fighting the Second Division lost nearly 7,000 men and the seven weeks of piecemeal attacks cost the A.I.F. around 23,000 casualties. As the official historian of the Great War C.E.W. Bean noted, the Pozieres ridge was 'more densely sown with Australian sacrifice than any other place on earth'. Consequently, many in the A.I.F. were outraged by Haig's widely reported communiqué which appeared to belittle their efforts: 'I attacked again on my Somme line. My troops with dogged persistence and bull-dog tenacity, captured and held Pozieres . . . Casualties almost nil . . . Australian troops also participated.' Haig's strategy, if it can be called such, was to wear down German resistance by hurling his troops against the well-constructed German defences in intense local engagements, but his reckless pursuit of that goal inevitably wore down his own forces as well. Finally, in November, Haig called a halt to the first Somme battle because the onset of winter made the battlefield an almost impenetrable quagmire.

In April 1917 the Allied offensive began again with an attack south of Arras which drove the Germans back to their stronghold of the Hindenberg Line. As part of this offensive, the Australian Fourth Division was detailed to capture Bullecourt, a fortified village forming part of that defensive structure. The assault was supposed to be assisted by British tanks, but in the event the slow, cumbersome machines proved ineffective and the Australians fought their way into the Hindenberg Line without artillery support. In the two phases of the battle of Bullecourt the A.I.F. lost 10,000 men. The 4th Brigade in particular was almost destroyed suffering casualties to over three-quarters of its combatants. Bullecourt was actually something of a sideshow. The main British offensive in 1917 was in the northern sector where a series of battles around Passchendaele cost nearly a million British and German casualties. The two Anzac Corps played a critical part in the battles of Menin Road and Polygon Wood, where fortuitously dry weather meant that the step-by-step method of heavy bombardment followed by an advance behind a creeping barrage worked to good effect. However, by thoughtlessly persisting with this method after the autumn rains began in October, Haig once more sacrificed Australian and British lives for minimal gains. When the battle ceased, the Australian Divisions had lost another 38,000 men. During the two months of the offensive, colonial units had served as the shock troops in nine out of the eleven attacks—the Australians led five and the Canadians four. While this was a direct acknowledgement of the superior fighting capabilities of the colonial forces, it also led to an increasing disillusionment with the British High Command which showed through in a number of ways.

The horrifying experience of the Western Front had one particularly significant outcome; it fostered the self-conscious development of a distinctively Australian identity. The grotesque mismanagement that the men of the A.I.F. endured at Fromelles, Pozieres and Bullecourt gave rise to an almost complete erosion of confidence in the competence and good faith of the British High Command. Many Australians felt that they had been badly treated by British generals and badly supported by British troops. They felt increasingly alone and alienated and, in their isolation, they looked to themselves for reassurance and inspiration. From late 1916, in self-perception if not in fact, the Australians saw themselves as a national force with their own standards, values and identity. It was for Australia that the men of the A.I.F. fought, suffered and died in such numbers on the Western Front. These sentiments can be seen quite clearly in the aggressively Australian character of the trench journals which will be considered at length later on.

In a very practical sense too, the Australian divisions were seen as a national rather than a colonial force. The Australian government, echoing the opinion of its troops, pressed the British to group the five divisions into a single corps, a de facto national army. In late 1917, after much opposition, the British grudgingly succumbed to sustained Australian pressure and the Australian Corps came into existence on 1 January 1918. Lord Derby, the Secretary of State for War, recognised the reality of the situation when he wrote to Haig, the Commander–in–Chief:

> I am having a great deal of trouble about [the colonial forces] at the present moment, especially with regard to the Australian Corps, and I am afraid, for various reasons, we must look upon them in the light in which they wish to be looked upon, rather than in the light which we should wish to do so. They look upon themselves, not as part of the English Army, but as Allies beside us.

After nearly three years of fighting, and after the combined disillusionment of Gallipoli and the Western Front, British–Australian military relations changed forever, and that change is well demonstrated in the trench publications by which the men far from home maintained and reinforced their Australian identity.

When General Ludendorff smashed through the British line in March 1918, driving a gap between the Third and Fifth British Armies, the Australian Corps was once more despatched to the familiar battleground around the Somme to stop the advance. Against all odds and expectations, the Corps first halted, then repulsed, the German force. Slowly the line was stabilised and the direct threat to Amiens removed. Throughout the spring and summer of 1918 the Australian Corps on the Amiens front was the most active force in the British sector; the 'live and let live' system of trench warfare common in other sectors was unknown to it. By vigorous patrolling and constant probing at the enemy's defences, the Australians established a psychological mastery over the troops facing them, and when the great allied offensive began they were the spearhead of the assault on the Somme. On 8 August the allies at last achieved the 'break-through' which had been sought for so long. For once everything went according to plan and in a co-ordinated attack the German lines were overrun and the enemy pushed back several miles. Towards the end of the month the Australian Corps under General Monash took Mont St Quentin and Peronne in a brilliantly conceived and executed campaign and by early September the Germans were once more

MAY, 1917.

FOREWORD.

The idea of this edition of the "Battalion Buzzer", is to ascertain if it is possible to start a real live paper for circulation amongst the 1st Battalion.

The Editor is convinced that there is enough talent in the Battalion to make the venture possible, and would like to hear from anyone with literary, artistic, or poetic aspirations.

Short, witty, and sensible articles are the main requirements. Any subject at all of interest will be promptly accepted; providing personalities are not indulged in to the detriment of anyones character or feelings.

Budding poets are welcome but sickly sentiment is discouraged.

Sketches will be accepted but owing to the limitations of the paper at present, all sketches must be on paper 6x10 inches later on the staff will deal with any size at all.

It must be also plainly understood that there will be no "Baksheesh" given for any effort however good the financial editor states that probably when the Buzzer reaches the million copies daily all contributions will be paid for however bad.

Do not hesitate about sending in your contribution, remember that all the leading lights in the literary line today started out in a very small way

Even should the "Buzzer" prove a failure our office boy has a good use for the paper

Buck up and let us hear from you

Yours Truly
THE EDITOR

(Australian War Memorial Printed Records)

back on the Hindenberg Line. The August offensive broke the will of the German High Command; Ludendorff wrote in his memoirs: 'August 8th was the black day of the German Army in this war . . . The 8th August put the decline of that fighting power beyond all doubt . . . The war must be ended.'

For almost four years the war on the Western Front had been deadlocked as both sides endeavoured to bleed the other dry of men and material. In many respects, the sacrifice and suffering from October 1914 to August 1918 was wholly wasted for neither side gained anything of lasting strategic value from the intervening slaughter. Initially the scales were tipped in favour of the Central Powers, but slowly the Allies recovered from their shock and unpreparedness and with the entry of the USA they gained the advantage. But even with the promise of limitless American resources, the stalemate continued until the August offensive. The fighting of August 1918 was critical in bringing the war to a resolution and, as they had been since 1916, the Australians were in the thick of it.

Field publications were slow to appear among the A.I.F. in France, although over twenty titles were published before the armistice. Only one paper can be dated conclusively to 1915 and that was *Honk*, the journal of the Australian Ammunition Park. *Honk* began life as the magazine of the Heavy Siege Battery and was produced on a press which had accompanied the unit from Sydney. For a long period this was the only press readily available and it was later used to print *The Rising Sun*, *Kookaburra* and then *Aussie*. Before the publication of *The Rising Sun* in December 1916, the only other trench paper to appear was *The Battery Herald* whose three handwritten issues in September and October were produced to amuse the men of the 14th Field Artillery. During 1916 several papers and magazines were started by units either training in England or located there for administrative reasons, but only one or two titles were continued when the troops crossed to France. On the Western Front more titles began in 1917 and 1918, but few enjoyed a long existence. The spectacularly short-lived titles were usually single-sheet papers of duplicated handwriting or typescript. These often represented the enthusiastic effort of one or two individuals, but such ventures were usually defeated by a lack of support or the sheer difficulty of production in a fighting unit. Private J. Duffy of A Company, 1st Battalion, launched *The Battalion Buzzer* to 'ascertain if it is possible to start a real live paper for circulation amongst the battalion', and later *The Sportsman* as 'the official organ' of his company. The former failed to generate a second issue and, although the latter survived for five issues, Duffy complained that they had all been 'practically a one-man effort'. Most field publications relied heavily on the energy, enthusiasm and literary skills of a small number of people, but even the most successful enterprises were beset by a range of production difficulties.

The most obvious problem was the near impossibility of putting a publication together whilst on active duty at the front. The solitary copy of *The Noreuil Noose* was typed and duplicated in the 14th Brigade Headquarters in May 1917 during the fighting at Bullecourt. The headquarters was in a gully which was heavily shelled and the target for over 3,000 gas shells on one night. The editors of *The 23rd* noted in the first issue that the battalion had been under fire every night since they started, but they persisted and managed to print twenty-four issues between September 1917 and October 1918. The 3rd Battalion was less fortunate; a magazine was planned but 'the line made constant calls and the rest periods were too short' for anything to be produced before August 1918. A similar story explained

THE RISING SUN

A Journal of the A.I.F. in France. (With which is incorporated "The Honk.")

No. 5.   SOMEWHERE IN FRANCE.   JANUARY 11TH, 1917.   PRICE ½d.

"ALL THAT HE HAD HE GAVE."

Straight from the open country life he came,
  A boy, clean hearted, simple, strong and fleet;
His world, a scattered township far from fame,
  His talk of football, and the price of wheat.

Yet to him also came his Country's call,
  Clear through the wattle and the gum-trees' shade;
Clear the long tale of wrong and murder's thrall.
  So leaving all beside, his part he played.

He offered all he had for human need,
  And his to make the perfect sacrifice,
Far on an alien soil his spirit, freed,
  Passed to the God who bought us with a price.

Just one more martyr for old freedom's cause,
  Just one more life laid down in youthful prime.
No need for tears; we hardly dare to pause,
  Or think in sorrow of a byegone time.

God grant us through all time that such as these,
  Men without fear who seek no meed of praise,
Brave simple hearts may bind our seven seas,
  So shall we banish fear and all dismays.

                    E. H. FERNIE.

OUR RAG.

We're really getting very smart in our Australian Army,
T'will help to give the lads fresh heart, and stop them going balmy;
For when they've read the Bulletin, and other news is done,
They say—"Before we all turn in, let's see the 'Rising Sun.'"

For Captains, Subs and Sappers too, as well as many others,
Will try what all their pens can do, to help along their brothers.
It isn't much to send along some little bits of rhyme;
And if it cheers a tired friend, its well worth twice the time.

Its only run to help us through, and not to make the cash,
The spending of a copper's not so ruinous or rash—
So we'll help along the paper—it shall get a decent chance,
For t'will help us through the winter—which we're fighting here in France.

                  Sap. H. J. GREENLAND

(Australian War Memorial Printed Records)

the interval of more than two years which separated the first issue of *All About It*, published while the 10th Field Ambulance was stationed on Salisbury Plain, from the second compiled in France but not printed until February 1919. Perhaps the most astonishing triumph of publication on active duty was achieved by those who put together *The Twenty Seconds Echo*. The paper appeared at fortnightly intervals even when the battalion was engaged in some of the fiercest fighting of 1918. The first number, on 1 April, was printed in Ploegsteert Wood and issued to the men in the La Basseville-Warneton section of the front line. Subsequent numbers were produced whether the battalion was in the line or briefly at rest. Number four was issued in the front line at Ville sur Ancre, numbers seven, eight and nine were printed in the Aubigny trench system of the Villers-Bretonneux sector, number eleven was produced during the fight for Mont St Quentin and number thirteen at Bullecourt on the newly re-taken Hindenberg Line. Sixteen issues were completed before the armistice and another five before the battalion finally left France.

Even when the editors of a field publication had sufficient material to fill a paper and the opportunity of producing one, they were often limited by the printing facilities at their disposal. The eight-page *The Twenty Seconds Echo* was printed on a hand-press that had been given to the battalion, but because of the shortage of type the sheets which were folded to make the paper had to be set up and printed one at a time. *Yandoo*, the publication of the 7th Field Artillery Brigade, consisted of six or eight sheets of duplicated typescript. With around 1,200 copies in each issue, the editors had to turn between 7,000 and 9,000 sheets through the duplicator. A further problem facing an editor of a trench paper, even if he was lucky enough to possess a typewriter or a press, was the acute shortage of paper. The editor of *Burnished Bits* noted that the lack of paper prevented the publication of all the pieces he had received, while *The Battery Herald* insisted that contributors supply 'at least one sheet of paper as owing to the war the paper is mostly used in the latrine'. Producing just a single copy for the first number of *The Sportsman*, the editor expressed the hope that for the second a copy might be prepared for each platoon. The exhaustion of their paper supply by December 1915 forced the editors of *Honk* to put a price of one penny on copies which had previously been distributed free to everyone in the unit. *The 23rd* appeared with a brown paper cover as a result of the shortage, but at the same time the number of pages increased and the price was halved in eloquent acknowledgement of the popularity of the battalion paper.

The field publications served three interlocking purposes. Their first requirement was to entertain in an alien and hostile environment. Without exception this was the principal goal of everything published for the soldiers themselves. The declared aim of *The Rising Sun* was 'to amuse Australians here by giving them something of their own production over which they can have a good laugh', and the editor of *Yandoo* believed that 'a little nonsense now and then serves to lift one above dull monotony . . . [and] alleviates the strain'. Beyond their value in providing momentary light relief for men facing enormous danger and discomfort, the trench publications acted as an historical record of their experiences and achievements. This second purpose was inseparable from the third which was that the publications might be used as a souvenir to send home. The editor of *The Twenty Seconds Echo* saw that the journal would be 'a regular chronicle of our daily doings on active service' and of interest to friends and relatives in Australia, a sentiment echoed in most of the less ephemeral productions. Commending their paper as 'a reference point' for both the troops and the folks at home, the editors of *The 23rd* left the bottom section of the last page blank with the injunction 'This space is reserved for YOU. Write a few lines home in it'.

Units that did not have a regular publication often managed a single souvenir edition. These were usually professionally printed behind the lines or in England and often ran to fifty pages or more. But in whatever form the field publications appeared, their editors were agreed on one point, they helped to cement loyalties within a unit and they fostered its esprit de corps.

The value of field publications to the morale of the troops, so regularly asserted by their editors, did not escape those in command and three semi-official A.I.F. papers were developed. *The Rising Sun*, whose masthead declared it to be 'A Journal of the A.I.F. France', was printed on the Ammunition Park press and absorbed its earlier offspring *Honk*. Edited by Bean, *The Rising Sun* lasted for three months over the winter of 1916–1917 and was part of the attempt to provide diversionary amusement for the troops who were facing the winter on the Somme. Compared with *Honk* and *Aussie*, both edited by Philip Harris, *The Rising Sun* was a dull, sober production and a poor imitation of a unit magazine. Even so, the nineteen issues printed between December 1916 and March 1917 were eagerly purchased by the troops who found in its columns a mixture of literary offerings and reliable news from Australia. The second attempt at a paper catering for all Australian troops followed the establishment of the Australian Corps. *Aussie*, with Harris as editor, was defiantly Australian, typically irreverent and exactly what was required. Ten thousand copies of the first issue were printed on the Ammunition Park press supplemented by a small machine 'liberated' from Ypres. Orders for the sixteen-page second issue amounted to 60,000 which forced the printing unit to look for a press which could print more than one page at a time. After much searching a somewhat damaged machine was located at Dunkirk, together with a quantity of type, and the second issue duly appeared in large numbers. The paper supply was always uncertain, but the fortunate discovery of ten tons in the cellar of a ruined printery in Armentieres meant that 100,000 copies of *Aussie* could be printed for the third issue. Eventually Harris persuaded the Deputy Adjutant-General for the A.I.F. to requisition three tons of paper per issue from the War Office in London. *The Digger*, the third of the A.I.F. papers, appeared for the first time on the fourth anniversary of the start of the war and circulated in the Australian Base Camps through which the troops passed on their way to and from the front. More like a newspaper than anything that had been published hitherto, its weekly mix of news, serious items and the typical nonsense of the trench paper helped to prepare the men for the end of the war and the slow process of repatriation.

In most respects the contents of the trench newspapers and magazines differed little from the pattern which had been laid down on the troopships and continued into the field publications of Gallipoli and Egypt. Gossip, humorous sketches, 'They Say' and 'Who Said' columns, sporting reports and absurd advertisements, with a leavening of verse and prose on every conceivable topic continued to form the bulk of the copy. But the French productions were different in three respects. They were more likely to include news from Australia, they often contained material of an historical nature and they were more stridently Australian in tone. One or two pages in each four- or six-page issue of *Honk* was reserved for 'News from Down Under' and *The Rising Sun* usually contained a page of Australian cables which kept the troops reasonably up to date with affairs at home. Although the supply of Australian news was obviously severely limited, the men at the front were kept informed about soldier settlement schemes, the conscription fracas, the prospects of repatriation, the scale of war pensions, and many less important matters.

With so many trench publications starting in 1917 and 1918, it was only to be expected

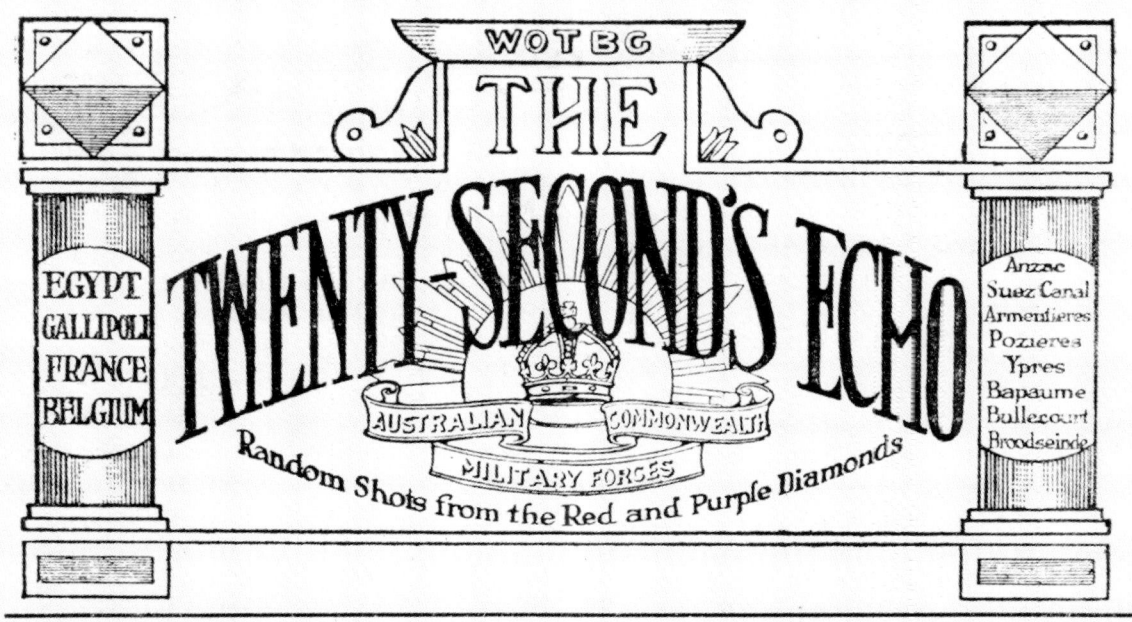

No. 3.   MAY 1st. 1918.   Price, Ten Centimes.

ANZAC DAY.

Once again the cycle of time has gone round and on the 25th. ult., we passed the milestone commemorating the third anniversary of The Landing at Gallipoli. We were unable to fittingly mark the occasion, owing to the Battalion being engaged in the business of Hun-strafing, but the anniversary without doubt has been duly celebrated by our friends "down under." On 25-4-15 Australian soldiers built for themselves a reputation as splendid fighters, a reputation enhanced since then on many a red field in France and Flanders and in the East also. It is a reputation that will endure for it was bought at the price of blood. Whether the Gallipoli expedition was a military failure or not, matters nothing now. What we will remember is that at Gallipoli the young Commonwealth took her place amongst her sister nations and emerged from her fiery baptism with honor unsullied and a pardonable pride in the exploits of her fighting men.

CORRESPONDENCE.

To the Editor.

Dear Sir,

The jaundiced remarks of "Ex-Bandsman" in your last issue were based on utterly misleading information, and are wholly unmerited. In the first place, the song "Good-by-ee" (the latest song out) has not yet been arranged for bands, and I doubt very much whether any band in the A. I. F. possesses this particular piece of music. Even if true the criticism is uncalled for on the ground that what is required is cheerful music and if "Ex-Bandsman" or any other man in the Battalion has any request to make, instead of hiding himself let him call round and see me, and we will be only too willing to oblige him.

H. J. Connell.

HONORS.

The Military Cross has been awarded to Lt. L. A. McCartin (wounded).

The Military Medal has been awarded to L. Sgt. P. Thurlow.

that many editors would use the opportunity to record the history of their unit to that date. The editors of *Yandoo*, who wanted to promote news 'of the Brigade for the Brigade', used each of the nine issues published between April 1917 and December 1918 to fill in the story of the Brigade's activities since the previous issue. These were either straightforward reports, limited only by the occasional omission of a place name to meet the concerns of the Censor, or presented in the form of letters to girls at home. Either way the effect was the same, the history of the 7th Field Artillery Brigade was recorded both for the folks at home and for posterity. Almost all the long-lived and souvenir-style unit publications attempted to give some account of their unit's adventures on active service. The two most successful battalion papers, *The 23rd* and *The Twenty Seconds Echo*, even included their battle honours in their masthead design as a very obvious reminder of their proud record. Two columns framed the title of the latter: on one side were the theatres in which it had served, 'EGYPT, GALLIPOLI, FRANCE, BELGIUM', and on the other the battles it had fought, 'Anzac, Suez Canal, Armentieres, Pozieres, Ypres, Bapaume, Bullecourt, Broodseinde'.

The recording of battle honours and the inclusion of unit histories in the field publications is evidence of the growing consciousness of a distinctively Australian identity among the men of the A.I.F. The most obvious manifestation of this came with the founding of *Aussie* as the magazine for the newly formed Australian Corps. Major-General C.B.B. White, the Corps' Chief-of-Staff who endorsed the idea, objected to the proposed name but the editor, Philip Harris, insisted and got his way. It was, after all, how the men referred to their homeland and he realised that they would more easily identify with a journal that spoke to them in their own 'slanguage'. Harris had used the approach successfully in *Honk* and had seen the life drain from its successor *The Rising Sun* under Bean's excessively literary and solemn editorial hand. Bean almost killed that journal in its tracks by his decision to use material left over from *The Anzac Book* to fill up several issues. White disliked the name *Aussie* and Bean was not impressed by the early contributions, but this merely demonstrates that there was a cultural gap between the literary sensibilities and taste of the higher echelons and the mass of the soldiery. Several journals actually urged officers to contribute, pointing out that most of the copy was supplied by the other ranks. Although Bean rather disapproved of Harris, referring to him disparagingly as 'a little Sydney Jew, not a bad chap—keen but no editor', he was ultimately forced to admit that Harris was right in his choice of name. And even though *Aussie* began under Bean's editorial supervision, he soon left it entirely to Harris who had risen through the ranks and was always more in touch with the sentiments of the ordinary soldier.

Like many of the other less well-known and less successful publications, *Aussie* was written in the kind of language the Diggers used amongst themselves. It was a distinctive mode of expression consisting of English enriched by Australianisms, flavoured with corrupted French words and phrases, and coloured by the peculiarities of military terminology. According to Harris, it was the result of 'continually borrowing, collecting and achieving new words and phrases'. 'Diggerese' set the Australians apart. Indeed, it was so uniquely characteristic of the Digger that after the war several little dictionaries of soldiers' slang were published to help the people at home understand the peculiar expressions of the ex-soldier. W.H. Downing, formerly of the 57th Battalion, published *Digger Dialects* in December 1919. He offered it as 'a collection of slang phrases used by Australian soldiers on active service', noting that during the war the men of the A.I.F. were isolated from 'the ways, the thoughts and the speech' of their normal existence. As a result, the Diggers developed their own vernacular but, as Downing observed, 'it savours of a new national type and its characteristics are the same'.

On the matter of both the magazine's name and its 'slanguage', Harris confronted his critics head-on in his second editorial:

> Some say that Aussie is not a nice word. But Aussie is the name that has been practically universally adopted by the Australian soldier for himself. 'Aussie' means 'Australian Soldier' and 'Australia'. It's short and friendly-like. One seldom hears the word Australia or Australian used over here in general conversation. Therefore it is not for AUSSIE to judge whether it is a good word or a bad one–whether it is a soul-stirring euphony or a lingual catastrophe. It is used by his cobbers and that's good enough for AUSSIE.
>
> Others don't like our slanguage. But AUSSIE would remind these friendly critics that there is a lot of slang in the talk of our Army. And whatever defects our Aussie vernacular may have it certainly has the virtue of being expressive. AUSSIE merely aims at being a dinkum Aussie—and a dinkum Aussie uses the language of the Aussie. He doesn't want to be a literary stylist. And, after all, the slang of today is the language of tomorrow. The history of the Aussie Army is being given by the Official War Correspondents. AUSSIE wants to give you its spirit—and that can only be done by allowing you to say the things you want to say in your own language and in your own way.

Harris achieved his goal; the magazine became the voice and the representation of the A.I.F. It amused its readers. As one contributor noted in April 1918:

> But when I reads the AUSSIE bloke, it always makes me larf,
> An' near forget there is a war. Oh strike me, yes, not 'arf!
> The things as some blokes writes about is real good dinkum mirth,
> An' I just take it into me just like for all I'm worth.

For a nurse serving on the Italian front *Aussie* was a profound psychological boost, 'it has as good an effect as the sight of one of our cocked hats'. It also reminded the Australian soldiers of their unique identity. Apart from the obvious significance of the title, the humorous paragraphs which formed a major part of each issue were grouped under the heading of 'Aussiosities', and in several issues there was a major section on 'Aussie Verse and Verse Writers'. The works of Patterson, Lawson, Quinn, Kendall, O'Dowd, Brady, Mack and others were reviewed with the implicit suggestion that the new nation in the south had poets who owed nothing to the Old World of Europe. And it is in the pages of *Aussie* and the other field publications that we find the clearest statements of what Australia meant to the men so far from its shores.

In much of the blatantly sentimental verse and prose Australia was still the land of sun and wattle blossom, but it was also a land of freedom, liberty, equality and social opportunity. Above all, it was a land utterly different from the stifling conservatism and suffocating smallness of Europe. Australia was young, new, open and free. According to a report in *Honk*, it was 'the greatest, grandest and freeest new country on the planet'. For an anonymous poet in *Ye Chatte*, Australia was the 'Home of immensities untold, / Land of resources manifold'. Others voiced similar sentiments in simple or pretentious phrases though few put it as bluntly as one contributor to *Aussie*:

(Australian War Memorial Printed Records)

> When God knocked off one night said He:
> "This world's a rotten failure."
> Lor Lumme, though, He'd let 'em see –
> Next day he made Australia.

But the consciousness of difference which the men of the A.I.F. had absorbed extended beyond the obvious, superficial features of weather and landform. Many of the humorous anecdotes in the field publications drew their meaning from the observed idiosyncracies of the British, their class-system, their accents, their stuffiness and their conservatism. It is, perhaps, hard for the modern mind to readily understand the deep emotional attachment which many native-born Australians had to Britain, and it is equally hard to imagine the uneasiness which must have accompanied their growing disillusionment with that country, its political and military leadership and its social system. A correspondent writing to *Astra*, the journal of the 3rd Australian Divisional Train in England, in October 1916 commented on a sign he had seen which advertised a 'School for the Sons of Gentlemen':

> School for the sons of gentlemen!
> And what is a gentleman pray?
> There are as many poor men gentlemen
> As sand grains round a bay!
> Away with your class distinctions!
> Away with your cold reserve!
> Give the poor men recognition
> And the credit they deserve!

Philip Harris, the editor of *Aussie*, captured the failings of the 'Old Country' and the promise of Australia in a single verse:

> The narrow ways of English folk
>   Are not for such as we;
> They bear the long-accustomed yoke
>   Of staid conservancy.
> But all our roads are new and strange,
>   And through our blood there runs
> The vagabonding love of change
>   That drove us westward of the range
> And westward of the suns.

The comparisons which were frequently drawn between Europe and Australia introduced a new dimension to the trench newspapers. As the war dragged on, the men of the A.I.F. were urged to think about the sort of nation they wanted to return to when the fighting finally ceased. The readers of *Ghutz*, the paper of the 1st Field Ambulance, were told that a social revolution was 'swiftly shaping' in which the old order would have to give way to the new:

> It is up to the survivors of the present great struggle, to thoughtfully consider, and to make war upon those systems that have in the past precipitated human world tragedies.

"I say digger"–stir yourself, and don't be prepared to go back to think the same old thoughts and countenance, without a protest, the same old wasteful, slip-shod methods in our governing and social systems. Too many are content to go onwards like so many smiling images pushed from behind.

The editors of *Yandoo* declared they were 'concerned to the heart about Australia'. Australia was their 'Idol' and their 'Ideal' and, while disclaiming any enthusiasm for party politics, they urged their readers to think deeply and carefully about the future. Readers of *The Jackass* were told that their slogan should be 'Australia first and all other things afterwards'. *Aussie* issued a simple instruction, 'You Must Cherish Australia'.

The growing Australian self-consciousness was displayed in many ways. The choice of names, masthead illustrations and cover designs of the field publications are all further testimony to the identity which Australian soldiers were forging on the Western Front. Not one of the papers or magazines produced by the A.I.F. in France or England contained a word or symbol on its cover that betrayed any attachment to Britain or the Empire. *The Rising Sun* with its masthead image of grinning soldiers within the half-halo of the sun's rays was obviously based on the Australian army badge. The symbol, well established in Australia since Federation and the birth of the Commonwealth, was that of a new dawn for a new country. Unit badges and mottoes were often incorporated into mastheads and cover designs, while titles like *Kookaburra* (used several times), *The Jackass*, *The Dinkum Australian*, *Aussie* and *Digger* were unequivocal in their origin. The first few issues of *Aussie* had a cover showing an Australian soldier on guard duty with his slouch hat at a rakish angle. But the soldier's face, much enlarged relative to his body, was formed from the map of Australia with Cape York as his nose. Although other covers were used, that image was an essential part of the magazine and was always used as the banner above the 'Aussiosities' column. It was also restored to pride of place for the celebratory Christmas issue of 1918. *Aussie* was, without doubt, exactly what Harris claimed it to be, 'The Australian Soldiers' Magazine'. With print runs of up to 100,000 copies, it circulated widely, drew the Corps together and helped to define the characteristic attitudes and values of the Digger and the force in which he served.

Australian troops were notorious for their general disregard for military etiquette and pointless discipline. They did not possess that unquestioning obedience they condemned in the gallant but docile Tommies. They were sometimes arrogantly dismissive of the armies around them, although the New Zealanders and Canadians were usually exempt from criticism. But the Australians had proved their effectiveness in action and it was the conviction that they could out-perform all others in any task before them which became the ethos of the Digger. There was also a degree of frustration at the constant obsession in Britain and Australia with the achievements of the Anzacs. The men on the Western Front were accomplishing herculean tasks and yet they were somehow always cast as second-fiddle to the Anzacs. The decision to issue a special 'A' badge, which Gallipoli veterans were entitled to wear, prompted others to call for a 'P' for Pozieres and this provoked the editor of *Ghutz* to complain of the 'degradation and imbecility' which these attitudes betrayed. But what angered the Diggers above all measure were those individuals who basked in the glory of Anzac at a safe distance from the front. For a correspondent writing to *The Rising Sun* in January 1917, the Anzac had become:

... a resident of England or of a Base Camp. It wears an Australian uniform but the habitat of the English variety is mostly in London. It invariably insults men on leave

(Australian War Memorial Printed Records)

from France, by asking them to which camp they belong; and feels insulted when the 'bloke' spoken to replies, The Somme. It wears kiwi leggings, an Officer's tunic, a wounded soldier's face, about 8 gold stripes, and a G.S. waggon load of ostrich plumes in its hat. Also generally wears the battalion colours of some unit which is doing its bit, but has long since forgotten that he existed.

The Diggers of the Western Front knew they were doing a vital task; they knew they were not Anzacs, but they believed they merited an equal respect on their own terms. Above all, they understood who they were. A poem written during the winter on the Somme and published in *The Rising Sun* of February 1917 acknowledged the Digger's strengths and weaknesses and shows how solidly the self-image was entrenched:

> He is not a peacetime soldier on an afternoon parade,
>   He's unused to clean a legging or a boot.
> And it beats him being questioned why he hasn't lately shaved –
>   But he's there when all the guns begin to shoot.
>
> He's a trifle rough and ready, but he's never known to shirk,
>   And although his manners are not quite refined;
> And his language may be awful, still he'll do the dirty work,
>   When iron things—not words are in the wind.

Endurance was, perhaps, the central element in the Digger's persona and there was much to endure in the hell that was trench warfare.

In the field publications, danger and discomfort were generally treated lightly. They could not be eradicated and were more easily endured if they provided an opportunity for humour and an encouragement to optimism. For men in the front line the danger from shot and shell was ever-present, but this attracted less direct comment than the discomfort caused by the mud, the lice and the fleas. Battlefields on the Western Front were often turned into quagmires by the effects of heavy bombardment and wet weather. The occasions when frontline soldiers were not soaked through and encased in mud were few indeed. The mud was so deep, so cloying, so sapping of strength and morale that it sometimes appeared in the field publications as an enemy more resented than the Germans:

> No, it ain't the blanky Fritzies that has got our danders riz –
> Nor his whizz-bangs, minniwerfers, nor his crump –
> And it ain't the vaunted Prooshan guards–I tell you what it is!
> Square dinkum, it's the MUD gives me the 'ump.
>
> You gotter wear these rubber boots wot reaches to the 'ips,
> When yer goes astrafin' Fritzies up the line,
> And fer five mile up the duckboard track yer shuffles, slides and slips,
> While the rain drops trickle slowly down yer spine.
>
> If yer slips into a 'dimple', yer disappears from sight,
> And if it should chance to be a Johnson 'ole,

> Then unless yer pals is 'andy, yer chance is pretty right
> Of appearin' on the *Herald's* honor roll . . .

The men in the trenches were perpetually damp, they could not wash or change their clothes for long periods and they sheltered in holes dug in the slush. The mud, awful though it was however, seemed a minor irritation compared with the body-lice and fleas which flourished in those conditions.

Few men escaped without an infestation and the unremitting war waged on these bodily pests was duly recorded in the trench papers and magazines. The first reference occurred in *Honk* as early as August 1915:

> Whilst seated one day on my lorry,
> Weary and ill at ease,
> I saw a Gunner scratching
> As though he was full of fleas.
> I asked him what he was scratching for,
> But his only reply was a long drawn sigh,
> And he carefully killed some more.

The louse was known in Digger vernacular as a 'chat'. This nineteenth-century thieves' word for a louse was used by the London Tommies and adopted by the Australians on arrival in the trenches. Lice and fleas flourished in the seams, folds, and crevices of the thick, woollen underclothes and uniforms of military issue. 'Chatting' became a social activity in the trenches and much humour was found in its dual meaning of idle conversation and the relentless pursuit of lice. Soldiers would sit down together to pick over a piece of clothing, or talk while each slowly inspected his garments and removed the offending presence. One of the most common sounds in the trenches was the crackle of exterminated lice as men ran a lighted cigarette along the seams of their clothing. Out of the line in the rest camps, the troops' chief concern was to rid themselves of lice and fleas. Mass bathing in huge tubs made from brewing vats was the first ritual in a process which involved the exchange of infested clothing for freshly disinfected and fumigated items. Clean and freshly garbed, even if their uniforms were patched and threadbare, the men of the A.I.F. were then able to enjoy the other limited pleasures of the rest camp.

Apart from the opportunity to rest, eat properly, and write letters, the camps offered organised diversions in the form of sporting contests and concert-parties. Although these events were well reported in the soldiers' papers and magazines, it is doubtful if they were as universally enjoyed as more illicit pleasures. Drink and sex, with the former being generally more available than the latter, were much sought after by troops out of the line. Liquor was readily found in the many informal cafes and bars that flourished in villages close to the front and there was no coyness in the journals about the consequences of heavy drinking. As described in almost every account, an *estaminet* was operated by a middle-aged woman who served beer and wine and cooked eggs and chips. These were certainly pleasures to be savoured in their own right, but the chief attraction in many 'staminays' was often the young waitress. Women were an extreme rarity in the war zone and many amusing stories were conjured out of attempted flirtations and seductions which were usually unsuccessful and always handicapped by language difficulties. While such accounts were fairly common in the field publications, there was scant acknowledgement

Concert parties provided entertainment close to the front for men temporarily withdrawn from the fighting. 'The Shrapnels' Concert Party performing in a barn at Maricourt, Somme, January 1917.
(*Australian War Memorial, Neg. no. E00099*)

In the rest camps sporting competitions were a gesture towards the soldiers' earlier civilian existence. The 4th Australian Machine-Gun Company Rugby team. (*Australian War Memorial, Neg. no. H02436*)

of the brothel-visiting which was almost as common as heavy drinking.

In France brothels were legal. The British military authorities had to accept the fact that most towns and villages in the base area contained licensed brothels. These premises came under the jurisdiction of the Town Major and, although they never received any official recognition, the soldiery always knew which were reserved for the officers and which for the other ranks. It will come as no surprise that this aspect of military service was not generally recorded in the trench papers, but it can be detected occasionally. In the 'We Want To Know' column of the September 1915 issue of *Honk* someone asked: 'Who was the first man to find out there was something wrong with the house on the other side of the railway bridge, thereby causing the place to be put out of bounds?' A mock advertisement in *The Noreuil Noose*, designed to amuse and embarrass, declared:

> JOY RIDES TO AMIENS
> The town of frills.
>
> I will personally direct you round to the 'Flappers'
> Prices to suit.
> BASIL

In another column of unit gossip it was noted that Amiens was out of bounds since Basil's last visit and that 'She got his last 50 francs'. This none-too-subtle reference to the purpose of Basil's visit and similar items in other publications suggest that the troops understood the code which allowed only oblique mention of this commonplace activity. Only one candid mention of a sexual encounter with a prostitute has been detected in the mass of material reviewed and it was made to serve a moral purpose. The first three lines declare 'I went with a Woman of Vice tonight/Whom I chanced to meet/In a Paris street', but the poem, entitled 'Remorse', tells how the narrator abandoned the encounter in the 'harlot's den' when overcome by a vision of a future wife and child in Australia. The sexual adventures of the A.I.F. were more usually acknowledged in the following manner:

> The Signal Sergeant went to Paris
> With a pocketful of dough
> And 'Done' the swellest cafes
> With a swagger dontcherknow
> He swears he had a good time
> Quite the one time of his life
> But I'll lay a franc or forty
> That he didn't tell his wife.

As that extract from *The Sportsman* indicates, some things were not to be shared with the folks at home; it was the one aspect of service life which was not fully and openly dealt with in the trench papers and magazines. The verse also draws attention to the soldier's most sought-after privilege, leave.

A combatant soldier in the A.I.F. lived in three worlds: the front line with its obvious dangers; the base area where the immediate discomforts were reduced and relaxation was possible within a disciplined military environment; and the streets of cities far from the front like London, Paris and Rouen. Only in the cities could a soldier escape, to a limited extent, from the war. Sightseeing and conventional tourist activities were undoubtedly pursued by most men on leave, but they were only occasionally reported in the unit magazines. Most of the adventures recorded and the humorous tales told incorporated one or more familiar elements—drink, women, and linguistic confusion. But without doubt the principal attraction of a leave spent far from the battlefield was the prospect of female company both platonic and commercial. According to an English officer, whose *Byways on Service* was published in 1918, French city shops were a popular place for arranging liaisons. He noted that all the shops were staffed by pretty girls who could sell anything to men starved of feminine contacts. Soldiers would enter the shops to look at and talk to the girls and possibly arrange a meeting:

> To the officer from the line feminine intercourse is reckoned cheap at the price of socks and ties. But there is more in it than that. Whilst he purchases he arranges a rendezvous. There are few girls who will not co-operate. Many of them regard employment in the 'Magasin' as a means to the end of driving a more pleasurable and lucrative trade.

That extract from *Byways on Service* was reprinted in *Aussie* and in the same issue the editor, writing on 'Leave-Making in Paris', noted that the Folies Bergeres was very popular with men on leave. The chief attraction was 'the sportive females' who attended for 'business motives', and Harris felt it was 'worth experiencing' the attempts of the 'laughing, ogling, lively girls . . . to cajole the male visitor to accept their company'. As in so many other matters, Philip Harris was a sensitive barometer of the attitudes and values of the Digger and his sympathetic account, devoid of moralising, recognised as a reality what most others sought to conceal.

The desire for social contact with women showed itself in another curious way. One of the benefits to be derived from sickness or a wound was a stay in hospital and the attention of the nurses. The blessings of a 'Blighty' wound which required treatment and convalescence were openly acknowledged in the field publications. A poem in *Burnished Bits* about the duties of a signalman during the battle of Messines ended with the verse:

> He thanked old Fritz with all his heart
> For that's what brought him Blighty
> Those two round holes bored in his arm
> Injuring him but slightly.

While no soldier in his right mind actually wanted to be injured, every man envied the fellow whose wound guaranteed an evacuation from the battle zone and a stay in the tranquil, feminine security of a hospital. And after a stay in hospital there was always the prospect of a recuperative period during which the soldier might be briefly reminded of his former civilian existence. Out of the line the men of the A.I.F. craved anything which resembled normality: the bustle of city streets; the peace and beauty of landscapes that were not barren wastelands of mud and death; and, above all, the opportunity to establish, however briefly, some human contact with people not wearing khaki. These sentiments are clearly displayed in the trench papers and magazines and through them we have a remarkable insight into nearly every aspect of service life on the Western Front.

THE MUDLARK

MEETINGS

4th M.G. Coy. R.L.F.C.

Lieut. Watts donated 40 Fs, 20 to the Club and 20 for a medal. It was decided that the medal be donated to the best forward player. The value of the medal was increased to 40 Fs. by Capt. Mitchell; the same Officer has also presented a new Football to the Club.

The Club now has 11 pairs of Boots.

4th M.G. Eng. Ass. F.C.

This Club gained a decisive, a decisive victory over the 16th Battalion at ████████ beating them by 10 goals to 1. The game was well contested in the first half, but goals came with monotonous regularity in the second half, when 9 were scored. Loar, Whittle and Caton were three of the best, but the whole team acquitted themselves well, especially the outside right.

At the initial meeting held, Lieut. Kirkland kindly consented to act as President. Ptes. Russell and Andrews were elected as Captain and Secretary respectively.

MUDLARK BALANCE SHEET

Receipts		Expenditure	
Capt. Mitchell	20 Fs.	15 Prs. Guernseys	2.8.9
Lieut. Langbourne	20	15 - Socks	1.5.4
" Dodd	20	Postage	2.8
" McGhie	20	5 Prs. Boots @ 11/9	2.18.9
" Kirkland	20	Postage	8.6
" Watts	20		£7.2.5
Serg. Clasper	10		
L/C. Raymont	5	Equiv. in francs	199
Mudlark Sales	36	15 prs. Shorts	67
Members' Subs.	125	Credit balance	30
Total	296	Total	296

Signed
W.G. Sevan
Secretary

A CATECHISM ON TANKS
For soldiers on leave.

Q. What are the Tanks like?
A. A monitor mounted on wheels.
Q. Do they do much damage?
A. Yes, they've destroyed a few German reputations.
Q. How do they destroy trees and houses?
A. Goanna Oil is injected and the Tank then tries to climb the obstacle.
Q. What are they armed with?
A. Greek Cognac and Australian centipedes.
Q. How many men does it take to man one?
A. Righto! There's my train now, bon jour, see you après la guerre!

CONGRATULATIONS

To Diver Jones on receiving the Military Medal. Who's the next?

AMBITION

Officer, to applicant for position of interpreter. "But are you a fluent French speaker?"
Applicant. Yes, I know a bit an' I think I could bluff the rest through with semaphore.

LONELY SOLDIERS?

A London paper printed display posters worded
CHATS WITH SOLDIERS
Now what does that paper mean?

THE SEVEN STAGES OF MAN.

1914. He was duty christened Peninsula Percys.
1917. He began to slope arms with a penny rifle.
1920. He was drafted into the Compuls. Cadets
1923. He was engaged on munitions work.
1926. He made the most of his single life.
1929. He married.
1932. He became a soldier —
    and ceased to be a man.

Fip-squeak.

CHAPTER SIX
'WE'RE HERE BECAUSE WE'RE HERE'

EN ROUTE: ENGLAND AND FRANCE

The sight of Plymouth... was to me at least, the most welcome since leaving Sydney Harbour. Hedged in fields and meadows extending to the very water's edge were most picturesque and quite novel. On the right were rows and rows of houses of even height and uniform design; in the central foreground throngs of people were taking Sunday afternoon relaxation on the lawns overlooking Plymouth sound, and directly ahead rose the tall buildings of Devonport....

On reaching Plymouth we boarded a waiting train and were soon being hauled through the city by two engines at express speed. All transport arrangements were executed with machine like precision. For my part, railway travelling is infinitely preferable to the ancient mariner stunt, and on sight of English lassies waving Australian flags I was so intensely excited that none other than the practised hand of the former ships police could have averted my precipitation through the window.

The train journey was a surprise and an education. I have seen great stretches of the verdant carpet on '4D' and waving crops of wheat on 'Prairie Lands', also travelled all day on 'Lake Victoria' station, but the idea that England with its huge population contained anything but backyards and congested cities with occasional estates, never presented itself to my mind. Imagine my awakening when the train speeded through expansive stretches of beautiful country...

At Exeter the Mayoress and ladies supplied us with tea and coffee on the station, which in addition to being very acceptable was an indication of the heartiness of our welcome to Old England.

We arrived at Amesbury at about 5 p.m. After marching through the villages and innumerable camp huts, we arrived at our future quarters. This place is a stunner. Dotted all over Salisbury Plain are similar camps containing thousands of men, and in spite of this, extensive stretches of open country are preserved for Artillery ranges, training, sports etc. We can walk through the paddocks (or meadows) in all directions for miles among grass, clover and wild flowers, or along the narrow roads with hedges and dense woods on both sides. The booming of large howitzers and field guns rattles the windows of our huts, an Artillery range being adjacent to the camp. The fire is directed by aeroplane, and scores of these machines fly over the camp daily from the aviation school a short distance away.

The provision for our comfort is astounding when it is considered that an army of millions has been raised in the brief period since the outbreak of war. The huts are most commodious; a building which in Liverpool would shelter 50 men, is here allotted to 30. Separate mess rooms are provided in addition, so that the huts are used for sleeping places only. Each man is furnished with sleeping boards and mattresses in fact we have all the comforts of home, except when Johnnie Horton is on duty in the boiler house and lets the fire go out....

Batches of Australians continue to arrive and I have looked up quite a host of old pals...

Yandoo, 20 August 1916

Somewhere in Australia
Midnight: Awake Jack? Awake... yes–me and the mosquitoes are!!! Why don't they civilise the pests here!!! Gorblimey its 'ot. Why did I leave old England–they've got the climate sensible there!!!!

Somewhere in Larkhill
6 a.m. By cripes Bill, its blanky cold! That the reveille? I've been playing the bones since about 4 a.m. Come on Joe the quarter call's gone. Orlright Bill, wait till I get my boots on. Cripes this here Pommyland will be the death of me.... Instead of

fighting for a confounded, cold, clammy, cow of a country like this they ought to give it to the Germans!
Yandoo, December 1916

31/12/16. Slept during transit across ditch and woke at 6 a.m. to tell French post card sellers to go to Holborn. Disembarking here (Le Havre) we collected drivers and horses who had already arrived, got aboard train with all paraphernalia and steamed out at 1 p.m.

1/1/17. Passed through the French towns of ROUEN, BOULOGNE, CALAIS, ST. OMER, HAZEBROUCK to BAILLEUL. When train stopped en route it was inevitably lined by French children calling for 'biski'. Several of our boys attempted conversation with them in French, but the youngsters did not appear to understand their own language. By the aid of acetylene lamps we emptied the train at 10 p.m. and during the 10 kilo ride to STRAZEELE a staff man found that to maintain a centre of gravity while asleep on horseback needs practice. Throughout the ride the roar of the guns was distinctly audible. Arriving at the village of STRAZEELE, horses were picketted, watered and fed, and we retired to the old barn which was to be our habitation. Pigs resented our intrusion, but the application of boot to bacon proved effective. Horse lines were in a cultivation paddock, and armed with shovels we slimily crawled there three times a day to dig the neddies out for their meals. We quickly located egg and chip shops, where the French scholars among us volunteered the information that "Je desire five oofs" meant "I can do five eggs." Happening to be eating eggs after hours one evening long after the '8 o'clock fini' I was saved from the clutches of the M.Ps. by the mediation of Madeleine. Fortunately W.O. Macartney and Sgt. Buckle were also there, and even if I had been captured I was not on my own.
Yandoo, 22 April 1917

IN THE TRENCHES

Mud
While we're fighting for the nation, in our present situation,
We've example in the good old common mud,
For it sticks with desperation and makes quite a decoration
Till a soldier man looks something like a spud.
When we meet an old relation, and he starts the conversation,
It's the same, —unless you nip it in the bud—
For we curse the whole creation for its slimy old foundation,
Drives a man to aviation—does the mud!
When with frantic jubilation we shall hail the termination
Of the war, then e'en forgetting all the blood,
As the train comes to the station we shall step in sheer elation,
To the land in which there's not a speck of mud.   *V.C. Walker, Sgt.*
The Rising Sun, 25 December 1916

The mud was as much an enemy as the Germans. 'Biscuit Trench' leading from near 'Cheese Road' to the front line on the Somme. (*Australian War Memorial, Neg. no. E00572*)

A Hymn of Hate
What is the thing of which I write
And execrate with all my might?
   The Mud.
What is the thing that sticks like glue
And covers France and Belgium too?
   The Mud.
What is the thing that makes us swear
And clings to everything we wear?
   The Mud.
What is the thing that blocks the Push
And stops us 'fellers' from the bush?
   The Mud.
What is the thing that spoils our togs
And keeps us wallowin' like 'ogs?
   The Mud.
What is the thing that makes us sigh
Far up in aeroplanes to fly?
   The Mud.
What is the thing (forgive the pun)
That makes us want *The Rising Sun*?
   The Mud.   *F.K.*
         The Rising Sun, 18 January 1917

The Mud He Left Behind Him
We used ter growl about the bloomin' sand in Sinai
   (Afore we crossed the sea to sunny France)
And weren't we pleased, not 'alf, ter leave the burnin' cloudless sky.
   I'd double back there now if I'd a chance. . . .

For four long days and longer nights yer does a bunny stunt,
   A-hiding like Brer Rabbit in a 'ole,
Unless yer on post freezin', and awatchin' Fritz's front,
   An' a-crawlin thro' the soup out on patrol.

Each thing you own gets covered with a coat er mud and slush,
   An' yer trench is runnin' like a bloomin' gutter,
Yer dug-out starts ter crumble, then comes down with a rush,
   Well I can't write here the 'blessings' that you utter.

If you wants a drink er water, you have gotter take a spade
   An' scratch the ice that on each shell-hole grows,
Then coax a 'Tommy Cooker' to boil it 'cos yer 'fraid
   That underneath's departed friends or foes.

At tucker time ol' Fritz 'e starts to chuck about the mud
   With his whizzies, or coal-boxes or a mortar,
You aint too pleased when on your bread and meat and only spud,
   Lobs 'alf er ton er muck and dirty water. . . .

Yes, I think I'd rather plod the burnin' sands in Sinai,
   Than this weary, soggy, land of slush and mud,
Where more bally rain 'as fallen from this dreary Froggie sky,
   Than when Father Noah arked it, on the flood.   *'Sacko'*
         The Rising Sun, 24 March 1917

"What about having a bit of a chat before dinner," said Bill to me. As Bill was a one-time shearers' cook, he spun some snifters when he got going. I followed him into the tent and asked "about what, Bill? Home and the sheds?"

"Sheds be--------; about the seams of me shirt!"

The Rising Sun, 25 January 1917

'A Little Chat—A Tale of High Life'
O! When you're tired, and full of sleep
And long to sink in slumber deep;
Remove your tunic, p'raps your 'strides'
And wrap your blanket round your sides.

'Tis then, my boys, around your back,
They dream they're on a cycling track;
A crawler stops to kiss and woe –
You quake and shudder, through and through.

The hours go by; you only doze;
You seem engulfed in all the woes
Of all mankind; you scratch and pitch,
And beg a pal to rub your itch.

Unrested, dull, Morn comes at last,
You're thankful that the dark is past;
Then slink away where all is still,
Unrobe yourself and start to kill.

You search your tunic, pants and shirt,
And marvel that such specks can hurt;
Determined-like, you search your hat,
And, shiv'ring, chase the wily chat.

A knavish chap observes you 'stark',
And sneaks along to have a lark;
And fellows laugh 'That's not a dud'
And o'er your back explodes the mud.

You turn and smile a sickly smile,
Yet keep on searchin' all the while;
With nettles armed, some 'creatures' rush
And stain your skin a crimson blush.

Some creosole you then purloin,
And wash each seam and shelt'ring join;
"At last," you cry, 'They're done, by Gad."

But nightfall comes–'life's' just as bad.

Alas! From chats you're never free –
They cling like Fate or Destiny;
But Peace and Change will come one day –
And jolly soon, we hope and pray. S.W.H.

Yandoo, September 1917

The Chat's Parade
When the soldier, fagged and weary,
In surroundings that are dreary,
    Aside lays his rifle and grenade,
Seeks solace in forgetful slumber.
From shell-crash and battle's thunder,
    'Tis then the 'chats' are mustered for parade.

At the double about his back
In a most irregular track
    They make for the parade-ground on his spine.
When there they will never keep still,
Undisciplined they stamp at will,
    And up and down they march in ragged line.

Round his ribs they do manoeuvre,
Curses issue from the soldier,
    There's divisions by the score, he declares,
Doing artillery formation
Without his approbation
    He wriggles and he twists and loudly swears.

Through long dark nights they carry on,
At charges they become 'tres bien',
    The soldier to disperse them madly tears
With savage fingers at his skin,
As he prays for the morning glim,
    In darkness, though, the victory is theirs.

The morn at last breaks good and clear,
Light is this 'Army's' one great fear,
    They retire to warm flannel trenches.
But not too long there they linger,
For the soldier's thumb and finger,
    Routs them out with unregretful wrenches.

But no victory is there won,
For again reinforcements come,
    And in darkness of night again attack;

Behind the front line, the Somme, December 1916. (*Australian War Memorial, Neg. r o. E00051*)

This church at Millencourt, thirteen miles from the front, was used as a hospital for men wounded on the Somme. (*Australian War Memorial, Neg. no. E00342*)

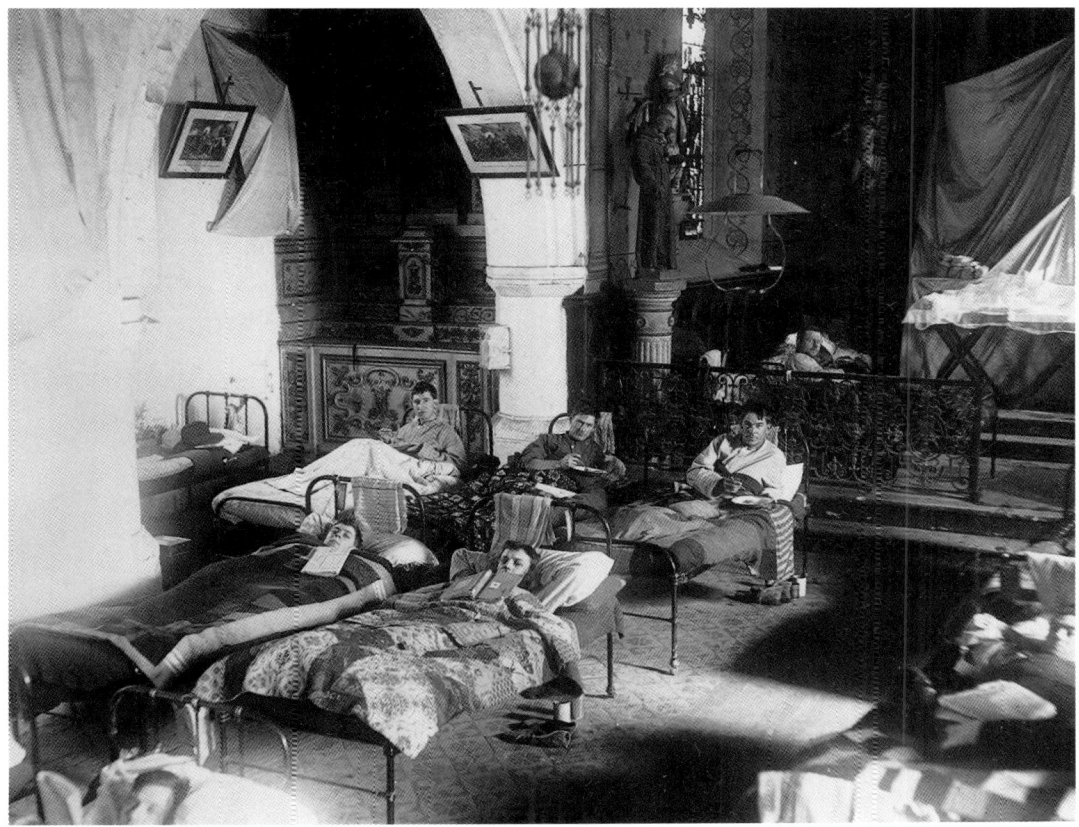

So the fight goes—on and on,
They are almost like the Hun:
   Their foul deeds are performed behind the back.
J.M. Harkins
Aussie, 8 March 1918

'Marching Song'
(*Sung to the tune of 'My Home in Tennessee'*)
Down in the old front line,
Oh, that won't do for mine,
Amongst the mud and slime,
Amidst the slush and grime.
All I can think of to-night
Is the parapet so white;
  Bombs are popping, shells are dropping,
No relief in sight.
The rum we ought to get,
We see no signs of yet.
You bet we'll get trench feet,
With nothing hot to eat.
There's tons of shells to chase us
And no dugouts to save us,
  Till we get back, till we get back,
Where there's wine and cheer for us.
Aussie, 4 April 1918

Up and Down the Duckboards
Up and down the duckboards,
  Up and down again,
Blinking at the star-shells
  Falling in the rain.

Thinking of the rations,
  If they're getting wet,
Thinking if there's any rum,
  How much will we get.

Thinking if a bullet hurts –
  If there's any pain.
Yow! Here comes a blanky bomb
  Up and down again.

Up and down the duckboards
  Screwing at the moon,
Musing on the bally strafe
  We got this afternoon.

Thinking how explosives
  Make you jump and shake and sweat,
Thinking how you duck and run,
  And hug the parapet.

Thinking of the next one–
  If it's joy or pain,
Hell! It's getting hotter!
  Up and down again!

Up and down the duckboards,
  Good and bad and worn,
From 'stand-to' in the evening
  Till 'carry-on' at dawn.

Thinking all the blooming things
  You never thought before,
Thinking of the stunt last night,
  And feeling pretty sore.

Thinking you'll chuck thinking up,
  Before you go insane –
Two whizz-bangs! A nine-two-eight!
  Up and down again!   *J.R.S.*
Aussie, August 1918

IN ACTION

Bullecourt
You boasted a wall of granite strength,
  Which nothing on earth could take.
The skill you learnt in forty years,
  You defied us blokes to break.

Four thousand men from the 'Southern Seas',
  In War but infants yet,
They crept grey-eyed from a sunken road,
  And through your barbed wire swept.

No guns to aid, no barrage long
  To sweep the wire away,
But a headlong charge of a thousand yards,
  And the blues they paved the way.

The first line through, the second held.
   They fought as strong men do,
'Hindenberg's Line' with its vaunted strength
   Was smashed by an Anzac crew.

No bombs to throw, no guns to speak,
   Nothing but lives to sell,
The 'Dark Blues' like a quivering wave.
   Fought through this infernal hell.

"Officers this way, the men go there!"
   The Hun O.C. called out,
But the men hung back as *men* will do,
   They broke—and a few got out.

There's a tale that is told in history,
   It's large on the scroll of fame,
Of a charge they made in the Crimea –
   'Balaclava' is the name.

But the charge we know and the charge we've seen
   Never from our minds will fade,
God speed the day we'll avenge those boys
   Who fell with the Blue Brigade.   '*Carey*'
Aussie, 16 February 1918

Extracts From My Diary
Ploegsteert. May 8th, 1917. A party of us have come to 'Plugstreet' Wood, to do some fatigue work in the trenches here. Today the guns are fairly quiet, and you can walk through the wood with all its fresh young growth of leaves—the elm, maple, honeysuckle, hawthorn, and oak, with fresh violets and cowslips blooming underneath. All the birds are busy with their songs, so that you can almost forget the roar and the 'crump' of yesterday, but we know that we insane human beings will begin the roar and 'crump' again to-morrow.
All Abaht It, February 1919

The Big Stunt. A couple of weeks elapse and the guns of the whole Brigade point ominously at the enemy from the vicinity of   . Something big is doing. Ammunition comes forward in unlimited supplies, and facilities for transport are being perfected. The roar of gunfire daily increases in intensity; tanks and heavy artillery continue to arrive. The enemy retaliates with his artillery, and from time to time tremendous explosions indicate that he has located one of our ammunition dumps. In spite of our suffering from enemy field guns, heavies, shrapnel and gas, it is obvious that Fritz is subjected to a bombardment infinitely more terrible. One night in particular will ever live in the memory of those engaged in this great attack. For 9 hours on this night we wore gasmasks with saliver accumulating within and the band pressing almost unbearably on the forehead. The gas on this night (3rd June) constituted an experience which tried the patience and nerves more than any other which has fallen to our lot.

Still we were ready for the Boche. Throughout the few days prior to the advance each man was confident and expectant. In the early hours of June 7th, tremendous explosions intimated that the mines had gone up, and the Infantry went over the top protected by a barrage which they described afterwards as a wall of steel. . . . In a much shorter space of time than had been allowed the important ridge where once stood the towns of Messines and Wytschaete was in our hands . . .

Shell Hole Country. After a few days the Brigade again went into action, this time in a position which was formerly enemy trenches. The landscape here is a perfect network of shell holes. Approaching the former battlefield, we notice ahead a stretch of devastated country of shell holes, mine craters, smashed dugouts, and annihilated woods. In the foreground is a strip of green grass, daisies, poppies and other wild flowers—the former site of No Man's Land. The scene behind is a contrast. Flourishing woods, verdant pastures, and red-roofed farm buildings enable us to comprehend what this country was like before the invasion by the Boche. Relics of the battlefield lie everywhere, among which are enemy rifles and ammunition which are useful for miniature rifle ranges in leisure moments. Little wooden crosses denote the last resting places of those who 'died that the nation might live.'

Fritz dugouts are constructed of reinforced concrete about 4ft in thickness, and even they may sometimes be seen hurled out of position by the heavy shells from our guns. Heaps of brick, and an occasional cabbage or turnip are all that remain of the former farm. In this locality we are enabled for the first time to note the results of our own fire.
Yandoo, September 1917

The human cost of any 'success' was enormous. Australian wounded returning from the battle of Menin Road, September 1917. (*Australian War Memorial, Neg. no. H00711*)

Infantry of the 2nd Australian Division at rest in the deep dugouts near Ypres, November 1917. (*Australian War Memorial, Neg. no. E01440*)

A Blighty
Twas one morning early before dawn on the Western Front
When there came a sound like thunder, the start of a blood red stunt
And out opened the batteries and shells went whizzing by
And many a square head German went for his morning fly.

We had a place to go to, a place of horrors and scenes
Twas just across a valley its name it was Messines
The first wave had started the second was on its way
Our own trenches we departed and taking his was play.

We gained our first objective by way of Avenue Farm
And sure the rest was easy for all the boys were calm
When the operator at the phone, showed signs of some dismay
For well he knew the trouble, our wires were cut away.

So twas linesman up and at it and mend those wires quick
For a message here is waiting so get up and do it quick
He started off at the double with knife cutters and tape
To mend the broken wires that Fritz put out of shape.

When he heard a whizzing in the air
And knew it to be a shell
So did not wait for it to strike him
As that's how many a man fell.

So for a shell hole he went sprawling
To get away from harm
When the blessed thing exploded
And a piece went through his arm.

He thanked old Fritz with all his heart
For that's what brought him Blighty
Those two round holes bored in his arm
Injuring him but slightly.

Burnished Bits, 1917

Notes on the Operation of October Ninth
We formed up in our JOT at 4.20 a.m. Fritz was fairly quiet; a good start was made at Zero hour. D company were followed by A C and B.

We got to our first objective with a good many casualties from machine gun fire on our right flank, and waited for our barrage to lift.

We reached the second objective alright, and dug a series of posts connecting up with the 5th Brigade on our left, but found we were not in touch on our right. . . .

It was trying work with one flank 'in the air', and our

boys did well to hang on until relieved about midnight.

It was very sloppy work down in the hollow, after getting accustomed to the (comparatively) dry sand up on the ridge.

On the whole it was a job of which the Battalion may well be proud. Our lads were not fit after days in the mud, burying cable and laying tracks, but it was a case of intense necessity, and they 'stuck it' as they have always done.

They were very tired indeed when they hopped the bags, but they 'got there' just the same, and hung on too. . . .

The 23rd, October 1917

Extracts from a letter from a Stretcher Bearer 8/10/17.
My job was to carry wounded from the advanced area to the first-aid post in the line of evacuation. It is no exaggeration to say that every inch of ground was a shell hole or rather a quagmire of shell holes. As the weather is rainy the bearers sink to the knees every step and progress is very slow. Never before have I seen so many dead. In many places we had actually to walk over the bodies, and the sights were sickening. I have seen pillboxes full of German dead, most of the bodies jet black through the effects of our gas. . . . The work at night is terrible. I was with a party for two hours, lost in the mud, with no idea of direction except that afforded by the Very lights. Floundering in the mud . . . we came across a Tommy officer sunk down to the armpits and calling for help. We had to lever him out of the mud with pieces of wood under his arms.

All Abaht It, February 1919

A Stunt
The afternoon preceding the night we moved forward witnessed a heavy thunderstorm. Terrific claps of thunder were followed by a torrential downpour lasting for a couple of hours. Late at night we moved to the place of assembly. The rain had made the going across country very heavy and slippery. A short rest and off again, this time to the tapes. Once in position, it was merely a matter of waiting for the signal to hop off. One's reflections were disturbed by the remark "A minute to go." Bang! Bang! Bang! The stillness is suddenly broken by the roar of many guns. Our barrage had opened. A few seconds to fix our bayonets and we were off. Just in front of us was our curtain fire, slowly advancing. Australians are considered by outsiders to be unhappy unless they are leaning against something. In this case, in the absence of lamp posts we leaned against the barrage . . . The main part of the job fell to our Battalion and we did it. When we discovered Fritz at the sunken road, he was a very surprised man. He eagerly loaded us with souvenirs, watches and revolvers being first favourites.

The Twenty Seconds Echo, 1 June 1918

Just a tiny bit of shrapnel fell from out the sky one day
And it smacked an Aussie soldier as in a deep shell hole he lay;
When the stretcher bearers found him, muddy, spent, but filled with glee,
He yelled "Oh! Ain't I lucky; this is a cert Blighty".
So they sprinkled him with iodine, they always do you know,
It's the only thing that saves us, it routs the septic foe.
They relieved him of his silver while he cursed to beat the band,
But they carried him to safety through that awful No Man's Land.   *J.O.D.*

The Digger, 11 August 1918

THE BATTERY HERALD

REGISTRATION AS A NEWSPAPER HAS BEEN REFUSED

NO. I. 25TH SEPTEMBER VOL I

SHIPPING NOTES.

The S.S. DEADSLOW will leave MARSEILLES on Saturday 30TH SEPTEMBER 1916 for Sydney and Melbourne. All men in posesion of week-end leave passes should book their passage at once.

The R.M.S. NEVERCOME owing to a landslide in the YARRA has been delayed indefinately with mails for Australian Troops somewhere in France.

Teeth repaired at shortest notice. F. CONRICK. DENTIST

BUSINESS NOTES.

All adverts for these colums must be in accordance with rules and must be accompanied by name and number of sender etc. NON DE PLUME only for Publication. EDITOR

WANTED. Man to interview all persons wishing to interview the Editor.

RETIRED. WOOLOOMOOLOO. Pte PREFERRED.

CHARWOMAN. To clean out the Telephone Pit, make beds, & be on hand when required by men. Knock, bell out of action.

Amiens, 1918
They shall not pass! The marshal said.
They shall not pass! The order sped.
The far-flung British battle line,
Facing odds of six to nine,
Was bending, but not broken.
Australian troops to man the line!
Australian troops to face the iron!
And Marshal Foch had spoken,
They shall not pass!

They shall not Pass! For all their boasts.
They shall not pass! For all their hosts.
Across poor tortured Picardy,
Imposing dev'lish tyranny
On villa, farm and town.
Australian troops to bar the way!
Australian troops to join the fray,
And strike the base invader down!
They shall not pass!

They shall not pass! We pledged our word.
They shall not pass! We drew the sword,
That Amiens and France might see
That Right would gain the victory,
And burst their bonds asunder.
Australian troops to face the foe!
Australian troops to lay them low,
And bring the tyrant under!
They did not pass!   *Sgt. E.S. Scott Holland*
The Tassie Times Magazine,
November/December 1918

A Record of Cumulative Honour
Beach Thomas' Verdict
In the course of a despatch to the Continental 'Daily Mail' Mr Beach Thomas, the famous war correspondent said:

'Yesterday's attacks rounded off the exploit, and the capture of Beaurehain by the Australians with 500 prisoners adds to a corps' triumph to which there is no parallel. The Australians drove the enemy from Villers-Bretonneux and saved Amiens over six months ago. They have never ceased fighting since. First a succession of small assaults near Hamel. Then the great battle and break through on August 8. Then continuous local attacks and patrol penetration that quite broke the nerve of the enemy. Then the snatching of Mont Saint-Quentin and heavy street fighting. Then the bitter and obstinate battle, first at the Hindenberg and then at the strongest and most wired part of the Beaurevoir line. Again recently, in company with a tank corps, whose dash and endurance they so admire, the storming of Beaurehain and the break-up of counter-attacks in which large numbers of the enemy were killed by very few Australians.

Is there any record in the war of such a six month's tale of unrelenting energy unbroken progress, and cumulative honour?'

The Jackass, December 1918

BEHIND THE LINES

Little trips to Amiens,
Little drops of vin,
Makes the gallant Anzacs
Think the war they'll win.
Big fat Tommy redcaps
Pinches them galore,
Lands them in the peter
"Straffe the ruddy war".

The Sportsman, July 1917

Extracts from My Diary
L'Estrade. March 12th, 1917.... Walk into Steenwerck, buy some odds and ends, and have some tea (eggs and chips) there. We walk back and look in to see Papa, Marguerite (Marry I) and Ginger in the capacious kitchen of the farmhouse, which does duty also as an estaminet. Papa is asleep in a corner of the room. Big stout Mama at a side table is also dead to the world. The room is full of our merry boys, and Ginger is busy filling up the beer-jug and collecting the francs. D----, with overflowing glass in hand, unwarily tilts back his chair just over the balancing-point. Though he, chair and all, goes toppling to the floor, he holds the precious glass so that not one drop is spilt. ...

I miss B----, but he is discovered down the cellar with Marguerite.

About an hour after 'Lights Out' we retire. Outside we discover that J----, who was somewhat 'estametic', has lost the road and found the ditch, wherein he has got submerged in its own peculiar mud and slime.

All Abaht It, February 1919

In Billets
Oh, it's red wine, white wine, beer and stout,
When the troops are back and billeted out;
For it ain't no fun when you're up the line,
Where guns go mad and bullets whine.

You say we're mad when we strike the beer!
But if you'd stood in a shivering fear,
With the boys who bring the wounded back
'Cross no-man's-land, where there ain't no track,

You'd read no psalms to the men that fight!
You'd take to drink to forget the sight
Of torn-out limbs and sightless eyes,
Or the passing of a pal that dies.

So drink with me, or I'll see you damned
With the German and his fatherland;
For it's red wine, white wine, beer and stout,
When the boys are back and billeted out.
G.C. Murray
Aussie, June 1918

From an estaminet one dusk of day
I watched the Mam'selles passing o'er the way
And shortly afterwards was heard to say,
"Deux Piquants garcon, toute suite s'il vous plait".

Come fill the cup. How oft must I repeat
Deux Piquants? Bring the bottle here toute suite
And now champagne. How much? Vingt francs!
   That's steep
But carry on, this Mam'oiselles a dinkum treat.

There with a lump of love in that Café
We drank beaucoup, and did in all my pay,
And then when I was broke, from o'er the way
A froggy bloke comes up HER FIANCE.   A.D.I.
The Digger, 18 August 1918

The School for French
One night I took a stroll with Bill,
   Along the Boulevarde,
And Bill, he said, "Let's have a pot" –
   He caught me off me guard.

So in we went: the 'staminay
   Was pretty full of cheer;
A couple of me cobbers too,
   Were pretty full of beer.

But Bill he strode towards the Bar,
   And called for "Two beers, quick" –
Just like he did at 'Mick Malone's' –
   The pub at Sandy Crick.

Ole Bill he ain't no 'ansome bloke,
   He's rough, but in his eye,
I guess a chap can always spot,
   A twinkle if he try.

Ole Bill, he sinks his glass o' grog,
   And winks at me for 'Toast' –
"And now I'll teach yer parleyvous" –
   He ain't no bloke to boast

Up came the tart to get the glass,
   So Bill most gravely said,
"Mam'selle vous promenade with moi"-
   She laughed and tossed her head.

So Bill he quietly lit a fag,
   He found behind his ear,
"I'll bet I make her parleyvous,
   Before I go from here."

So Bill he called the tart again,
   And swore he'd make her 'bite' –
"Deux beer, encore, please sil vous plait
   I'm talkin' French tonight."

"Deuz oeufs and chips, vin rouge & blanc" –
   He couldn't go too fur –
She laughed at him, she liked ole Bill
   "Yes Bill, apres la guerre.'

So Bill he shouted once again,
   And Marie came once more –
"Nous promenade la Wagga Hay,
   Et Coogee, Borenore."

Them Marie looked a bit non-plussed
   While Bill began to yell –
"Vous compree Bourke, Wallerawang,
   Gibraltar, Spain or 'ell?"

Out of the line men were able to shed the mud and vermin of the trenches and prepare for good food and drink in the estaminet. *The Yandoo*, July 1918. (*Australian War Memorial Printed Records*)

Still Marie stood with puzzled air,
   While Bill's voice rose in fury –
"Vous compree Dubbo, Booligal,
   Balmain or Toohey's brewery?"

Just then mam'selle began to speak
   "Now boys, thank you, good-night."
And "Finish, Eight o'clock" rang out
   Before he'd made her 'bite'.

Then Bill, tho' beat, just drained his glass
   "No stoppin' after hours,
I couldn't pick their lingo up,
   I'll teach the Frenchies ours."

The Baths

A bath is a luxury. A man who claims a bath as a right would expect sugar in his tea, meat in his stew, or 'thank you' from his Sergeant. Seldom is a man heard to complain that he is detailed for a bath out of his turn.

A march of 4 miles over cobbles, and the N.C.O. halts his party outside an old distillery, from which volumes of smoke pour through a tall chimney stack. Parties of Australians, Canadians, New Zealanders and Tommies belonging to Artillery, Engineers, A.S.C., A.M.C., and Inf., all wait their turn. That the baths are well within the range of Fritz's shells troubles them not at all. The establishment of baths so close to the trenches is typical of the many wonderful provisions that are made for the comfort and well being of the troops.

   "What are you, Cpl?" queries the doorkeeper.
   "Umptyumpth Battery."
   "How many men?"
   "Ten."

The doorkeeper counts the ten men as they pass, but when inside the addition of several 'hoggets' has unaccountably swelled the party to 14. Here an Orderly, like the almost extinct town-crier, monotonously bellows–"Turn your tunic and breeches inside out and hand them in at the first window for brushing. Leave your hat, gasmask, jack-knife, boots and other valuables at the second window. Nothing must be left here as you go out another way."

Scantily clad figures with 'valuables' dockets hanging beside identity discs, rush along the duckboards to a large steam-clouded room. Here they transfer remaining garments to their arms, are glanced over by an A.M.C. man and enter a race with bins on either side. Casting dirty clothes to left, they receive clean ones from the right. After pigeon-holing the latter according to number or docket, over go the troops into a large wooden vat of 4ft to 5ft of hot disinfected water. Like the occupants of other tubs in the large room, they flounder about, duck one another, and perform the almost impossible feat of holding one foot above water level during soaping operations. As one by one they clamber out, they present a tempting target and bearing numerous impressions of the red hand, rush for their shirts.

"Good-oh" a grinning gunner grunts, "the towel I chucked in was one I picked up, the shirt had the tail clipped off for harness cleaning, and the other clobber came from The Warren."

                    Yandoo, July 1917

Those early French baths were no gentle white-tiled luxuries; but small drippings from leaky taps on to wooden boards dirty with the tread of many army boots. The taps warned off from the inquisitive gaze by a wall of thinnest hessian that quivered in the icy December wind. The water may have been warm when it left the tap but by the time it trickled down your back it had a glacier touch. Ugh!. But things improved. There did come a time when the trickle became a spray, and real live hot water descended on your crouching back. What a delightful sensation. Three weeks in the line, caked in mud from head to foot, chatty and irritated by many torments and then this exquisite freshness and the removal of a leaden weight. And with luck the baths soon improved. Barns were utilised. Turned into bathrooms by the energetic Australians. And clean linen neatly stacked in bundles at the side. A strange thing that a man should grow accustomed to the idea of handing over his inner clothes in exchange for others–washed certainly–but worn previously by some other person. How many of us would have endured the thought in civilian days.

It must be confessed that victory has its disadvantages. Baths suffer. The uncertainty of the established line means that proper accommodation is not easy to obtain. And so we find ourselves back once more to the hessian sense of decency and the

After bathing to get rid of vermin the troops were issued with clean underclothes and uniforms. The Divisional Baths, Daours, May 1918. (*Australian War Memorial, Neg. no. E02314*)

The troops in France voted against conscripting men to join them. Men of the 3rd Battalion resting at Samer record their votes, December 1917. (*Australian War Memorial, Neg. no. E01400*)

trickling tap. "Now, boys, all under together and we'll turn on the water."

The 23rd, 15 October 1918

The Ablution Shed
The joys of an ablution shed
Perhaps are known to you;
In case they're not I'll go ahead
And tell you of a few.

Its size is sometimes large enough
To hold about five men,
Though signs display in words of bluff
There's 'Washing space for ten'.

Inside the shed the ten men get,
Though how you don't quite know,
While one man washes, nine get wet
While standing in the row.

With soaking clothes and sodden boots
To shave you then essay,
While at the glass four other coots
Shove faces in the way.

You then attempt your teeth to clean,
Around the tap you crush,
When finished that you find you've been
And used your cobber's brush.

At last your toilet is complete
You then wish to get out,
You push and shove through legs and feet
For half a mile about.

These inconveniences are just
A few you have to stand,
So take my tip if wash you must,
Try doing it in sand. F.U.N.

The Jackass, September 1918

The Field Vaudeville Theatres have become a recognised feature of our soldier life. . . . *Aussie* intends to give a short description of each of our Field Shows dealing with one each issue. On this occasion, dear brethren, he will make a few remarks about that cheerful collection of mirth-producers, 'The Senti-mental Blokes', who belong to the Division of the horizontal oblong.

'The Blokes' specialise in comedy. The combination includes a number of clever comedians who serve up good, humorous patter and songs, which never fail to produce the loud laugh that denotes the happy mind . . . Their trump card is their 'Girl'. She's a dear. *Aussie* has seen a lot of girl girls not nearly so girlish as Pte. V. Kemble's impersonation. Before he got mixed up in this international argument, the writer's job brought him pretty closely into contact with Australian histrionics, but he has never seen a better female impersonation than that put up by Kemble. He shows up best in 'Grow, little Mushroom, Grow!' and 'China Town'. Driver R. Cerise issues a liberal ration of really funny gags mixed with an assortment of more or less comic songs. . . . Pte. A.D. Bett has a well-trained tenor voice and puts over popular stuff in good style. Lieut. W.M. Blake specialises in things like 'Burlington Bertie' and makes a good job of them. Driver R. Glenister can emit a good basso song, and does well in acting parts in short sketches. Sergt. W.J. Goodall is 'The Blokes' star 'monologuist'. As an ancient Aussie in 'Snail's Aeroplane Tours' he is the Big Noise of the Show. Pte. Anderson mostly ragtimes and does it in a cheerful manner. As Charlie Chaplin conducting the band, he threatens to outchaplin Chaplin. Sapper R. Smedley tunefully agitates the mandolin to everybody's satisfaction. Pte. H. Marther puts a lot of humour into 'The Soldier's Story' and other comic items of that kind. . . . As a conjuror and balancer Corporal R. Davy is 'out on his own'. The risky things he does as a juggler of bayonets gives one the impression that when he wants a rest from nerve strain he goes up into the front line. ...

Aussie, 8 March 1918

NEWS FROM DOWN UNDER

The Conscription Referendum
Australia is now at a critical stage of her national life. The conscription turmoil has shaken the fibres of the Commonwealth from the 'Gulf Country' to Gippsland, 'The Speck', and across the 'Never Never' to the Western state. The momentous question is about

to change the whole aspect of Australian politics, and who knows what the future may bring forth? Certainly political parties had reached a dead-lock, and the desirability of a party of a broad national character to intercept the futile 'Redrag—bloated Capitalistic' wrangle, has long been felt. The Conscription disagreement will be the clarifying factor.

Australia, like other parts of the Empire, is fighting for her existence. Those who know, pronounced the voluntary system of recruiting inadequate. The majority of those to whom patriotism and honor appeals, are already doing their share; the minority are covered by the liberal exemption clauses in the Conscription Bill. Others, eligible soldiers, are among the agitators in the present disgraceful coal strikes, and in the crowds which assemble at any spectacular functions in the vicinity of the city.

Probably, the most potent argument against Conscription, is that Australia has sent her quota of troops, and the remaining men are required at home to back up the army, and assist in the sustenance of the Empire by primary production. A logical contention, and one not lost sight of when framing the Conscription Bill.

German newspapers, of course, make much of the Australian Referendum figures. They acclaim an indication of the disintegration of the Empire. Therein they err. The difference of opinion lies solely in the method of procedure. . . .

Anti-Conscription leads with 1,102,227 against 1,033,753. With Conscription discarded—which seems a likely contingency—the task before Australia to keep up her forces at the front is a tremendous one. . . .

Yandoo, November 1916

The Referendum—A Conscription Symposium
How did you vote on this matter?
Is a question asked by all.
Some of us voted with reason,
Some with no reason at all.

Yet, still in their huts they will argue,
And fight and kick up a great din.
Some say the Allies are 'home on the bit',
There's no doubt they are going to win.

Then why bring our mates from Australia?
Is the answer of voters for 'No.'
'Twill be funny if in the near future,
For reinforcements they look - and a 'Blow'.

The boys in trenches are waiting
For our help to pull them through.
Good luck, Third Australian Division,
Your hope of relief is quite 'Blue.'

That, sure, will be the outcome,
Should conscription lose the day,
But with Anzac heroes we'll do the share
Of those who are staying away.

I voted 'No' on this question,
(The greatest our Nation will ask),
For the reason that the Anzac
Has volunteered for his task.

We have argued it here in the Division,
With language full of force and 'go',
But some have just come to a decision,
That is answered with a simple 'No.'

There are some who stay behind,
With their reasons good and sound,
And yet we're urged to make them fight,
For reinforcements must be found.

Over here in England
We have learned what Conscription yields,
And then we have to pause and think
Of our pastures and agrarian fields.

How can we help the Empire
If our wool and our wheat be lost?
Surely, surely, we're helping,
In paying the terrible cost.

We had a chance of spending Easter
At home, you'll all confess,
But it was outed for good on polling day,
By those who did not vote 'Yes.'
                                                       J.M.R.

And if, were our last man conscripted,
And our land were a prey to the Orient,
You'd then rue the day that you voted
That all men in Australia be sent.
                                                       W.S.
                                All Abaht It, November 1916

AUSTRALIAN CABLES
AUSTRALIAN GOVERNMENT ELECTIONS LIKELY IN MAY
AUSTRALIAN NATIONAL PARTY FORMED
MR. HUGHES DECISION

The Times states that Mr. Hughes has finally decided not to attend the special War Conference in London. He proposes to devote his whole energies to launching his new National Party. Melbourne, Jan. 13.

Sir William Irvine in a letter to the press contends that Australia must be represented at the Imperial Conference, which in his opinion is the most important constitutional development since the granting of responsible Government. Melbourne, Jan. 11.

A general election for the Australian Federal Parliament is likely to be held in May. Its object is to clear the political atmosphere. Melbourne, Jan. 11.

At a meeting convened by Mr. W.M. Hughes at the Melbourne Town Hall it was unanimously decided to form a new association of Australian nationalists. The object of this association is to set the winning of the war before party issues . . . and to ensure that the Parliament and Government of Australia shall reflect the determination of the Australian people in these directions. . . .

The following platform has been adopted by the executive of the new Australian National Party . . . who are prepared to unite upon a common platform for:-

1) Winning the war and maintaining the Empire's solidarity.
2) An effective repatriation scheme for returned soldiers and sailors and their dependents.
3) The maintenance of responsible Government.
4) The settlement of disputes by conciliation and arbitration.
5) Upholding the White Australia Policy.
6) Organisation and development of Australian national resources and ensuring of absolute free trade within the Commonwealth. . . . Melbourne, Jan. 11.

The new recruiting campaign is now in full swing throughout Australia. Sir Munro Ferguson, the Governor General, speaking at the opening meeting of the Victorian campaign . . . said that the rejection of the compulsory system involved a responsibility for making the voluntary recruiting system succeed. One might say that Australia had staked her honour on the outcome. She was pledged to make it a success.
                                    The Rising Sun, 15 January 1917

WAR PENSIONS
Commonwealth of Australia

In the case of a loss of a leg, or foot, or hand, or arm, the rate of pension payable is to be the maximum for six months, and thereafter three quarters of the full rate. For the loss of an eye, the soldier is to receive half the maximum rate. For the loss of both legs, of both feet, of both arms, of both hands, of an arm and a leg, of a hand and a foot, of both eyes, of an eye, together with the loss of a leg, foot, hand or arm, the payment is to be the maximum rate for at least six months, and thereafter subject to reduction to seven-eights of the maximum rate if and so long as the member is capable of earning at least 6s. a week.
                                    The Kookaburra, April 1917

A SENSE OF IDENTITY

We are Australia's representatives in the field in France. In Gallipoli, our Australian comrades have made tremendous sacrifices in order to prove to the world the fact that the Australian is not inferior to others in stamina and fighting qualities and that he is entitled, by the sacrifices of wealth and blood he is prepared to make for it, to the possession of his vast continent of the South. It was the first time that History had favoured him with an opportunity for conclusively establishing that claim, and judging from the praise that his achievements have won for him in England, he has not been weighed in the balance and found wanting.

Honk, 12 August 1915

A Word To Our Friends
There's the *Times* and there's the *Herald*.
Daily Telegraph and *Mail*,
And there's stacks of other papers
Harping on the same old tale.

The same old tale about us;
What mighty deeds we've done,
How we scaled the cliffs at ANZAC,
How we made the Turks to run.

How we tickled up the Kaiser
Since we landed here in France;
How we're terror to the Boches
Whom we lead a fearful dance.

How at POZIERES we conquered,
At ARMENTIERES made good,
How we're fond of facing danger,
How we've always firmly stood.

But though it's nice to listen
To this literary praise,
Still we know no earthy reason
Why a difference should be raised . . .

So now when you read about us,
And think p'raps there's too much fuss,
You know we're not the authors and
    WE ARE FED UP, ALL OF US!   *B.M.M.*

Somme Sketches
It is wonderful how, in spite of the real inner change wrought in a man by military life, bush types persist. Just note the man driving that G.S. waggon. He is going up to an advanced dump with rations. Brown mud and watery desolation surround him. No environment could be more unlike his own hot, dusty roads, bordered by eucalyptus. Yet does not that hunched back, that pipe standing out clear against the skyline, that rather bored, fixed expression on the immobile face speak of long solitary journeyings in the bush. Should a shell intrude on his meditations, he will indicate the fact that he has noticed it by spitting on that side when next, in the fullness of time, he has occasion to spit. Should several arrive, and his mature judgement tell him they are meant for his piece of road, he will stir his heavy laden horses to a faster walk. But no observable change of expression will cross his face . Should he be splashed, he will content himself with one terse verbal comment on his enemy's pedigree. How many keen, highly strung minds in positions of leadership and responsibility would give all that they had for that driver's nerves; his heritage from the bush.

There are obviously three Australian privates coming down from 'the line'. But I had to rub my eyes, to clear them of the impression of three bushmen humping their swags.
    There was no N.C.O. The strain of several day's intense discipline had slackened for a moment; they had been left behind for some purpose or other and were 'drifting' back to their battalion. So they moved abreast instead of in single file. The 'tin hat' instead of being worn flat, was tilted slightly backwards, both hands in the pockets, shoulders stooped, a swag up, which included tin utensils, knife and fork, rolled blanket, and they swung along with a rolling unmilitary stride, legs wide apart. O, Gippsland, when the mud of Picardy is washed away, thy children shall return to thee unchanged.

The Rising Sun, 22 January 1917

Reinforcements
Many Australians fight in France
(You could not tell 'em at a glance
At hardened chivs and grimy paws),
Who never fought on Anzac's shores.

When Woolly Bears burst overhead,
All look the same, alive or dead;

Chats from the Somme, as well as Turkey,
Find all their garments just as lurky.

Over the bags they go as fast,
Where Fritz or Abdul sends the blast;
While guns behind bark just as hot –
Dinkums or Anzacs matter not.

Lone Pine and Mouquet both took toll
Of boys who sought the self-same goal,
We're going till we have strafed the Hun,
And where? Well, what cares anyone! *'Dinkum'*
The Rising Sun, 24 March 1917

For the benefit of budding poets it must be thoroughly understood that jingoism and mushy sentiment is severely discouraged. 'The Gallant Anzac and the Love-sick Tabby' is played out—dead as meat.
The Sportsman, May 1917

Theoretically every soldier before a stunt should become meditative, devout and concerned with things that are not of this world. In actual practice, however, the reverse is the actual case, and the average soldier is never so inclined to levity and lightheartedness as just on the eve of battle.

Which recalls the experience of an ardent moralist who approached a little group tempting fortune with the inevitable pennies.

"Before action," he said to one of the group, "You don't, of course, go in for this do you?"

"No," replied the lad slowly, "before a stunt does make a difference—then we double the bets."
The 23rd, May 1918

While the programmes presented by ... our Field Theatres are very attractive and very highly appreciated, a few more typically Australian items would make them still more acceptable. AUSSIE feels that the wish of the majority of the members of this Aussie Army of ours is being expressed when the suggestion is made to our Field Shows to try to create a strong Australian atmosphere in their programmes by the inclusion of songs, recitations, etc., of Australian origin.
Aussie, June 1918

Almost unnoticed in the travail of this world war there is a nation that is approaching full consciousness of its purpose of living and shedding many old ideas. Australianism is the new cult that is displacing all other old dogmas, creeds and theses. Australians are now learning the dignity of nationhood, are leaving that provincial outlook with which, hitherto, they approached many questions affecting their own country. It is not now the advantages of Sydney over Melbourne; the respective merits and demerits of each separate state. Every man now is an Australian living and thinking as best he knows how, as an Australian. This comparatively sudden awakening to a new national ideal has been brought about by many causes, but the one which appears to have exercised the most potent influence is our sojourn here in France.... [It's] good to be an Australian these days, good to realise this warmth of sentiment that is growing amongst Australians. A firm conviction in the eternal destiny of our country to be a leader amongst the nations, a country of rational freedom, where everything may flourish, where men may lead logical lives free from the old narrow-mindedness of sect and politics. 'Australia first and all other things afterwards' should be our slogan. It is a new religion, a logical purpose for living that we have in this new cult of Australianism, a new incentive to give of our best, because it is ours to make it the leader of civilisation in the Southern hemisphere. An Australian Gambetta is wanted to make this cult that of every Australian; to give a new meaning to the word for many thousands of men; to raise the fiery cross of intense Australianism, so that we may all live better and die better for having realised the dignity and the purpose of our inheritance and responsibility as Australians. *Picken*
The Jackass, July 1918

During the ... time we have spent in France, our boys have adopted many French expressions ... One of the most popular phrases in use, and which few of us are likely to forget, is 'Ca ne fait rien' meaning 'It doesn't matter.' A simple everyday saying this, yet underlying the simplicity there is a depth of philosophy in the remark, as used by the men who are taking part in this struggle for freedom.

A fatigue party may be staggering along under heavy loads in the mud and darkness ... Some of the men are on the verge of despondency, when one of the hardbitten Billjims, with the nearest approach to jocularity that circumstances will permit, in reply to an outburst by another member of the party, remarks–"Ca ne fait rien–C'est la guerre." The saying almost seems to electrify the men, who carry on with renewed vigor.

In all of the many trials encountered in the course of duty, the same remark can be heard, and it indicates a philosophic spirit in adversity which will surely endure.

If a man can face the trials of life in and around the Trenches with unquenchable optimism, there is not the least doubt that he will rise superior to any of the comparatively petty troubles of civil life, and in the years to come will meet misfortune with a shrug and the old familiar by-word "Ca ne fait rien."

The Twenty Seconds Echo, 1 August 1918

Cobbers
Have yer ever had an 'ead,
When yer get up from yer bed
Like a grammerphone wot's playin' outer tune;
And to get off for the day,
You would give yer socks away?
   I 'ave.

Have yer ever done yer brass,
With two pennies on the grass,
Backin' 'eads when 'Micks' kept showin' orl the time;
And yer didn't 'ave a brown
For a tram ride into town?
   I 'ave.

Have yer ever made a splash
On yer leave with tons of cash,
And the pay-book lookin' 'ealthy for a score;
And yer last day been so broke
That yer 'ummin' for a smoke?
   I 'ave. . . .

Have yer ever thought how much,
Cobbers, diggers, mates and such
Can mean in this 'ere rotten game of war?
You'll 'ave found this brother'ood
Is the one thing any good.
   I 'ave.   *F.J.D., The Jackass*, August 1918

AUSSIOSITIES

Two English Privates were sitting in an estaminet t'other evening conversing loudly in French. A couple of Australians at an adjoining table decided that they were not going to allow themselves to be out-swanked. So one, who came from N.S.W., remarked excitedly to his companion:

"Wagga Wagga walgett woolloomooloo wee waa wallerawang woolgoolga yarramalong."

"Woollongabba," replied his comrade who came from Queensland, "Cunnamalla toowoomba toowong thargomindah indoroopilly camooweal goondiwindi."

"Bondi coogee maroubra," said the other with great determination.

It made the Englishmen slew round and take notice.

"Excuse me," said one, 'but what language is that you're speaking?"

"Oh, that's our Australian language," he was told. "We learnt English before we came away, but we always prefer to speak our own language among ourselves."

Honk, 29 August 1915

The Convenient Commandments
Thou shalt not covet thy neighbour's wife
His ox thou shalt not slaughter
But thank the Lord He did not say
Thou shalt not covet his daughter.

If you are a good soldier you will treat your rifle as you would your wife.
   Rub it over each night with an oily rag.
The Battalion Buzzer, May 1917

He was from a part of the camel country where they only heard there was a war on in 1916, and until an affable R.T.O. consigned him to a lonely terminus in France, about the only foreigners he had met were the boys at his station. So, standing lonely amid his kit in the aforesaid French terminus, he shouted to the astonished porter: "Hi, you pfeller! You bin take it mi pfeller kit, put him longside pfeller cab, me bin gib it tickpence!"

The Rising Sun, 29 January 1917

It occurred on the Somme. A Billjim, new to traffic control, received instructions to divert traffic along another road. This did not suit a particularly famous British regiment, and the C.O., after expostulating, wound up with "but don't you know we are the Guards". Quick came the reply, "I don't care if you're the blanky engine drivers; you can't go this way." They didn't.

The 23rd, 15 November 1917

The idea of the camp I speak about was to give the 'war-worns' a rest—at least, that is what we were told. This haven of delight was situated near a village in France. Anyhow, we were a happy family and our lives would have been *quite* free from anxiety if it had not been for those eternal fatigues. The C.O. was typically English, some went so far as to say that his symptoms were even more obvious than that; in short, that he was a 'squire'. Whether this was the truth or not, the fact remains that the unfortunate colonel will long remember the colonials under his charge. Making his round of inspection one day with the Orderly Officer, 'the old man' asked a certain mess the usual question about complaints, evidently expecting the usual answer. Did he get it though? Well, hardly. An Aussie was present, you see, and Aussies will talk so. "The bacon is short again, sir", the Billjim said with great feeling. (One desires nourishment even in a rest camp, they say.) The squire blinked in amazement and then replied impressively; "My dear young fellow, considering that there are so many submarines about, you ought to be thankful to get even the smallest piece of bacon! Report to the Guard Tent!" Amongst many titters and more or less sympathetic remarks, the Australian went outside and accosted the guard, saying thusly: "Say, digger, have you any bacon to spare?" "Aye, choom, 'ere you are," and the poor innocent handed over a liberal supply to the master criminal who promptly 'beat it'. ...

Sgt. McGregor M.M.
The Jackass, July 1918

The great Australian game of 'Two-Up' has been played in some queer places, and under strange conditions. Recently, one of our patrols was considerably overdue, and I was detailed as one of a search party. We dodged about evading flares and shell-holes for some time. Suddenly we saw the shadowy figures of a number of men standing silently in the darkness. "Fritzes!" said someone, and we all ducked into shell-holes. Fritz's next flare revealed a small party, all stooping and gazing intently on the ground. Then one of them cried softly and exultantly, "Two heads are right!" picked up the pennies and pocketed his winnings. It was the lost patrol. They were making their bets and tossing the coins in the darkness, and then waiting for the light from a Fritz flare to see the result.

Aussie, August 1918

"We'll have that movement again!"
An R.C. Padre was tripping gaily along somewhere near supports, when he noticed a burying party, just putting the finishing touches to the graves of four of their comrades. He pulled up, and finding that three of them were of his creed, asked who had read the service. "Some Tommy C. of E. Padre, Sir" was the reply. The R.C. Chaplain asked nothing more, but walked straight to the graves, and, in a voice like a sergeant-major, gave the order—"Numbers 2, 3 and 4—As you were!"—then proceeded to re-read the burial service.

The Third Battalion Magazine, August 1918

A DIGGER was smoking one day in a non-smoking compartment of a London Bus and the conductress was quite willing to let him break the regulations, but an old gentleman objected and finally threatened to report the conductress if the soldier wasn't ejected.

Faced with the prospect of dismissal, the girl went up to the Aussie and said in a timid whisper "Would you like to ruin me?" and the reply came back, quick as a flash, "My oath Miss, what time do you knock off?"

Brain Wave, August 1918

The monocle is still popular. As the English Johnny Captain stretched himself in his hut (a cow shed) he knocked his head against a beam. "Oh, ---- it. My bally glass has broken." The officahs monocle had fallen with the bump. He had a box full by way of reserve. This same officer who was all monocle, cane, and expansive breeches, visited the Australian officers mess one night and "Ah ah" and "haw hawed" with no success. Billjim officers were once Diggers, coves, blokes, coots, or Aussies, and it was too much for them. About twelve secured monocles, or rather identification discs, and brown paper discs, and "hawed" to some order. The officer has not been seen since.

The Digger, 4 August 1918

When we were in supports at Villers Bretonneux, we found several cases of champagne in an old Fritz dugout, evidently pinched from one of the *Estaminets* in the Fritz-blighted town. Next day we were ordered to go into reserves, but were loath to leave the unexpended portion of the salved joy-water for the newcomers, as it would be likely to bring about conduct to the prejudice of good order and military discipline. So in the best interests of the Army and ourselves, we decided to bury the stuff until we returned, which we knew would be in about a fortnight. Nearby was the grave of a dead horse with the regulation sign on it: 'Foul ground. Dead horse buried here.' We dug a hole near this, buried the champagne, and then took the sign from the dead horse grave and placed it over our live champagne grave. When we returned about a fortnight later, a Tommy Battery was at the spot. We immediately secured a spade and energetically set about the exhumation of our buried treasure. "Hi! Choom," said one of the Tommies, "there'll be a 'ell of a stink if you dig up that dead 'orse!" "That's alright," replied a Dag, "it's suspected that this horse met its death from foul play, and the body is being exhumed to hold an inquest on it." You could have knocked those Tommies' eye balls off with a stick when we produced the cases of cham. We gave them a couple of bottles and advised them to dig up the other grave if they wanted more. They wanted more, alright. The bunch made a combined attack on the dead horse grave, and we gathered up our liquid life and carried out an orderly retreat before the stench from the dead nag became due. A.E.T.

Aussie, December 1918

Whilst walking down a street in a town in France, my attention was drawn to a notice in an estaminet window, 'English spoken here—Australian understood'.

To the uninitiated, the Australian Soldier has a language all his own—he calls it 'Dinkum Australian'. It has three very marked properties— Forceful, Expressive, and Unprintable.

All Abaht It, February 1919

LEAVE

C.B.
I ain't a bloomin navvy, and I ain't a bloomin' mule,
But I'm just a blessed soldier what 'as been a bloomin' fool, . . .
Yer want ter know what stroke of luck 'as landed of me there.
It's all because a blue-eyed girl a-whispered in my ear.
I 'ad a bloomin leave pass that only went till eight,
But it must 'a been at midnight that I left 'er at 'er gate.
I sneaks along to barricks, and I tries to dodge the guard,
When I 'ears a voice say "Who goes there," I says, "It's me, old pard."
'e takes me to the sergeant who shoves me in the klink,
And all because I dallied with a bit of skirt in pink. . . .

The Rising Sun, 25 December 1916

There was a young lady from Kent
She knew just what everything meant
She was asked out to dine

Private room—lots of wine
She knew what it meant
So she went. *The Sportsman*, May 1917

Respite from the fighting offered the chance of female company. *The Twenty Third*, November 1918.
(*Australian War Memorial Printed Records*)

(*Australian War Memorial Printed Records*)

Square the Dink
When an 'Aussy' goes home on his ten days leave;
He's the time of his life no doubt.
The first days has 'tabbies' and taxis galore.
"Come on, have a booze?" he will shout.

His ticket is made out for Scotland 'tis true,
But the only Scotch he sees is whisky,
And, accompanied by 'cobbers' from
    Woolloomooloo
At times he'll get rather too frisky.

He may get a bit rash and blow up his cash;
Even get stiff and might finish in clink;
Still he's had a good time—a 'bonzer' big dash—
Keep on smiling boys—"Square the Dink".
                The 23rd, October 1917

London—An Appreciation After the Line
One day I lived where Death had broken bounds
The next I travelled on the Underground
Sheer delights to me were common sights and
    sounds.

The red and green lights letting trains go through
The rush of passengers as evening grew
The neat advertisements that all eyes drew.

Dear little child going your East-end way
What pleasure in your gurgling laughter lay
After the drumming of the guns across the bay.

I saw a lady angry with the mass
Of hurrying scurrying thoughtless lad and lass
Fleeing monotony ere the day should pass.

I thought how she would like a lonely trench
With dead for company—and all the stench
The loss of friends—and all its awful wrench.

An old and stately man in corner placed
Frowned at a couple with hands interlaced,
How dare they show their love so open-faced.

He should have lived where womanhood we miss,
No touch of hand, no soft caress—no kiss,
Only the memories of such eager bliss.

Oh, wan conductress, working wearily,
Opening and shutting doors so drearily,
As though life held you so contrarily.

I'd change your place for joy it would impart
Of riding close to London's mighty heart
As thro' and thro' it with the trains I dart.   *L.G.S.*
                The 23rd, January 1918

The Leave-taking of Leave
The world, includin' Blighty, 'as gone grey,
There's nothin' much to live for. When the clues
Give me the glad, I look the other way.
I 'aven't got the 'eart, somehow, to booze,
I've 'ad enough 'o theatres an' plays.
The Strand might just as well be miles away.
I got the indigoes because today's
    The 14th day.

I've 'ad a slashin' time, an' done me tin,
An' it was worth the fifty quid I 'ad;
Me an' me cobber would a got shot in
Only we dooked the John a 'alf a Brad.
An' now it's fini—like me bloomin' cash,
'Ope the ship sinks before we get 'arf way.
I've come er gutzer, digger—done me dash ...
    The 14th day.   *H.F. Winters*
                Aussie, 4 April 1918

"They carry this ticketting business too damn far in London," said the tall, hard-faced digger, as he looked for his meat coupons. "Last night I struck a dinkum little tab and route-marched her to Hyde Park. We sat down on one of the chairs—one chair—to try and forget about squad drill, and managed bonzer. She was one of those sort of girls that seems to know how to appreciate all the kinds of kisses a man learns through fighting in many countries; and things were just getting interesting when a bloke in uniform lobs up alongside and says: 'Have you got your tickets?' I told him that if they like to put that sort of thing on ordinary citizens they weren't going to carry out rationing like that on an Aussie, and you can bet he cleared. Tickets!" he snorted in conclusion. His illusion seemed too good a joke for me to tell him that they make a charge for the use of the chairs in Hyde Park and that he was being asked for

Leave offered the prospect of adventures which lingered in the memory. *Diggers' Doin's*, Troopship *Valencia*, 1919. (*Australian War Memorial Printed Records*)

a ticket for the use of a chair, and that kissing was one of the few things for which you do not require a ration-ticket in London. '*Hamer*'

Aussie, December 1918

A sensational sequel to the strike of the Metropolitan Police in London was a traffic 'hold up' in the Strand last Saturday, instituted by two Canadian soldiers who commenced a two-up game. Soon, about five hundred Aussies joined the ring with the result that all traffic was held up. Bus drivers hurled anathemas at the school, pedestrians and motorists moaned something about a terrible war. There were no police to give the 'move on' order.

The ring grew and the centre called for big money and the scene soon attracted a few MPs to the spot, but their orders to a mixed battalion were hurled at deaf ears and the game went on.

Members of the police force stood amongst the players. They wore civie clothes and took a keen interest in the proceedings—perhaps they took part—who knows?

A group of digger officers plead with the gang to cease their illegal public gambling escapade and advised them to go anywhere else they desired and carry on with the business, but let the congested traffic untangle itself.

In spite of all efforts to bust up the school, a hoarse and tired voice yelled—"Quids in the centre".

The Digger, 8 September 1918

Billjim was on leave and the damsel sitting opposite him in the railway carriage was flighty. She ostentatiously adjusted her skirts, leaving on view about 12¾ in. of stocking. After a short interval there was a sound of agitated lingerie, and he turned his head just enough to ascertain that the silk stocking visible had increased by a couple of inches. The train sped on and the contest continued, the lady making no attempt to camouflage her sentiments. Although he could not resist an occasional glance opposite, Billjames's attention was mostly concentrated upon the landscape. When his station was reached he explained his position. "You have put up a dashed good offensive mamzell", he informed her; "*but my 'obby is beer!*".

The Digger, 1 September 1918

A Paris Flutter

. . . Arrived Paris at 9 p.m. All the khaki was yarded and Char-a-banc(ed) to Pepiniere Military Barracks where the passes were checked and initialled. Then came the inevitable lecture by a humorous Canadian M.O. on 'what to do and what not to do' while in Gay Paree. This over, the Y.M.C.A. attended to the inner man with a good supper, and the progress of the fork from the plate to the gap was accompanied by a Ladies String Orchestra. Ye Gods! What a treat, Yep! Farmer's and the A.B.C. all over again.

Our hotel being central, all sights were within easy reach. Firstly we made our way for 'A Corner of Blighty in Paris' a soldiers' club presided over by Miss Butler ably assisted by a number of ladies, some being 'Ossies'. 'Blighty' is a fine idea, as it is there expressly for Tommies and Overseas Troops who want to see Paris . . .

The Army and Navy Leave Club was next on the list. This is also a splendid institution where meals are served very cheaply and beds provided. It is a curious fact that the majority of our men from 'down under' do not patronise these places for board and lodging as much as one would expect. It is due no doubt to the sight of khaki being continually before their eyes in the war zone. Therefore the Hotels and Restaurants draw the crowds despite the high tariffs. Of course one's pay-book must show a healthy credit.

That night Follies Bergeres, a fine theatre, with a wonderful promenade and 'wonderfuller' women, was visited and much appreciated after the long months in the line, where theatres and women were non est.

The troops not being 'skanky' bought promenade tickets at 3 frcs. each, which entitled the holder to wander any old where. A pleasing feature was that 'Gladeyeing' did not come under the censorship laws and as Billjim knew the fine points of the game he soon made a host of–er friends (Now then you Ossie girls, don't get the wind up, Paris isn't in Scotland!).

On the morrow we saw historic Paris under the excellent guidance of Miss Butler. First the Roman Palace, now the Cluny Museum, . . . The Roman Amphitheatre was inspected . . . Notre Dame was next . . . The sight which takes the bun is undoubtedly the Palace Versailles and the grounds. . . . Palace Fontainbleu . . . Napoleon's Tomb and The Invalides

... The Louvre, Pont Alexandre, L'Opera House, Hotel de Ville ...

After being seven days in an atmosphere of heavenly bliss we were brought to earth with an 8" thud (not a dud) by suddenly remembering that the old war was still in progress. So beaucoup au revoirs occupied the last day and there was much rivalry as to who would have the greatest number of mam'selles at the station to say good-bye to. Gnr. Ken Grieves (26) was an easy winner.

The long hours of the journey back to home sweet home ???? were passed in holding posts mortem on each others doings. However, we arrived at Bailleul at 5 p.m. next day, and the tramp to our billets through yards of mud soon damped our spirits ...

Still, Paris leave is not a bad stunt, is it?

Yandoo, January 1918

WILL IT EVER END?

The Sweet Bye and Bye
A little happening in the future, if the peace that is wanted does not turn up. Time—about 1937.

The cold drizzling rain which had poured incessantly all day had temporarily abated, and, with an effort that in the language of the times, deserved a V.C., old Sol forced his way from behind the still lowering clouds. For the first time in many days his rays played pleasantly down upon the muddy trench. Suddenly a waterproof was snatched aside from the entrance to a dreary looking dug-out and a second or two later a figure coated with mud appeared in the opening. This on second glance proved to be a sergeant of the A.I.F. who had emerged from his sloppy shelter determined to obtain the fullest benefit from the sun's welcome rays.

Taking out his pipe and tobacco, he sat down contentedly on an upturned biscuit tin some few yards from the dug-out. Hardly had he commenced to smoke when he heard footsteps in the next traverse and a second later there appeared before him a tall, handsome stranger, whose apparently new uniform contrasted strongly with the sergeant's much worn apparel. The new arrival introduced himself as one of the 210th Reinforcements and after a few generalities the Sergeant asked "who keeps the estaminet in Sydney now?".

The newcomer thinking this one of the Sergeant's stock jokes, ignored the question but on it being repeated for the third time, stammered, "I do-oo-don't know."

"Don't know," said the Sergeant, "Gawblime." Then he added, "perhaps you're a teetotalor, in that case you can tell me who runs the canteen."

"Canteens!" gasped the astonished recruit, "there ain't no canteens there."

"Then wot the 'ell do you do for a booze," queried the N.C.O.

"There are the pubs," the new one murmured.

"Pubs –PUBS–PUBS," roared the Serg, " Wot-in-'ell are Pubs". Then as memory came faintly back he said, "They're boozin' joints aren't they. Can you get vin rouge an' vin blanc an' champagne in 'em?"

"No–I don't think so, only whisky and beer".

"Beer"–the Sergeant spat contemptuously—"and whisky, wots whisky."

The definition of whisky was too much for the newcomer so he held his peace. The Sergeant seeing this said "how much is a dixie of beer, anyway."

"Threepence a glass," said the lad. The Sergeant scratched his head and after a little thought replied, "I suppose you mean half-a-franc. Whose the Town Major?"

"There's no Town Major over there," exclaimed the now bewildered newcomer.

"What! No Town Major! Then wot kind of billets do you have for Gawds sake," roared the gallant Anzac.

"Billets!" We-we-don't live in billets", mumbled the lad.

"Don't live in billets," shouted the old warrior now thoroughly aroused, "why you must be getting regular savages out there now, why do——"

At this point a 5.9 lobbed close handy and the latest addition to the battalion took to his heels and scampered to safety. The Sergeant then leisurely arose and among the screech of shells and the rattle of machine guns could be heard mumbling. "No estaminets–no vin blanc–no Town Major–no billets–no champagne. Damn it all I'm not so sure that I want to go home. I don't——". Further soliloquy was cut short by the sudden pulling of the waterproof across the dug-out's entrance. The rain had started again.

The Sportsman, July 1917

The feeling that the war would last forever was widespread. *The Dinkum Australian*, January 1918
(*Australian War Memorial Printed Records*)

At the advanced age of 94, Major Kumagutzer, the last of the 'Original Anzacs', who as a youth of 17, enlisted in the year 1914, has been killed in action while leading his men in an attack by the Huns against Marseilles.

Another aboriginal rising is reported from Queensland. The Bullenbeefery tribe is heading the revolt, which is expected to last for a few years. The natives are said to be equipped with 23in. and other large guns, in addition to petrifying gas, electric death currents, and other fruits. Anzacs willing to serve at home send their names to the Editor. On Sunday last many Hun planes were observed over Sydney Harbour, evidently mistaking it for a shell hole. They then attempted to bomb the city, but without material result. The Gothas then proceeded to drop bombs on Melbourne without effect, owing to Percy Brunton and his peanut cart obstructing observation.

The 23rd, 15 November 1917

War Ends 1960
According to home papers just to hand, Bdr. Kirby, quill pusher for No. 2, has won third prize in a patriotic raffle, the prize being an armchair. Oh! Ye optimists! Doth your hearts sink at this news? Armchairs for the troops! Ye Gods! Latest maconochie re the above. The Comforts Fund have ordered 200,000 of these chairs, contract stipulating delivery somewhere about the year 1960. Cheerio. *La guerre tres bon!*

Rueteen Awders
- After April 1st, 1925, all men who joined up between 1914-1916 will, in future, be allowed to grow beards (length not to exceed 14 inches), and hair as far down as the shoulders. Curling tongs may be had on application.
- Chats are on no account to be destroyed, but handed in to the Q.M.S. who will forward them on to the Divvy boiling down works. The fat extracted there-from is found useful in the making of munitions.

The Kookaburra, June 1918

The following is a letter from an ex-soldier to his grandson, a member of the 17569th reinforcements, on the eve of the son's departure for active service abroad on the Great War:-

My dear Jack,—As you are now entering on your life-work, I feel it my duty to put you wise to a few wrinkles. As you know, both your father and myself were superannuated at the age of 85. The discharge age will probably be extended by the time you reach that age, so you have to look forward to many years of useful service. Still I have no wish to discourage you. As for me, now the Food Controller has decided to debar discharged soldiers from obtaining the anti-age inoculation, I cannot last many more years. ...

Here are a few hints which may be useful to you:

Keep your kit complete when behind the line. Inspections have been known to occur at such times.

Never miss your rum ration. If possible compliment the sergeant on his fairness in issuing. This is generally sufficient.

Should you report sick, be careful to tell the M.O. that you do not want to leave the battalion. Usually this will get you evacuated.

If you are ambitious, conceal your ideas. Deny yourself, and give your sergeant your rum ration. Also remember your officers are invariably right, and be eager to take the blame for any mistakes. It's your fault anyway, for being a soldier.

If you attain to Lance rank, yell like hell when any officers are about. When they go, abuse them to your squad. This pleases both.

If you get leave—but no, that will not interest you for some years yet.

Finally my son, set your mind on becoming a Q.M. Thus will you make provision for your old age— Your affectionate Grandad. 356545758595 Pte. Rein.

Aussie, 16 February 1918

IN MEMORIAM

In Picardy
Have you seen them march to battle
   In Picardy?
Heedless of the rifles' rattle,
   In Picardy.
Have you seen them leaping, crashing,
(Muscles taut and good steel flashing)
Through the leaden Hell, and dashing
   'Gainst the foe in Picardy

Have you heard the great guns crashing
   In Picardy?
Shrapnel hail the air a lashing
   In Picardy?
Have you seen the air craft winging
Through the sky, and swiftly flinging
Devils playthings, ever bringing
   Hell and death in Picardy?

Have you heard the south wind calling,
   In Picardy?
Have you seen the red leaves falling,
   In Picardy?
Have you heard the elm trees sighing
Requiem for the dead and dying,
On the cold white earth low lying,
   Anzacs slain in Picardy?

Have you seen the poppies waving
   In Picardy?
Blood red poppies dew a'laving
   In Picardy?
Have you seen them at the dawning
Droop their heads to make an awning
Guarding 'gainst the mists of morning
   Anzac graves in Picardy?   *Coy. Sgt. Major Geddes*
          The Rising Sun, 25 December 1916

"No Bon For Soldats"
It is chalked on an old rusty German shell which lies wickedly sideways. Does it thrill you to realise what a world of human feeling is concentrated there—and mixed in with it the everlasting touch of humour which helps men through their trials. Do you think of the soldier who wrote it? How he emptied his pocket and opened his soul at the estaminet stoveside, and tasted the wine when it was red, and likewise the lips of the dear little demoiselle; how they both compromised the two old languages till they both compreed exceedingly well. How he marched and billeted, and marched and 'bivvied' and toiled on till at length he came within sound of the big doors banging, and of the little birds whistling at night from the crackling 'Emma Gees'—and then he fought the mud, and fought his disgust and his fears, and perhaps he hopped over and fought the Hun. And maybe he saw one of the big doors slam on his mates, and when he got a chance he scratched his story on the vicious looking dud in four words.–"No Bon For Soldats." I wonder if it was his epitaph?
          The Rising Sun, 8 January 1917

Night Piece
. . . I lay by his side in the white flares light,
And his hands were cold and his face was white,
And the beauty of all things woke in me,
As I lay in the rich dead company,
As I lay by his side in the night. . . .
          Ghutz, February 1918

Somewhere
Somewhere a gun lies red with rust
   And there 'mid the trampled clay
The bones of the gunner will turn to dust
   That the March winds waft away.

Somewhere a mother's eyes are red
   As she weeps for her only boy
Who sleeps at peace in his muddy bed,
   Out by the Corduroy.   *J. McHugh*
          Aussie, 4 April 1918

This is absolutely dinkum, for it was seen by one of our old friends—Roy Levine. During an advance not very long ago, he came upon a grave with a cross over it bearing the following inscription:
   Here lies a Fritz
   Who met an Aussie.
   Don't know his name,
   But this is his possie.
          The Jackass, December 1918

The Dying Anzac
The lights were shaded, no sound was heard
In the silent ward where the wounded lay,
Save now and then when a patient stirred,
Or a footstep echoed and died away.

Here in this chamber, so sad and still,
With feeble pulse and with faltering breath,
Languid and slow lay the maimed and ill,
In the shadowy valley 'twixt life and death.

The nurse, she pauses a moment's space,
Beside the bed of a wounded man,
Flashing the light on his haggard face,
Ghastly pallid beneath its tan.

She smoothes his pillow, she strokes his brow,
Did he feel the touch of her soft, cool hand?
She wondered, what was he dreaming now,
This long lean son of a Southern land!

What were his thoughts—in the crowded trench,
Did he stand again midst the maimed and dead?
Rifle in hand midst the mud and stench,
The thunder of guns and the hiss of lead?

Ah, no, for the smile on his face portrayed
No hint of sadness, no thought of strife;
Back o'er the ocean his thoughts had strayed
Back to the scenes of his early life. . . .

Then he chuckled softly, and crooned a verse
Of an old bush ballad, uncouth and strange;
She bent above him—this English nurse—
But the 'Aussie' had ridden across the 'Range'.

T.W.
Ali Abaht It, February 1919

Men of the 28th Battalion training in Flanders before the renewal of the Ypres offensive, September 1917.
(*Australian War Memorial, Neg. no. E00685*)

Peace at last! *The Jackass, Aussie Xmas Number*, December 1918. (*Australian War Memorial Printed Records*)

CHAPTER SEVEN

GOING HOME

At the war's end around 180,000 Australians were serving overseas. The armistice meant that all of them, long-service men and recent reinforcements alike, could look forward to going home. For most of the A.I.F. the attraction and romance of foreign parts had long since evaporated; there was a universal desire to leave the cold and mud of Flanders or the heat and dust of Palestine at the earliest opportunity. Repatriation, however, was a huge undertaking. It was self-evident that it would take many months to transport so many men and even before the war ended demobilisation schemes had been put in hand. In the event, the repatriation process was one of the logistical triumphs of the war.

Against some determined opposition in high places, General Monash insisted that the key principle in repatriation should be a man's length of service. The government wanted to bring the A.I.F. home in its regimental units, the units which had won such fame on foreign battlefields, but the troops had a less sentimental, more industrial expectation that the men with the longest service would go home first. Monash knew that the soldiers' instincts were right and eventually he secured the support of the Prime Minister. Orders were issued to draft the troops into quotas, one thousand strong, on the basis of length of service. A quota was usually sufficient to fill both a train and a ship. The repatriation process, however, necessarily cut across unit loyalties which had been forged in desperate circumstances. This was noted when the first draft left the 40th Battalion in France: 'it was only then that we realised that this brotherhood of men existed no longer as a battalion of infantry'. Because of the dislocating effects of the quota system, efforts were made to create a temporary esprit de corps by providing each quota with a band and an education staff to keep the men amused and occupied.

Repatriation usually occurred in three stages. On the Western Front units were withdrawn from the front line to bases in Belgium and France before proceeding to holding camps in southern England, from whence the quotas were assembled for the voyage home. Almost no Australians were used in the army of occupation in the Rhineland and the bulk of the A.I.F. was moved across the Channel at the earliest opportunity. In part this was because Monash recognised how eagerly the troops wanted to leave the scene of struggle and suffering and begin the journey to the Southland, and in part it seems likely that the British High Command was nervous about holding the Australians on pointless, time-wasting duties. Consequently, the troops were moved through the transit camps as quickly as possible and in May 1919 the last of the A.I.F. arrived in England. By then the camps on Salisbury Plain contained around 80,000 men, but quotas were filled and despatched with such efficiency that by September 1919 only 10,000 remained. In the Middle East, the defeat of Turkey accomplished, the mounted troops rested from the rigours of the campaign and recovered from the debilitating effects of malaria and other diseases in camps near the coast around Tripoli in Lebanon. Early in 1919 they moved to the old base at Kantara in Egypt and from there to the vessels for embarkation. By May most of the Light Horse had been withdrawn and by the end of the summer the Australian presence in the region was at an end.

The men on the Western Front knew they were on their way home when their draft was ordered to proceed to the Australian Infantry Base Depot at Le Havre in the Lezarde Valley. The base had been enlarged early in 1918, when there were around 90,000 Australian soldiers in France and Belgium, after Prime Minister Hughes insisted that the 1914 men should have leave in Australia. Following the armistice it was laid down that all infantry quotas should pass through the depot before proceeding to England. The base was set up to handle five quotas for delousing, refitting and recuperation, but at times had more than twice that number. To accommodate the extra men a tent city was set up beside the hutments. When the system was in full swing several thousand soldiers a week were moved on to England until the last quota passed through the base. To entertain the troops during this frustrating period a sportsground was laid out, a theatre erected, and a newspaper established.

The Digger, the paper of the Australian Bases in France, first appeared in August 1918 on the fourth anniversary of the outbreak of war. The Commandant, Colonel Davis, in his foreword to the first issue acknowledged that such publications helped the Australians cope with the fact that they were so far from home. A paper with the very familiar features of trench and troopship literature, 'teeming with the humour that is . . . a marked characteristic of nearly all Australians', made life in the Base Depot a little easier to bear. And after the armistice, according to the official historian, C.E.W. Bean, *The Digger* comforted the troops 'during these rather slow months'. Published weekly at the price of a penny a copy, *The Digger* announced itself as 'a paper by the Diggers, of the Diggers, for the Diggers'. The chief purpose of the venture was to record the events occurring at the Depot, but as the editors noted there was plenty of room for 'Australian yarns and jokes'. Above all, the paper was 'essentially Australian' and the editors declared they would 'take a strong stand against anything not Australian in character'. This edict meant that the paper contained the usual humorous material, but throughout its existence, which came to an end in May 1919, *The Digger* contained far more direct news than any other field publication. This was especially important after the armistice when it kept the troops at the Depot fully informed about the repatriation process and the educational opportunities available to them as they waited their turn.

Before they were ordered to Le Havre, units were held in bases throughout Flanders. While most unit publications had ceased before the end of the war, one or two appeared in that anti-climactic period after the fighting ended and before repatriation began. The 17th and 18th Battalions both produced a journal while they were held first at Walcourt and Charleroi in Belgium and later at Montigny in France. In January 1919, the first handwritten number of *The Waiting Times* rejoiced in the fact that the 17th Battalion at long last had its own paper. The crippling paper shortage meant that only one copy of each issue was produced and these were placed in the unit library. Even after it appeared as a duplicated typescript, *The Waiting Times* was a poor imitation of earlier unit publications. But although lacking the vitality and humour of the typical field paper, *The Waiting Times* and the *Deesweet Despatch*, the 18th Battalion paper, are valuable in one important respect. They show us how men tried to cope with the agony of waiting to go home.

In the week which marked the appearance of *The Waiting Times* the men of the battalion had a range of diversions when their day's work was finished. Two card tournaments, two inter-company debates, a mock election and a fun night were held in the camp's recreation room and three performances were staged in the theatre by the Green Diamonds Troupe who offered an 'Entertaining Melange of Mirth, Music and Mystery'. The snow which blanketed Walcourt in the early months of 1919 restricted some outdoor activities, but a few football matches were played and snowball fights offered an occasional outlet for repressed high spirits. In the 17th Battalion there were regular debates which addressed a range of propositions. The abolition of state parliaments, six o'clock closing, prohibition, trade unionism, the system of territorial mandates proposed by the peacemakers, and the introduction of licensed brothels in Australia were among the topics discussed in the Diggers' Parliament. These were well-supported meetings with upwards of a hundred votes being cast on some occasions. Serious pieces in *The Waiting Times* on the folly of war, the housing problem in England, the class war, and prostitution focussed readers' attention on other weighty matters. Many of the publications produced during the homeward stage reveal the soldiers' deep concern for a future in Australia which would be free from the folly and contamination of Europe.

Australia's destiny and the responsibilities of ex-soldiers in shaping it were common themes in this period. Even before the war had ended a leading article in *The Digger* speculated about the nature of Australian society and its future prospects. The paper maintained that the men passing through the Depot were keen to go home because Australian ways were fundamentally different to those of the European countries:

> Hence the longing of the Australian soldier abroad for his own country, because his methods of living are based on ideals different to [the] European. He has not the centuries of custom, method and class to live down. Old world traditions do not appeal to him. They annoy him and he cannot understand why the people live so crowded . . . and have so many customs which are offensive to his sensibilities. The fact is there is a great deal of difference between the ideals of the modern and old worlds.

The article ended with an exhortation: 'Australians! realise what your duty will be when you return.' A correspondent took up the challenge in a later issue and advised readers to 'remain an army after the war, an army of voters: a solid wall of determination to get fair play'. Australian soldiers had proved themselves overseas and at home they needed the same commitment if they wanted to save the nation from the grasping self-interest of politicians and profiteers. The concern that the men of the A.I.F. preserve their unity of purpose in a domestic context and act as a force for change was echoed in subsequent issues of *The Digger* and in many of the returning troopship magazines. This awareness of the role that returning servicemen might play in Australia's future was also reflected in the provision of educational opportunities designed to equip the soldier for a life out of uniform.

Plans for an A.I.F. Education Service had been laid early in 1918, but little was achieved before the armistice. The end of hostilities was a great spur to the appointment of education officers for every unit and the provision of classes and lectures in every camp. In addition, arrangements were made for men to attend courses at educational institutions in Great Britain or train with British employers, and an education officer was appointed to most returning troopships. As befitted a unit which aimed to assist soldiers in their return to civilian life, the Education Service offered a wide range of vocational training as well as more narrowly educational subjects. *The Fiveaustra*, the journal of the Education Service circulating in the Westham, Littlemoor, Monte Video and Wyke Regis camps in England, recorded the popularity of the more practical courses. Motor engineering, driving, electrical engineering, carpentry, shorthand and typing, wool-classing, book-

Horseferry Road, London, was the Administrative Headquarters of the A.I.F. and for most men English leave started here. (*Australian War Memorial, Neg. no. D00796*)

Most men going to or returning from the war on the Western Front passed through the camps on Salisbury Plain. The writing room at the YMCA Sutton Veny, Wiltshire. (*Australian War Memorial, Neg. no. H02059*)

keeping, telegraphy, and various agricultural activities were all well supported. The editor noted that there were other subjects 'too numerous to mention', adding that the same was true of every other depot in England. The courses held in the camps in France and England were undoubtedly appreciated by some men, especially those who intended to resume a course of training when they got home, but it is doubtful if more than a third of the A.I.F. took advantage of them. Most men probably idled their time away in an assortment of fairly frivolous activities while they waited in a lather of anticipation for their inclusion in a quota and the start of their journey homeward.

The chief diversions in the camps in France and England were concert parties and sporting contests, but there was almost no limit to attempts to keep the men amused. At Le Havre an evening route-march was organised once a week to visit the local historic sites around Harfleur. It was not uncommon for 250 men to assemble for the seven-mile march. Astonishing as that might seem, it pales into insignificance besides the folk-dancing classes arranged by the redoubtable ladies of the English Folk Dance Society. The thought of battle-hardened soldiers in heavy boots attempting the steps of the Morris or a sword dance is faintly comical and it is unlikely that too many attended the classes in the Geelong Hut of the Y.M.C.A. It is also hard to imagine that many would have turned out to the weekly meeting of the Library Club where Colonel Merrington read a paper on 'Psychology and War' and explored the mental and moral effects of war on the nation. Sporting contests, boxing, wrestling, football and hockey, probably attracted more participants, and even more observers, but there is little doubt that most men were occupied with nothing more demanding than killing time. A correspondent to *Yandoo* noted how his camp in Belgium grew increasingly dull as drafts were withdrawn from the artillery unit to fill various quotas. Increasingly the troops were left pretty much to their own devices:

> Dancing in the estaminets with the Belgian 'tabs' to the rasping strains of automatic 'blood organs', hopping the tram to Anderlues to the colliery baths, where one enjoyed a first rate hot shower, and consuming 'oeufs and chips' were our chief pastimes. The 'Heads' gave us a very fair 'burl' as far as buckshee leave was concerned.

In such circumstances trouble was bound to occur, but overall there were relatively few problems and they were usually the result of an evening spent in an estaminet. Two soldiers who were refused drinks in a Le Havre café soaked the proprietor with a soda syphon and then smashed a window. Another group thought it was amusing to steal a weight from a grocer's shop and when the owner protested they helped themselves to a considerable amount of food and drink. Incidents of this sort were not uncommon. Although basically trivial, they were a slight tarnish on the reputation of the A.I.F. One can sense the relief in the French newspaper which reported that 'two regiments of Australians marched through the village this morning. So far nothing has been reported missing'. To preserve the good name of the Australian force and forestall potential difficulties, the troops were moved from their camps to Le Havre and from there to England as quickly as possible. On the last day of April 1919 a draft consisting of artillery and signals units was trucked out of Charleroi for Le Havre. After going through a delousing camp, the draft entered the Base Depot where it remained for four days playing the national game of 'Two-up', exchanging old uniforms for new, and receiving new underclothing. On 6 May the draft crossed the

Channel and a week after leaving Charleroi it marched into camp at Sutton Veny on Salisbury Plain in Wiltshire.

The camps where the troops waited to be called to their port of embarkation were cheerless places despite the best efforts of the Salvation Army, the Y.M.C.A. and the Education Service. Sutton Veny consisted of 'acre after acre of corrugated iron huts, concrete pathways and ragged cabbage patches'. The little town of Warminster was only two miles away but according to one soldier 'after spending an afternoon there one was quite fed up'. For many men the highlight of their final period in England was the fourteen days leave granted before embarkation. Apart from that, the couple of months spent in camp were probably both depressing and monotonous. Spring and summer in the English countryside might have appealed to those with an interest in landscape and rural affairs, but for the majority the days to departure dragged. Sleeping, eating, gambling, with occasional visits to the public house, all unimagined luxuries during the bitter trials of fighting, were soon tedious time-wasters that simply filled up the days until a quota was notified of its boarding date.

Repatriation voyages generated more publications than any other phase of the war. Over one hundred titles have been identified and it is probable that there were others that have not survived. To some extent it would seem that the service publication had become a habit; it was expected that the final stage of the 'Great Adventure' would be commemorated in the familiar way. As literary ventures, however, the publications of the returning troopships are rather disappointing. They are not without value as a guide to the mindset of the returning troops and a record of the time spent on a transport, but they are much less interesting to read than their predecessors. In general the papers and magazines seem rather laboured. Compared to the subject matter of previous chapters they appear tired, as if the genre had simply outlived its usefulness. Trench and troopship publications had been a proven morale-booster since 1914, but perhaps they lost their point once the war ended and the soldiers knew their ordeal was over. The established, familiar features of the unit paper were still there, but because the quotas drew men from many units the publications often lacked coherence and purpose. The officer commanding the quota on the *Port Napier* noted that the variety of units in the draft had made it impossible to produce anything more substantial than a booklet since leaving Charleroi. There was also a consciousness that these final productions would inevitably be read by family and friends which undoubtedly affected their tone. The editor of *The Denison Quoter* warned his readers 'that the contents of this journal are going to be of such a nature that it can be perused by our mothers and sisters in dear old Aussie'. Consequently, many titles took the form of well-printed, polished souvenir editions designed, as Lieut. Colonel Travers remarked in his foreword to *The Maltese Roller*, 'to remind us that one of the happiest times of our soldier life is the Coming Home'.

The souvenir edition was often derived from a shipboard paper. Privates C.E. McGill and E.H. Partridge produced a weekly paper which provided the basic copy for the souvenir *Bakara Bulletin*. *Our Homeward Stunt* was similarly based on the weekly paper produced on the *Port Macquarie*. The souvenirs were sometimes printed at ports on the journey home and sometimes after arrival in Australia. *Karmala Kuts* was issued as a typescript sheet on the vessel, but was printed into a souvenir in Cape Town; the thirty-two page *Homing Aussie* was printed during the three-day stop at Durban. Some were printed on arrival in Australia and posted out to subscribers. The *Karoolian* was printed in Sydney,

(Australian War Memorial Printed Records)

the *Runic Rag* in Bendigo, *Our Homeward Stunt* in Brisbane, while the *Final Objective* announced that it was 'Written at Sea: Printed in Adelaide: Cherished at Home'.

Most shipboard publications appeared originally as duplicated typescripts. This restricted the size of each issue and on many transports the quota's paper was produced in limited numbers. *Imshi*, the weekly typescript journal of the *Karoa*, was printed in sufficient numbers to issue only one to each mess, although a souvenir reprint was planned on arrival in Australia. The continuing paper shortage was a further constraint on shipboard editors. Over two hundred copies of the first issue of the *Berrima News* were sold on the stage between England and the Cape, but a lack of paper was reported in the second, and a third number depended on the availability of paper at Cape Town. The editors of *The Borda News*, a bi-weekly paper, solved a similar dilemma by placing a few copies on each troopdeck and arranging to have more professionally printed at Cape Town. Sometimes the stay in port was too brief to get any printing done. For that reason the editors of *The Austramic* had to abandon any idea of a souvenir publication falling back on the duplicator 'and the good-natured co-operation of the office Staff'. Some quotas were lucky enough to have access to a printing press. *Homeward Bound* was printed by the A.I.F. Printing Section travelling on the *Nestor* and the editors of *Norman News* were able to use the ship's press. Yet even when a vessel had printing facilities, circumstances could frustrate the shipboard editor. On the *Wiltshire* the troops had the use of a Y.M.C.A. press, but a lack of paper meant that production of the *Ocean Echo* was limited and copies had to be posted at various points throughout the ship. Publication of the *Cape Verde Clarion* was planned for the last leg of the journey from Colombo to Australia, but a lack of paper and the discovery that the press would not work in the heat of the tropics frustrated that scheme.

The troopship papers issued on board or printed at a port of call were an attempt to lighten the monotony and frustration of the slow voyage home. The trip from England to Australia usually took about sixty days and every effort was made to lessen the tedium and minimise the discomforts. The Australian Comforts Fund and the Red Cross continued to care for the welfare of the troops with as much enthusiasm and commitment as they had shown in the field. On almost every ship the two funds supplied extra comforts, chiefly in the form of little luxuries. On the *Port Macquarie*, for example, the Comforts Fund supplied 112 cases containing tinned fruits, condensed milk, cocoa, cigarettes, tobacco, socks, shirts, writing paper and envelopes; the Red Cross added another 75 cases providing, among other items, fruit, jam, chocolates, biscuits, sweets, jellies, malted milk, coffee, beef extract and items of clothing, including dressing gowns for the hospital patients.

The Y.M.C.A. was also a presence on most of the returning troopships. The representative on board was equipped with a standard issue to help him in his task of arranging entertainment and diversion for the quota. Over sixty items went into this essential kit, including a stock of one thousand books, costumes for a twelve-person concert party, items of sporting equipment, and a case of prizes, like cigarette cases, razors and hairbrushes, for the competitions held throughout the voyage. On the *Friedrichsruh*, a German ship handed over under the terms of the armistice, the Y.M.C.A. representative organised 15 concerts and 10 song-services, 30 contests and fun-stunts, 10 chess and draughts tournaments, 36 card competitions, 7 Diggers' dances, and a range of other activities such as debates and lectures. The Y.M.C.A. also had staff in the principal ports where troopships docked. The Cape Town office was particularly busy. During the stay of the *Denison* it arranged for 600 men to visit Cecil Rhodes' estate at Groote Schuur, while another 400 went to Camp Bay and Hout Bay on coach excursions. The 'Y Emma' also had its own comfort fund and before the *Denison* sailed for Fremantle it sent on board 20,000 cigarettes, a hundredweight and a half of sweets (75 kilos), 100 packs of cards, 40 cases of raisins, 1,000 newspapers, and two cases of magazines and repatriation pamphlets. It also had the ship's piano tuned. Many of the returning troopship publications contained a tribute to the work of the Y.M.C.A. and the other organisations, but a thorough history of their role in supporting the A.I.F. has yet to be written, whereas the role of the Education Service has been well documented.

The Education Service, whose particular role was to help the troops prepare for their return to civilian life, provided a small staff on most transports who organised classes on many topics. Some were taught by the education officers, but others drew on the expertise found among the members of the quota. On most vessels it seems that classes were quite popular, although enrolment figures tend to exaggerate the numbers taking part because a man might enrol in several classes. Enrolments reached 700 on the *Nestor* and nearly 800 on the *Euripides*, but on the *Denison* 410 men enrolled out of 1,300 on board. Most vessels had some purely academic classes, but they were significantly fewer than classes with a commercial or occupational focus. A soldier on the *Euripides* could choose from twenty-six classes which in the business sphere included commercial arithmetic, book-keeping, accountancy, business correspondence, and shorthand. On all troopships there was always a demand for classes in various aspects of practical agriculture. Aboard the *Kanowna* there was even a Farmers' Club that met on the boat deck three times a week to discuss practical issues like soil fertility, dryland farming, maize growing and dairying among other things. This 'Cockies' Club' provoked a prize-winning poem:

> If you find the voyage dreary, and are feeling dipped and weary,
> Just hop up to the Boat Deck, where the Cockies hold their class:
> There you'll gain much information how to run a farm or station,
> And they'll argue any subject from harvesters to grass.
>
> If you've got a hungry yearning for a living to be earning,
> From a fertile patch of good Australian soil,
> You will find them optimistic, and in language most artistic
> Will promise you a fortune, with a minimum of toil.
>
> You will hear them curse the rabbits and their devastating habits,
> And how it's best to battle with the curse,
> Hear them spout of fertilisers and of wily advertisers,
> Who are out to make a fortune out of poor old cocky's purse.
>
> Listen to their views on marriage and the ruinous cost of carriage,
> How to build a barn or haystack, and how to hang a gate;
> How by courage and hard working, and not by shiftless shirking,
> You can conquer nature's curses, and be master of your fate.

Even though the classes and meetings occasionally provoked some mild amusement among non-attenders, they indicated that many men on the transports were setting their gaze on the future.

Most vessels had programs of lectures and discussions on a range of topics and many had a regular schedule of debates. The common thread running through these activities was

Some of the wounded returning aboard the *Star of Victoria*, 1918, gathered for an event on the well-deck.
(*Australian War Memorial*, Neg. no. H02024)

Concert parties relieved the boredom of the voyage on the *Shropshire*, April 1919.
(*Australian War Memorial*, Neg. no. H041650)

the emphasis on Australia and its future. The Chaplain on the *Port Lyttleton* gave a series of lectures on Japan's rise to world prominence and the threat this posed to Australia. The peopling of Australia's empty spaces, especially its northern border, and the admission or exclusion of coloured labour were topics discussed in the Diggers' Parliaments convened on many ships. These gatherings were taken very seriously. The Parliament on the *Mahia* debated whether preference in employment should be given to unionists and Asiatics admitted into Australia without an education test, while that on the *Themistocles* considered the use of indentured coloured labour in northern Australia. The men on the *Port Macquarie* discussed the merits of 'State Control *versus* Private Enterprise', a topic frequently aired on the homeward vessels, and came down solidly in favour of the former. The *Euripides* had a Diggers' Parliament which met each Monday evening after leaving Durban, while on Saturdays there was an open forum on any Australian subject. The serious-minded concern for the future demonstrated in the choice of subjects for discussion and debate was also fully reflected in the troopship publications.

One of the most significant ideas manifested in the service publications was the realisation that Australia had an independent destiny. The vast, resource-rich and empty land was young, modern and different. This awareness had developed during the war; it was very obvious in the aggressively nationalistic tone of the trench journals of the Western Front and was equally evident in the publications of the final phase. Shortly before the war ended a leading article in *The Digger* pointed out that Australia was more like the USA than any European country. Australia had borrowed much from the Old World, but had to construct its own destiny. Above all, Australians had to shrug off the inferiority complex which would always hold them back. The Diggers were instructed to 'champion everything Australian', they were never to think 'that anything foreign is better than Australia or Australian goods'. *The Homing Aussie* reported that Captain Potter, one of the quota on the *Euripides*, was vigorously applauded by the well-deck meeting devoted to the question 'How can we help Australia' when he insisted that 'Australia should not be developed according to European ideas' but should develop its own national standards and values. The editor of *The Boomerang* suggested that the 'wonderful future' and 'marvellous possibilities' facing Australia would be realised because the nation had 'thrown off the shackles of caste and conventionalities'. In another issue he insisted that the war had done a great deal of good by eroding state parochialism and 'welding Australia together in a big brotherhood'. It was commonly asserted that the war had helped to make Australia a nation, and the central agency in this realisation of a national identity was the brotherhood created by the A.I.F. It is not surprising, therefore, that many troopship papers discussed at length the role to be played by returned servicemen.

The most frequently expressed belief was that the ex-soldiers could be a powerful social and political force. According to an article in *Homeward Bound*, the 'Destiny of Australia' lay in their hands. Returned servicemen had the opportunity to be a 'dominating influence for good':

> It requires but little knowledge of society and history to assure us of the strong, permeating, invisible influence upon society at large of any body of men of clear thought, strong conviction and disciplined conduct.

The war had broadened the minds and experience of the men in the A.I.F. and many writers echoed the sentiments voiced in *En Voyage* that, as a result, they were better equipped to face 'the real test of citizenship' and fulfil their 'patriotic responsibilities'. The emphasis on new responsibilities was very strong. Australia's soldiers, declared *The Shropshire Blimp*, were physically and intellectually the best of the nation's manhood and no one could doubt their ability 'to assume . . . great national responsibilities'. The foreword to the journal produced on the *Dunluce* reminded readers that as members of the A.I.F. they were 'the best and most virile in the country'. They had performed great deeds as soldiers and in civilian life they faced new and daunting challenges:

> We organised and sacrificed ourselves to smash down the Hindenberg line. Now let us get busy and fight for a better Australia, for greater efficiency and economy in our Government departments, for a higher standard of living and comfort and improved education.

The big question, of course, was how the ex-soldiers could make their influence felt and on this point there was little agreement. While most journals contained material which pointed to the belief that the soldiers had a positive duty to shape Australia's future, few followed this up with precise recommendations of how it was to be done.

Some, however, believed that the returned servicemen could be an active political force. *The Digger* reported the foundation of a Soldiers and Citizens Political Party in New South Wales. The goals of the organisation, which stressed that it was 'DISTINCT FROM ANY PARTY AT PRESENT IN EXISTENCE', were to protect the interests of servicemen and their families and 'to provide a purer form of non-class Government for the people of Australia'. The paper did not suggest that Diggers should join, but the disillusionment with the party system that aligned Liberal against Labor and capitalist against worker indicated in the new party's platform struck a familiar note among the troops. The men of the A.I.F. had a poor opinion of politicians. A contributor to *The Shropshire Blimp* suggested that 'the parties have served their purpose and the old order must go'. The future lay in co-operation and the spirit of tolerance which had forged Australians together in the A.I.F. Others thought that the Diggers could be influential at the ballot box. A soldier who signed his article 'Ex-Democrat', reminded readers of *The Digger* of the eternal truth that 'politicians sell their souls daily for your vote and mine'. This, he continued, could be a source of power and he urged the Diggers to 'remain an army after the war, an army of voters' who would be 'a solid wall of determination to get fair play'. By exploiting the name, the fame and the numbers of the A.I.F., soldiers could hold the key to the future. That was also the opinion of the officer commanding the quota on the *Katoomba* who declared to the men assembled on the main deck that returned servicemen 'should rule Australia when we get back'.

Some advocated a social and moral role for the ex-soldiers. The Diggers' Parliament on the *Karoa* discussed the future role of the Returned Soldiers' Association and in particular whether it should become politically active. The troopship paper *Imshi* reported that the participants were almost unanimous that the R.S.A. should not become a political body but should act as a watchful guardian of servicemen's interests. In *Back to the Bush* Major Bean of the Medical Corps proposed that the Y.M.C.A. set up a 'League of Active Service' to keep up the social contacts between ex-servicemen and focus their energies on bettering Australia along non-party lines. Most publications acknowledged that the immediate problems of reconstruction were considerable and recognised that the nation had to confront a range of issues before its future was assured. Among the most important were immigration, the mechanisation of industry and agriculture, the creation of a reserve army,

(Australian War Memorial Printed Records)

and improvements to education and social welfare. Although the solutions discussed in the pages of the troopship papers varied enormously, there was a universal conviction that returned servicemen had the power to make things happen and a duty to do so.

For some of the returning A.I.F. the most immediate issue was not a matter of grave national importance but a pressing personal one. They were concerned about the welcome awaiting their 'Anzac brides'. Several thousand soldiers had married during the war and the number increased significantly after the armistice and the withdrawal to England. In the early months of 1919 around 150 men a week were marrying English girls. Many of these marriages had already produced children and in 1919 alone over 15,000 wives and children were carried to Australia. The delicate matter of the Anzac brides surfaced even before the war ended. In August 1918 *The Digger* reported the unsavoury scenes which occurred as the first English wives arrived at Port Melbourne. They were met with catcalls and boos, savage comments and even violence. On one occasion some factory girls confronted the new arrivals on the landing pier and set about them with sticks and stones. The police did not intervene and one policeman inferred that the English girls got what they deserved, 'after all weren't there plenty of good girls in Australia without going to England to look for them'.

These reports, which alarmed both the soldiers and their wives, generated considerable comment in the service journals. Some contributors denounced the 'cad' who betrayed a sweetheart at home, others defended a man's right to marry whomever he wished. One humorist suggested in *The Digger* that the government pass a Compulsory Bigamy Act requiring every sound man under forty-five to have two wives. This, he argued, would compensate for the men killed overseas and guarantee every Australian girl a husband. In the main, the troops were critical of the ungenerous reception accorded to the initial Anzac brides; a long poem in *The Dinkum Gazette* ended with a gentle reprimand:

> Sigh not, ye local young ladies and sob,
> Complaining they diddled you out of your job:
> Greet not the fair maidens who've captured your sparks
> With lemon-faced glances and catty remarks,
> But brandish the olive branch, let loose the dove,
> Remembering all's fair in war and in love.
>
> The woman the Anzac has claimed as his bride
> Now standeth as sister-in-law at your side.
> So 'can' all your cattiness, finish your fuss
> And let us remember she's now one of us.
> Wives, wives, welcome the wives,
> Here's luck to Bill Anzac and all of his wives.

As the process of repatriation accelerated, wives often accompanied their husbands on the transports. Not surprisingly, this led to some amusing gossip and comment in the ship's paper. One can imagine the embarrassment of the soldier who recognised himself in the *Bremen Babbler* as the man whose wife followed him into the hospital bathroom and 'sat there while the poor henpecked creature washed himself', or the unfortunate soul whose wife was overheard telling him not to drink his tea from the saucer. Some writers showed that the affectionate couples lurking in dark corners of the ship strained their good nature, some simply resented the lucky men who had female company. The journey home also prompted many correspondents to reminisce about the girls they had encountered overseas, acknowledging that on their return they would have to be discreet in recounting some of their wartime adventures. There was no shortage either of sentimental verse trumpeting the virtues of the mothers and the attractions of the wives and girls who would soon welcome their loved ones home. For these men, who were probably in the majority, the journey could not pass quickly enough.

Few regretted leaving England. The editor of *The Boomerang*, produced on the *Aeneas*, announced that 'this paper does not regret leaving the country of snobs'. Another piece in the same journal described England as the tail wagging the imperial dog and anticipated the time when the Empire would wake up and 'wag its own tail'. While most of the souvenir editions commented on the events surrounding the vessel's immediate departure, fond reminiscences of England were strikingly few. The 'chains of blood' which featured so prominently in the outward-bound troopship papers were rarely mentioned in those of the return. Perhaps they had been much corroded, if not dissolved, by bloodshed. While England was virtually ignored, the ports of call provoked much comment.

Exotic locations like Freetown, Cape Town, Durban and Colombo offered the prospect of shore leave, alcohol (for many ships were 'dry') and female company. They also frequently gave rise to patronising reflections on the character, behaviour and physique of the native peoples. In this respect the homeward-bound journals were no different from their predecessors. *The Rag Bag* warned the men about to go ashore at Colombo to behave themselves lest they 'lower the prestige of the ruling race'. A day ashore in Durban was remembered by a contributor to *The Boomerang*:

>Swift the gaudy Zulu
>Lopes a giddy pace
>While the sweat is pouring
>From his ugly face.
>Girl, she sits beside you
>Holding hand in hand
>As you sit up closer
>Everything is grand.
>Prancingly the Nigger
>Pulls his old Ricksha
>Wearing gaudiest costumes
>That you ever saw.

Shore leave, however enjoyable, amounted at best to three or four days in the eight- or nine-week voyage. For the rest of the time the troops had to seek diversion in shipboard sports and entertainments.

There was little room on a trooper for physical activity, but it was a rare voyage that did not include a couple of boxing tournaments fought for money prizes and various improvised sports and games. Concert parties and band performances, often arranged by the Y.M.C.A. representative, together with debates and discussions completed the range of organised recreational activities. But without doubt the most widely enjoyed activity was gambling. Two-up and Crown and Anchor were popular, but 'Housey' outstripped both and attracted the widest comment. According to some verses in *The Lytteltonik*:

> Of pastimes on board there are many
> From two-up to 'Anchor and Crown',
> But the favourite one with the pure mugs
> Is 'House, get ready! Eyes down!'.
>
> They roar it, and scream it, and sing it,
> In science it reaches a height,
> From its 'clickity click' in the morning
> To its last legs eleven at night.

Simple and easy to play with a winner every time, 'Housey' offered the enterprising banker a chance to make some money. It was played on all the vessels by many different groups at once and often every space was crowded with participants. Although it was a popular diversion, for some 'Housey' became a torment, cutting across all other activities. This was certainly true for the soldier on the *Karmala* who penned a verse on the obsession:

> "Who'll have a card?"
> From early morn till late at night
> The 'house mob' sing with all their might;
> 'Till in my dreams I seem to see
> Hundreds of cards,—and all 'buckshee';
> And when I leave this bunk of mine
> They're shouting, "Penny, single line!"
> Another week and I'll go daft,
> For they pursue me 'fore and aft;
> No chance have I to read in peace,
> "House, House!" they cry and never cease;
> But one hope still remains with me:
> When we have sailed across the sea
> I'll hop out to the 'Never-Never',
> And say good bye to 'House' forever.

No doubt there were many other frustrations to be endured on a troopship, but they all faded as the vessel drew closer to Australia and home.

The imminent return to Australia prompted many versifiers to reflect on two related themes: the land and loved ones awaiting them and the sacrifice of those who would never return. Memorial verses of many sorts appear in the troopship papers, but they are not as numerous as might have been expected. It is probable that those who had survived knew how lucky they had been and had already started to distance themselves from an experience most chose to forget. There was no point in dwelling on losses that could not be repaired and the joy of homecoming would have been marred by an excessive concentration on the fallen. But when those who had died were remembered, their sacrifice was often measured in terms of the loss felt by their loved ones. An anonymous author on the *Friedrichsruh* finished a poem entitled 'Coming Home' on just that note:

> There are some we'll leave behind us as we steer across the waves,
> And the crosses glimmer whitely over countless comrades' graves,

(Australian War Memorial Printed Records)

> And our thoughts go out in sadness to the mothers and the wives
> And the sweethearts with the sorrow pressing darkly on their lives;
> Little use for us to tell them that they died like heroes there
> Their's alone the awful sorrow that no other heart can bear;
> But the thought will live eternal, shrined within our memory's tome,
> Of the mates we leave behind us, Coming Home, Coming Home.

The troopship journals also contained occasional reminiscences about major battles and the lives they cost, but it is significant that such items were outnumbered by humorous recollections about leave-time escapades and encounters with girls. Although the dreadful experience of war could never be forgotten, it is clear that the returning soldiers were determined to look forward not back, and to take comfort in the fact that they had survived to go home.

There was a remarkable consistency of imagery in the trench and troopship literature throughout the war whenever 'home' was recalled. Australia was a land of perpetual sunshine, silence, waving grasslands, wattle groves, eucalyptus-scented breezes, shady billabongs, verandahed homesteads and patiently waiting loved ones:

> Oh! To be nigh that soft-breathed sigh,
> The myst'ry and spell of the bush:
> With the tops of the tall trees whispering
> In the stilly church-like hush!
>
> So Billjim sighs for his Austral skies,
> With a love that none can sever.
> Once gripp'd by the charm of Australia's bush—
> The spell of the Never-Never!

If the contributors to the journals were to be believed, everyone in the A.I.F. lived and worked in the bush. In fact, the men who filled its ranks were drawn chiefly from the cities because that was where the bulk of the population lived. But when the soldiers overseas constructed their identity they chose to think of Australia not in terms of the city but of the bush. This phenomenon has been extensively discussed by historians of Australian cultural identity but to date few have investigated the rich source contained in the trench and troopship publications. The material would repay detailed analysis, however, for it demonstrates the Australian soldiers' deliberate choice of the bushman persona and a vision of a home that was always rural and never urban.

The experience of the A.I.F. in the four years of war was often bitter and bloody. The 'Great Adventure' quickly became the 'Great Trial', but through it all the prospect of eventually returning home gave men hope. They had seen what England and Europe had to offer and they were conscious of the failings of the Old World. With a new-found confidence and a pride in Australia they knew that their country was very different. They knew they had been lucky to survive and return to 'God's Own Country' and they would have endorsed the fervent benediction printed in *The Lytteltonik*:

> Australia is the cleanest, sweetest, healthiest, sunniest, happiest, and everythingelsest country in the whole blooming world. Amen.

(Australian War Memorial Printed Records)

CHAPTER EIGHT
'THERE'S A LONG, LONG TRAIL A-WINDING'

FAREWELL

On March 19th and 30th, 1919, quotas 19 and 25 respectively representing various units of the Fourth Division assembled at the Australian Corps Reinforcement Camp, situated in Charleroi, Belgium, in an old factory . . . It was the day which all had been looking forward to for some time. We were "homeward bound" at last! However, the quotas did not leave Charleroi for some days. The 19th entrained at the Charleroi station, the train leaving there shortly before 10 a.m. on the 24th, and the 25th followed . . . arriving at Le Havre two days later. As usual we travelled in goods wagons (or "side-door Pullmans", as the Diggers call them—*hommes* 40, *chevaux* 8), but on the whole we had a fairly good trip, owing to the provisions made for our comfort, which were greatly appreciated. For them we are indebted to our people at home, who, through the channel of the Comforts Fund, provided Xmas parcels and a plentiful supply of cocoa and milk; and to the military, which contributed its share by way of fuel for the stoves in the wagons, also plenty of rations, and, last but not least, an issue of rum. During the journey we passed through Mons, Douai, Arras, Doullens, Vignacourt, and the outskirts of Amiens; thence through Romes Camp, a large military railway depot, to Le Havre. Halts were made, when necessary, for meals, and during these stops the Aussies' "national game" was played with the enthusiasm and varying fortunes characteristic of it. At Vignacourt, where there is an Australian military cemetery, the train happened to stop, and a good number of the boys made a hurried search for graves of their friends. However, not many of them could have been successful, as the stop was, unfortunately, very short. During the journey from Romes Camp to Le Havre the French railway employees along the line received a barrage of empties. The boys bombarded everyone they passed, and the accuracy of their aim put the "wind up" a good number of the "Froggies".

Owing to the late hour of arrival at Le Havre the night was spent in the train, and early the next morning we marched to the A.B.D. Camp at Rouelles, about five miles from Le Havre. Whilst at this camp, much to our relief, rifles and equipment were handed in, and, after passing through a well-organised bathing system and receiving new clothing, we moved to another camp. From there the quotas proceeded to England going by bus to the docks at Le Havre, and thence by the transport *St. David* to Southampton. The boat left Le Havre at 3.15 p.m., and (the voyage taking about six hours) thus did not reach Southampton until after nightfall, so we had to sleep on board overnight, disembarking next morning. After being provided with breakfast on the wharf, we travelled by train to Fovant, near Salisbury, and from Fovant marched to the camps . . . The day after our arrival there the "good oil" was given out that the quota was to march through London on Anzac Day to represent the Division, and would not be given leave until after the event. This news was not favourably received, but, however, another quota was chosen for the job, and a few days later we commenced our leave, which expired on April 28th. It must be assumed that everyone had as enjoyable a time as possible, the natural aim of all whilst on leave. On May 3rd, about twenty-five per cent of the quota took part in the overseas troops' march in London. One would not imagine that the Diggers were a serious-looking crowd, yet during the march they were frequently appealed to for a smile; still, five miles is a long way to keep up a happy countenance, but I don't think any of them failed to comply with the request, especially when it came from one of the fair sex. The spectators certainly did their best to show their appreciation with cheering, etc., and, during halts, with smokes, chocolates, and other sweets. It was a tiring day, but well worth while. The remainder of our time in camp before leaving England was uneventful, excepting for the usual every-day occurrences. The quotas embarked on the *Port Napier* at Devonport on Monday 12th May, and the voyage back to Australia was commenced the next day.

Four Guineas
Four bloomin' guineas. Well! Gawd spare me days,
I thought the blanky war was won, and now
They 'ops it over on a bloke like this,
And pays him 'cos he's going on leave, the cow.
    Total, four quid . . . .

And then to make it worse they want your fare.
Eight bob it is third class to the big smoke.
That leaves you wond'ring how much can you spare
To buy some Kiwi, khaki shirt or tie.
    Result, three quid . . . .

A few refreshments at the camp canteen,
A little game of 'eads which turn up tails,
A cobber broke appears upon the scene,
He wants a bob to get his washing back.
    Remains, two quid . . . .

The city reached, you saunter down the Strand,
Look in the windows, lean against a post,
A "tabby" chips you, talks about a band,
A "jazz" or something. She interests you, you go.
    Next morn, one quid . . . .

One bloomin' note, and thirteen days to go.
The War Chest claims you, one more tourist still,
One of those ornamental coves, you know,
Who sit along the footpath day by day.
    But you've one quid . . . .

The days go by, you've seen some of the sights.
You've slept for breakfast, dined at one or two,
And on occasions grown reckless quite
By having just a booze or two at times.
    Cash, arf-a-quid . . . .

Ten days you do, chuck up the bloomin' game,
Return to camp and loaf around the huts.
Most of the boys are back, but life is tame,
No smokes, no booze, and, crowning all, your book's
    In debt four quid.   R. Owens, 1st Fld. Amb.
Coming Back, June 1919

Pleasant indeed are our last memories of Blighty. The morning of July 9th 1919, was the opening of a typical English summer day. The sun shone brightly from a sky of pure blue. The waters of the bay danced gaily at the bidding of a gentle, refreshing breeze. The hills beyond made a gorgeous background of verdant green. We hung over the railings to drink in this final view of England, and it will form a picture ever pleasing to dwell upon when, in years to come, we search in the memory's treasure house in quest of happy reminiscence. The bustling, radiant port of Devonport constituted a glorious setting for one of the memorable, red-letter days of our careers in the A.I.F.

Memorable it was. The day before, we had embarked on the *Friedrichsruh*. We were actually going home. We were happy in a vague, well-satisfied way, but few of us were capable of properly realising the actual fact. It was hardly comprehensible. For months and years we had been cherishing dreams of the day when we should set our faces Aussiewards, but they were vague, intangible visions. Now even the days of expectancy were over. It was an established fact—we were on our way. And yet so hard to believe, because so good.

It was a royal send-off. The band that played superbly on the quay, the dock-workers who roared so lustily, the spick and span naval boys who formed up on the decks of the men-o'-war as we passed slowly down the long sea-lane of giant fighting ships, and cheered by numbers, yet with great gusto . . . Dear old Blighty! Land of many doings—some fit for publications, some hereby relegated to the darkness of oblivion—place of memories that will last a lifetime.
Homeward Bound, July–September 1919

The thoughts that ran through peoples' minds as the *Katoomba* lay off the white cliffs of Dover . . . were of a varied character, for the *Katoomba*, a troopship, contained a mixed complement. But in addition to being a troopship, she was a family ship conveying hundreds of young English, Scottish, and Irish girls from the lands of their birth, from their own family associations, to be soon thrust into unknown adventures of life in a foreign land. These young people naturally looked upon the scene with feelings of sorrow, but others admired them for their courage, and hailed them as new British Colonists worthy of their fathers and mothers who had gone out before them, and who had helped to make Australia what it is today. The troops on board perhaps looked upon the scene in a different light. England to them had been a home it is true; but it signified many and terrible experiences for them. They had been exiled from their homes for years, had fought in the most terrible war in history, and now they were leaving all that behind them—their work was done, and they were finally on their way to the shores so dear to them. So, as they looked upon those cliffs of Dover they felt that behind them lay buried those unpleasant memories, and they rejoiced that they were homeward bound. The passengers, it is presumed, felt no feelings of regret, for they were Australians fortunate enough to have been detailed for the boat after many weeks of waiting. As the ship steamed away one naturally watched the brides. Their eyes remained on the shore in solemn thought. "Would they see those cliffs again?" was, one thinks, their principal thought. That, this journal ventures to say, will depend upon themselves. Let them prove themselves worthy Colonists, and Australia will afford them good opportunity for a return voyage to see their homefolk. We wish them all the success we can, and commend them for their fortitude.

The Katoomba News, August–September 1919

The Light Horseman's Farewell
To Jericho and Rafa,
Jerusalem and Jaffa,
We have said good-bye and left with hearts so glad;
Of Beirout and Tripoli,
Or the sea of Galilee,
No memories will ever make us sad.

And of Jordan's holy stream,
If perchance we ever dream,
No angel's wings will brush our sleepy heads;
Though heat devils through the haze
Of those thirsty, dusty days
May dance a devil's hornpipe on our heads.

Port Said we'll no more see,
Of Cairo we are free,
For it's finish "Bints" and "Backsheesh" ever more;
For biscuits of Moascar
We care not one piastre,
As our good ship heads south-east for Aussies's shore.

To the horses left behind
We pray the fates be kind
And save them from the gharry neddy's toil;
And for mates we held so dear
We will shed a silent tear
When once again we tread Australian soil.

'3352', 8th *L.H.*
Demosthenes Souvenir, January–February 1919

THE VOYAGE

The *Karmala* jerked up the old 'mud hook' at noon and passing through the breakwater faced the open sea, and we drew deep breaths of fresh salt air and said to one another "At last we're in the straight". The shores of England slowly receded and by five o'clock were out of sight.

Today is our tenth day on the bosom of the mighty deep, and with the exception of a distant view of the Canary Islands no other land has been sighted. For the first five days we had a calm sea and a stern wind and our old packet (beg pardon Captain Armitage) bowled along at a great rate, the log one day registering 349 knots. As we neared the Equator the weather changed and on the afternoon of the 10th we bumped a bit of monsoon but this blew itself out in a couple of hours. Each day was increasingly hot, but a strong head wind followed the squall and somewhat cooled the atmosphere. Our troopship is excellently fitted up and the 'tucker' well-cooked and good. Military discipline is to a great extent relaxed and after the morning parade we are free to do as we please. The Y.M.C.A. provides the troops with a library and the canteen with luxuries. There are educational classes on a score or more subjects and these and deck sports fill in the long hours of the day. We have to thank the

Quota Orchestra and the Divisional Concert Party for some very pleasant evenings. Take it from me there is nothing like a bit of music to help gladden the heart. The mere fact of being homeward bound should be sufficient to fill our hearts with joy, and if there's any Digger with 'the skanks'—well he may as well join the porpoises, the 'Quack' cannot cure him.

Each night we dance, at least some of us do, the others try. On the morning of the 12th July we crossed the line and that evening those on board celebrated the event by holding a Fancy Dress Jazz. The promenade deck was alive with gay colours and here let me whisper that the dances were not all buck sets for we have with us ten of the sweetest, dinkiest, 'ikkle Sisters you ever saw. Oh, la la !!!

Yandoo, July 1919

What We Suffered Each Day
The throb of the engine is all that can be heard in the early morn, until our Bugler, with his melodious call of "Get out of Bed", breaks the stillness. The remarks of all and sundry are worthy of George Robey. There are other forms of hardship inflicted upon us to get us to rise, to wit (other than the bugler), a few spare Sergeants. Such nice tones are used, and they have a wonderful musical command that usually sends you to sleep again. Then the offensive of the wash. You have no trouble in obtaining this, and the objective is usually gained after an hours barrage, followed by a charge at the slow crawl. That is, of course, if the water happens to be on. Those sleeping on deck usually kill two birds with the one stone; sleep in until the decks are washed down—this takes the place of bugler, Sergeant and wash. Knowing fellows! Cookhouse at 7 a.m. is answered promptly, and the one desire of each man is that half a dozen or so will be seasick. Parade (?) comes on somewhere about 10 a.m., and between times the games indulged in are varied, "2 to 1 he finds the 4", "I hide 'em and you find 'em", and "a dollar wanted in the kick", being among the best patronised. Usually nobody is a winner, but the old cry of, "What about a bit for the Y.M.C.A.?" is never left out.

Afternoon—ditto; with a variation in the way of sports. The "cool" places are very well patronised, and after tea the Digger has a great knack of finding a burrow, or, if not, of annoying somebody who has one.

You choose your own bedtime, a great liberty; and it's then that those at home have our entire thoughts.

The Bakara Bulletin,
December 1918–February 1919

(*With apologies to Kipling*)
If you can keep your feet when all about you
Are losing theirs, and cursing themselves blue.
If you can sleep in comfort when she's rolling,
And make allowance for her pitching, too,
If you can fall and not be bruised in falling,
Or, being heaved about, don't heave in turn—
You're just the man that's wanted on the Malta,
The ship that puts to shame a floating churn.

The Maltese Roller, August–September 1918

Sausages were the favourite breakfast dish at our table until Trooper Woolcott discovered a dead bullock's eye embedded in a conglomeration of stale bread and minced meat. We completed the meal hour leaning far over the lee-side bulwark.

    The sausage was a ship's one,
    The outside was all skin;
    The inside was a mystery—
    A bull named "Brindle Jim".

(*With apologies to R.K.*)
If you can sweetly smile when those around you
Are feeling just like ninepence in the quid;
Can lightly step while angry waves surround you,
And threaten on your can to put the lid,
If pitching gives you an immense sensation,
And rolling means for you ecstatic life;
If you can meet with calm imperturbation
The height of nature's oceanic strife;

If you can dine on pork without a quiver,
Assimilate the greasiest of food,
Nor get a swift rejoinder from your liver,
But still feel hard as nails and twice as good;
If you had never known just what delight meant,
Till in the Bight you heaved for seven days,
When Ocean's wrath provided mild excitement
And nothing more, nor made you change your ways;

If gastronomic worries never get you
When shipping seas right o'er the fo-c-sle head;

If groaning, sea-sick shipmates cannot fret you,
Nor make your innards feel like lumps of lead;
If you can keep your grub down when you get it,
And of life's joys take out a further lease,
Then—if with health your heart is not besotted—
For God's sake let the others die in peace!
'Junior Engineer'
The Morvada Magazine, July–August 1919

Once we got properly out to sea and found the elements so gracious that none but those with the most fertile imaginations (and the unfortunate passengers aft) could possibly think of being sea-sick, we stowed our glad rags and ki-wied boots and leggings, donned baggy slacks and roomy shoes, looked just as unsoldierly as possible, rejoiced in the novelty of being able to have a blaze of lights o' nights, and in the absence of the submarine guard, breathed deeply of the fresh ozone, and then started to look around for something to do. The search was not in vain. The Y. Emma, with Capt. Forrest, ever after known as 'Bro', at the helm, Padre Rentoul, counsellor, critic and staunch friend of everybody under a slouch hat; Sergt. Quartly, with a band that perhaps was a bit wheezy at the start, but which developed into a really fine musical combination long before the finish; Lieut. Steber, with his troupe of Pierrots who could (and did) put on a show that was absolutely dudless from overture to 'God Save'; and finally, Lieut. Symonds, with a staff of teachers positively bulging with brains, all had their plots wherewith to beguile the time in pleasure and improvement. Concerts, fun-stunts, dances, sports, sing-songs, card tournaments and classes in everything were forthwith arranged and duly carried out. We lazed through the hot, steamy days approaching the line, stirring only at stated intervals for meals, but woke up to a full appreciation of life and good wholesome fun when the sun . . . had plunged into the sea.
Homeward Bound, July–September 1919

When I've rolled me bloomin' hammock,
Got some porridge down me neck,
   And I ain't on piquet or on bloomin' guard,
I do me constitutional,
And all along the deck
   It's "Housey! Housey! Have a buckshee card!"

As I'm eyein' the Atlantic
Churned up by the old 'Eurip',
   An' I've got me brain-box set for thinkin' 'ard,
Of Aussie folk, an' civvy life,
I plan me future life
   To "Housey! Housey! Have a buckshee card!"

When I've peeled the steamed pertaters,
Got some cove to pass the salt.
   And I'm sortin' out the soft peas from the 'ard –
Meals is ticklish on a troopship,
And they ain't improved at all
   With "Housey! Housey! Have a buckshee card!"

Now the long, long day is over,
An' I'm swinging in me bunk,
   An' the old boat's set for Aussie good and 'ard,
I close me bleedin' blinkers,
But, faintly in me dreams,
   Comes . . . "Housey! . . . Housey! . . . Have a buckshee card!"   F.W.
The Homing Aussie, September–October 1919

On 20th July, we sighted land and the same day entered Table Bay. It was a fine clear day and camera fiends were busy all over the ship snapping different views of Lion's Head and Table Mountain as we slowly passed into the Harbour. Eventually we tied up to the wharf and about 3 p.m. word went round that leave was granted.

Everyone at once hopped into their 'Glad rags', in fact I think many of them got dressed overnight and wandered about the ship 'All dressed up and nowhere to go'. We remained at Cape Town until the 24th and had general leave each day till midnight. For the first two days we had torrential rains, so we made the rounds of the Theatres and Cinema shows, but immediately the weather became [better] we set out to see the country. Two of the most popular trips were to Cecil Rhodes' Estate and Memorial, and to Camp Bay. At least 50% of the troops on the *Karmala* visited these two places—maybe the other 50% had appointments to keep, appointments made during our stay at the Cape whilst *en route* for England and The War. What oh those Aussies.
Yandoo, August 1919

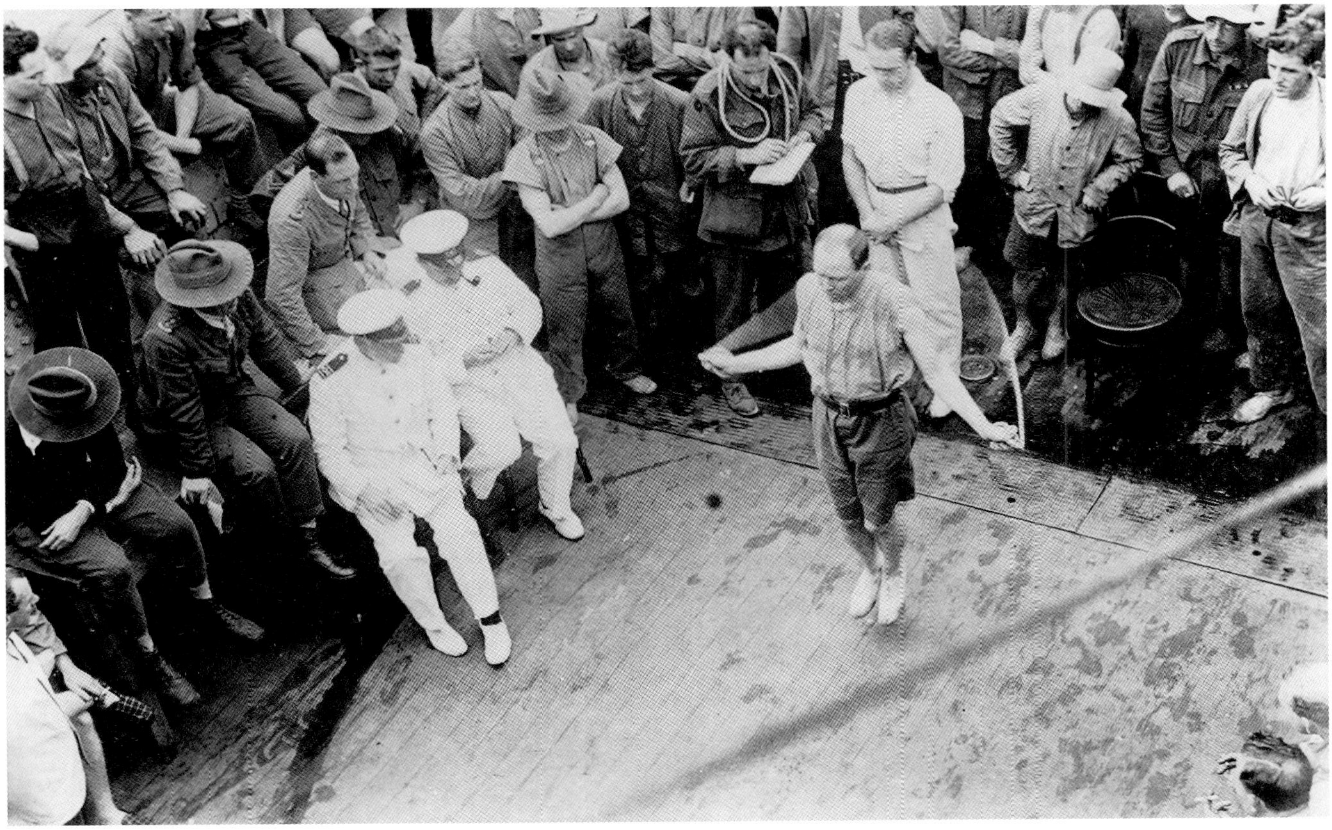

Shipboard entertainments on the *Aeneas*, June 1919. (*Australian War Memorial*, Neg. nos. H15557, 15558)

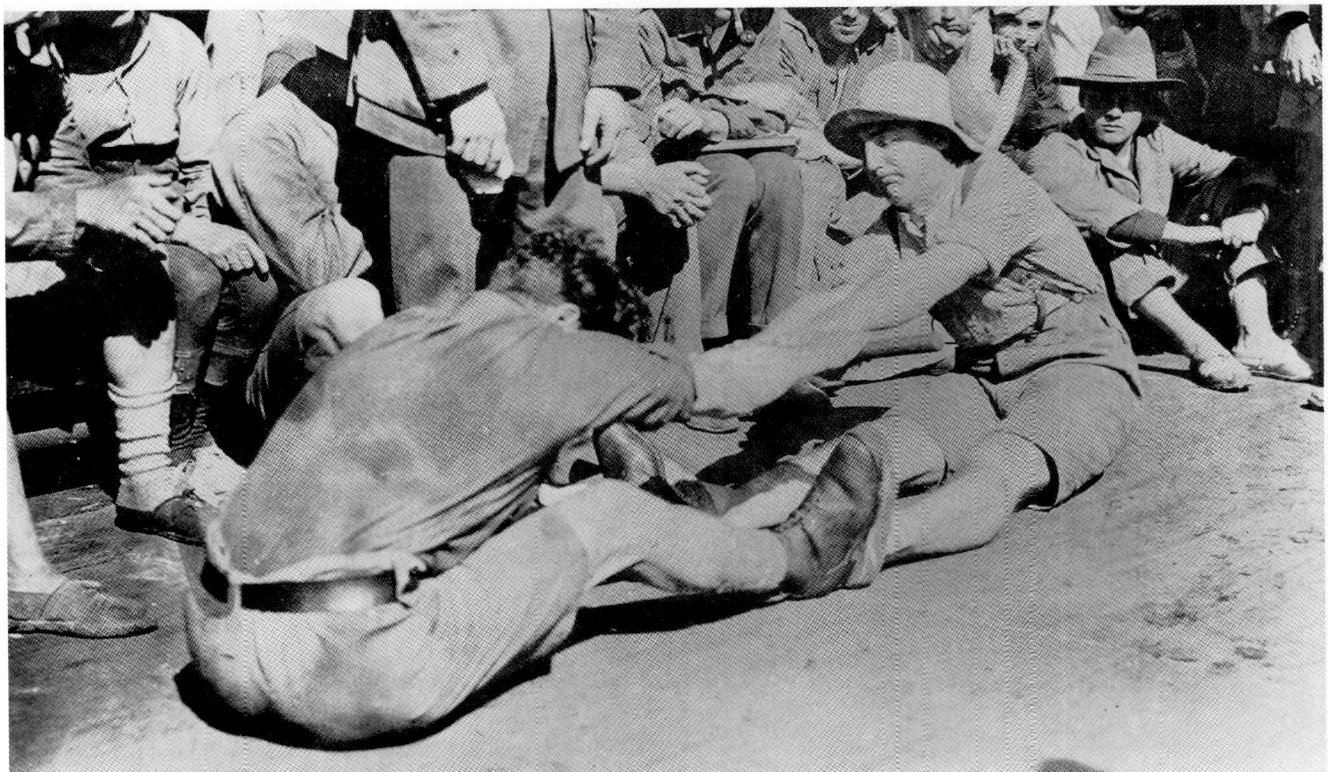

Our Next Leave
Just listen to me digger, as your going on leave,
There are things go on in Cape Town which are hard to believe.
A dusky little tabby will meet you in the street,
Her smile, her manner charming, her dressing rather neat.

She'll tell you she is lonely, she loves Aussies too,
She hasn't had a sweetheart since the last boat passed through.
But, get me digger, it's kid stakes and rotten to the core,
The same old yarn is spoken to soldiers by the score.

So take a tip and feed your mind on all that you can see,
You can still improve your intellect no matter who you be.
A girl is splendid company if you know her to be straight,
But cut the dusky street tab out when you reach the Cape.

Bak-Ara, No 3, August–September 1919

April 19th—From a vague outline of coast land Colombo began to make itself visible at 7 a.m., its vivid colours making a pleasing picture. By 8.30 we had passed the breakwater and were safely moored. . . .

During the day a rumour that shore leave might be granted secured circulation, and before long a good half of the troops were all dressed up and nowhere to go. The news that leave was to be given on the morrow from eight o'clock in the morning created intense satisfaction. This was an excellent arrangement, as, if leave had been granted on this day, the Troops could not have proceeded to the shore before three o'clock, and their time must have been limited to at most a couple of hours.

April 20th—The Colombo hop-over commenced with reveille at 5.30 a.m., and an early breakfast; and at 7.30 the Troops moved from the vessel's side into the barges waiting for them. They were in bottle order, thirsts worn at the alert. The incidents in Colombo were various, but the Troops had a good day, and the casualties were slight. The objectives were Good Time Farm, a Skinful of Booze Estaminet, and Souvenir House; and having attained all these, the Troops returned to ship in good order; although at least one man, who had discovered that it was good sport to chase Niggers through the water, got slightly damp.

Imshi, 24 April 1919

Recipe for Osterly Omelette
To one deck chair add two people. It is essential that the chair should be a strong one and that the contents should be of opposite sexes. Add a good portion of darkness and cover well with a layer of thick rug. Shake into a comfortable position and allow to settle for half-an-hour. When contents simmer, covering should be removed and chair mended.

This dish is specially recommended for the Red Sea and other tropical places.

The Dinkum Gazette, February 1919

January 1st (New Year's Day) was celebrated on board with a programme of sports. The weather being ideal, and everyone by this time having well passed calling forth "Europe" over the side of the boat, entered into the day's events in a true sporting manner.... As one walked along the deck, passing from one group which seemed to be interested in the ordeal of trying to pick up a collar stud by standing on their eyebrows or elevating their front teeth, to another group who were enjoying themselves at the expense of one, who, blindfolded, was trying to place the tail on the pig, and so on. I think the most interesting event in the sports—one which caused the most amusement—was the pillow fighting competition on the cross-bar. It was a case of "He that thinks himself most secure, take heed lest he fall". The tug-of-war competitions were thoroughly enjoyed, and to crown the events of the day, we were entertained with a good concert to bring to a grand finale the close of a very pleasant day....

SPORTS PROGRAMME

1. Tug-of-War
2. Pillow fighting on spar
3. Potato race
4. Orange-eating
5. Cock-fighting
6. Scratch pull
7. Bull-board
8. Skipping
9. Placing stud
10. Placing tail on pig
11. Wheelbarrow race
12. Guessing number of peas in jar
13. Memory test
14. Fancy dress
15. Sack race
16. Reveille race
17. Weight-guessing
18. Recovering coin from electric tub

The Final Objective, December 1918–February 1919

HOMEWARD BOUND

Homeward Bound
Ended is the raging conflict,
   Foes are conquered, victory won;
Hearts are lighter, spirits brighter,
   For our work is done.

Thoughts will traverse miles of ocean,
   Back to those who gave their breath;
For their Country's freedom dying,
   Faithful unto death.

Hidden is the nearing future,
   Of our prospects little known;
Hope is present, courage needed,
   In the land we call our own.

Fathers, mothers, wives and sweethearts,
   Waiting there to greet their boys;
Anxious for the grand re-union,
   And its many joys.

Soon we'll reach those shores delightful,
   Speeding onwards o'er the foam;
Land of sunshine, dear Australia,
   Home, Sweet Home.

Homeward Bound, 1918

Shipboard entertainments on the *Aeneas*, June 1919. (*Australian War Memorial, Neg. nos. H15559, 15561*)

Homeward Bound
Oh! It's good to smell the briny, and to see the seagulls wheel
O'er the long-drawn wake of swirling milky foam,
And the good ship's throbbing, throbbing from binnacle to keel,
    Going Home!

Full many weary months have pass'd—we've done our little bit
From Gallipoli to Ypres and the dreary, muddy Somme;
But cast our cares behind us, recking not how hard we're hit,
    Speeding Home!

Soon we'll see them in the distance—sweethearts, wives and mothers dear—
Stretching out their arms in welcome o'er the foam:
And we'll hear the shouts of greeting resounding from the pier,
    Nearing Home!   *E.P.H*
                  The Final Objective, December 1918–February 1919

Across the Line
The Southern Cross is in the sky, Australia lies ahead;
My heart is like a feather now, where once it seemed like lead;
A few more leagues of water and our journey will be o'er,
We'll ring the joy-bells madly when we see Australia's shore.

The sad old world lies far behind, and all its troubles too;
The days of bully beef are o'er; (likewise the days of 'stoo');
We've crossed the Line and soldier Jack thinks fondly of his Jill,
At last we're on the straight for Home, we're going down the hill!   *P.J.B.*
                    The Khyberian, 28 April 1919

Going Back
Steaming back to Aussy, thro' the dancing sea,
    Churnin' up the ocean, happy you and me
Nearer to our mother, sweetheart, wife or son,
    What a glad reunion now the war is done.
Times we've sat a-thinkin' would Fritz sell me a pup
    While the shells were screamin' and the 'wind was up',
But strike me blue an' happy, gone is war an' pain
    We're breakin' blanky records we'll soon be home again.
Wave adieu to Blighty and the firin' line
    Ever south we're headin' and the weather's fine,
Nothin' now to stop us, see the creamy foam
    Swirlin' in the back-wash now we're headin' home.
Blighty has its pleasures, booze and ladies fair
    Goodbye Piccadilly, farewell Leicester Square,
Au revoir to Paree, never more we'll roam

Unless its with the missus waitin' there at home.
　　　When we're back in Aussy, when we've lost the knack
　　　　　Of twirlin' up the pennies or stoushin' up a Jack,
　　　Won't we be respectable in civies and straw lid
　　　　　Strollin' with the missus and carryin' the kid.
　　　Blime Dig we're lucky, ain't the weather grand
　　　　　Ham and eggs on Sunday, 'Aussie bon' brass band,
　　　And we're gettin' nearer every blanky day
　　　　　Nearer to old Aussy, hip hip hip hooray.　　F.P.B.
　　　　　　　　　　　　　　　　　　The Nest of News, May 1919

Der Tag
For we've talked of the day, and thought of the day;
　When we shall sail back home once more.
And the eleventh of May was the happy day
　When we started for Aussie's shore. ...

And as these shores are drawing near,
　On the serious side we'll dwell:
For we must all have a tale prepared,
　For our wives and sweethearts to tell.

For we one and all, at times back there;
　Lost our hearts to Yvonne or Suzanne,
So if you are asked: "Were you true to me dear?"
　How will you answer, young man?

Le Guerre finis, and we are home once more,
　How you will think of those times, par bonne,
But we'll never forget the girls we met,
　While on the "Continong".
　　　　　　　The Borda News, 21 May 1919

Homeward Bound
'Homeward Bound', oft have we dreamed of,
Thought of, prayed for this great day;
When to war and all it stood for
Glad farewells we each could say.

'Homeward Bound', but many comrades
Homeland's welcome n'er can share;
Sleep they 'neath the soil of far lands,
Men whom Homeland ill could spare.

'Homeward Bound', their voyage ended,
Ne'er forgotten shall they be;
Age on age shall tell the story
How they died to keep us free.

'Homeward Bound', with true hearts waiting
Us in outstretched arms to take;
They who bore the pain of waiting
Cheerfully for love's dear sake.

'Homeward Bound', speed on Kanowna,
Quickly we would reach our shore;
Golden, sunny, dear Australia,
From her we will sail no more.
　　　　　　Cpl. W.M. Doig, 5*th* Div. Sig.
　　　　　Souvenir of H.M.A.T. Kanowna,
　　　　　　　　August–October 1919

OH WHAT A LOVELY WAR

Officialdom has never been able to thoroughly overawe the wearer of the 'Rising Sun', and the solemnity of the occasion has not prevented him from exercising his ready wit even on those in high places.

　At Loere, on one occasion, a Brigadier-General was engaged in the apparently to him congenial task of distributing medals to a couple of deserving cases. He had the unfortunates providing the amusement in front of him, under the admiring gaze of the parade of their comrades, and during his eulogy of their behaviour which had earned the distinctions conferred upon them, he held the medals in his right hand. During the display of oratory he turned over the medals once or twice, and the proceedings were

With his distinctive uniform the Australian soldier on leave was a very visible tourist.
(*Australian War Memorial, Neg. no. D00710*)

Soldiers visiting Hampton Court near London. (*Australian War Memorial, Neg. no. D00635*)

interrupted by a general burst of laughter when one of the boys in the ranks, probably as a result of a misspent youth, yelled, "A bob he heads 'em".
The Home Trail, October–December 1918

My Desire
I want to bash a Gyppo,
He seldom hits you back;
I want to plant my horny fist
In something brown or black;
But every man within my reach
Is strong and rather white,
So I must keep myself in check
Because I cannot fight.

O! would I were in Egypt,
Where slender Gyppos dwell—
I've often heard a soldier say
The place resembled hell;
But when you've bashed a Gyppo,
And cinked his ugly face,
You've helped to swell the glory of
The great Australian race.

The word "tallaheena"
Rings like a clarion call;
It promptly brings a Gyppo
Around your boots to crawl;
But somewhere in Australia
Where I may shortly be,
Life will be sad without a "Bong"
To take a punch from me.   *Blue Stripe*
The Morvada Magazine, July–August 1919

Jim's girl was tall and slim, My girl was short and thick-set; Jim's girl wore crepe-de-chene, My girl wore flannelette; Jim's girl was sweet and bright, My girl was pure and good; You think I'd change my girl for Jim's?—Well, you're darned right—I would!
Homeward Bound, 1918

Girls
Oh, London girls are sporty girls, and Cardiff girls are sweet,
And the dark-eyed girls of Charleroi are dainty and *petite*,
But now I'm on the track for home the only girl for me
Is the homespun, all-wool, dinkum girl who's waiting on the Quay.

I've had my fun, I must admit, and made the money go,
For the sheelahs know the Aussie hat, from France to Scapa Flow.
There was Maisie down at Margate, there was Maggie up at Frome
But I'm forgetting all the lot, now that I'm bound for home.

'Twas "Hullo, Aussie" everywhere, and girls have saucy eyes,
And most of them have little throats just made to swallow lies
Of emu-farms in Footscray and sheep-ranches in Balmain …
But I will quit romancing when I lob back home again.

Oh, London girls are sporty girls, and Glasgow girls are neat,
And the black-haired girls of Froggieland can lead you on a treat,
But now I'm on the homeward track one face comes back to me,
   The dinkum girl, the only girl,
The dyed-in-the-wool, unshrinking girl,
The girl I never quite forgot when I went oversea.   *Vance P.*
The Homing Aussie, September–October 1919

The Aussies' Farewell
We came from Australia to help to beat the Hun,
We came on business only—not expecting any fun;
But when we got to 'la belle France' we found you M'amoiselle,
Intending, if we did this work we'd have some fun as well.
You flirted, danced and sang with us—taught us to 'parley-vous';
Life would have been so rotten if it had not been for you.
But now 'la guerre' is over and we're going home again;
But tho' we're glad we're going the parting gives us pain.

   So farewell, M'amoiselle; M'amoiselle adieu!
   Tho' we're going home again our hearts will be with you;
   When we settle down in Aussie, and have wife and kids as well,
   Vous n'oubliez jamais votre chere M'amoiselle.

Now, when we came to 'Blighty' first, to spend our ten days' leave,
We didn't feel quite sure what kind of welcome we'd receive.
We'd heard that English girls were cold and froze one with a glance,
But we found you just as loving as the M'amoiselle of France.
By your barrage of beauty caught—we yielded to your charms;
The war was quite forgotten when you nestled in our arms;
But now we're off to Aussie with some of you as wives,
And the rest will be a memory to cherish all our lives.

   So good-bye, Blighty girls, Blighty girls good-bye!
   Altho' we're glad we're going home we leave you with a sigh;
   Your winsome ways, your faces sweet, your dinky little curls,
   Are twined around our hearts forever, dear old Blighty girls.
Homeward, 1919

The Anzac and his Girl
There's a chap they call the Anzac
   You can see him up in town,
With his smartly fitting tunic
   And his face of sunny brown;
And although he's but a stranger,
   He's as proud as any Earl,
If you leave him to his hobby—
   Trotting round some pretty girl.

Then in hospital you'll meet him,
   And the symptoms here are seen,
When his boots he dabs with polish,
   And his hair with brilliantine;
Some scented correspondence
   He'll at intervals unfurl,

Then you know that he has found her
   That the Anzac's got a girl.

But his dinkum girl, why, bless you
   Is at home; and then perchance
The maiden has her own boy,
   Fighting somewhere out in France.
So they're feeling rather lonely;
   Don't reproaches at them hurl,
For they have to keep their hands in—
   The Anzac and his Girl.
The Homeward Trail, n.d.

Some very strange stories of the reception accorded to wives of returning Australians have been heard; but we think that our fair adopted daughters will find their sisters in the new homeland can quite appreciate the fact that Cupid shoots his arrows promiscuously and that after the barrage there is nothing more to be said on the matter.

The Bremen Babbler, 12 July 1919

Modern Nursery Rhymes
Sing a song of happiness
The diggers and their wives,
Sailing out to Aussie land
To recommence their lives.
When the steamer reaches port
The Aussie girls will say—
"Alas we should have leg-roped them
Before they sailed away".

Poor Miss de Vere,
Rushed to the pier
To welcome her dear Aussie back;
But when she got there
A Wife did appear
So she came a gutzer, alack!

Berrima News, 5 October 1919

THE FUTURE

Thoughts for the Future
The time will soon come when we shall reach our own land, and we shall be happy—for a while—then the desire to fight on may return to us and with it discontentment.

It must be so to all those who have their Country's greatness at heart, and there are many. There is something within us that makes us strive to do our best. We may growl and find fault, but we uphold Australia's name, and our prayer is "Thank God we are Australians". We have risked our lives for our country and we desire our country's greatness before all other things.

Therefore, let us strive to have all the questions that concern the health and well-being of the coming generation brought forward and discussed.

Let us realise that in the physical health of our children will lie the future greatness of the Commonwealth, and that we cannot do better than have our children say: "Thank God, we are Australians".

Boonah Boomerang, July–September 1918

Effects of the War on Australia
In the minds of all the thinking people of Australia today, the question "What is to be the result of this war to our Homeland?" recurs with almost annoying frequency. All who have the interest of their own country at heart, admit freely that "the old order passeth", but, few among them really exert themselves to mould the NEW. Rather, they drift on a sea of indecision, and Micawber-like, wait for "Something to turn up". . . .

From this distance it is hard to get any definite information on the matter of what is being done to stop this "drift", but a step in the right direction has been made in the establishing of a Repatriation Board. Here is an organized body with funds at its disposal, the nation at its back, and a supply of first-hand information to work upon, ready and anxious to place all its resources at the disposal (practically) of returning Australians. I have qualified the word "disposal" because it will be easily realised that in a great number of cases, demands could not be ACTUALLY met. But in such cases, the Board does "the next best thing". The benefit of all this, is that it is not so much for the individual as for the Nation. The idea is, I venture to say, to save the individual from "drift" so that the Nation itself may be saved. . . .

A great demand for organized and efficient labour has been created by the loss of many of the most virile of Australia's sons. This situation MUST be boldly faced and handled if our country is still to be successful in competing in the world's trade. . . . Australia's resources are unlimited: we need unlimited labour to make the most of them. So let us get on with immigration. Would it not be reasonable to suggest that a part, if not the whole of our share in the indemnity might be paid by over-crowded Britain to her under-populated colonies, in manpower? But, here is the need for care of the strictest kind! Let us have no journeyman immigrants but finished tradesmen! Not the superficial clerical man, but the man whose qualifications cannot be questioned!

Australia, as a country, is one of the best; therefore it behoves us to receive none but the best. Only thus can we ever hope to attain again the high standard of efficiency that was ours before the world-war and regain our place in the world's markets.

So, to us, returning citizens all, comes the lesson of the ages, "don't drift: PROGRESS".

The Dinkum Gazette, February 1919

The men of the A.I.F. are composed of both sides of politics—Liberal and Labour. But in the future we will not be concerned about these differences. It is the co-operation of both sides which made the name of Australia famous on the field of war, and we can, by the same method, make history in the field of politics. . . . No one will challenge the unanimous verdict that the Parties have served their purpose and the old order must go. A new state, compatible with the huge sacrifices that have been made to attain it must be built up. Let us for a moment consider what responsibilities we have. The first is to our 58,000 comrades who are with us no more, but to whom a solemn promise was made in life. The second is to their parents, wives, brothers and sisters who are suffering the agony of grief through irreparable loss. Thirdly, to ourselves to see that their sacrifice has not been in vain.

Surely no one doubts we have the ability to assume these great national responsibilities. We have in the A.I.F. the best of Australia's manhood, physically and intellectually. No job was considered too big for us. It is not too much to ask that the future of the homeland should be entrusted to us.

We have an immense chance to show our worth. We have public opinion with us, and the whole of our island continent. The war has taught the value of every man and woman. A country can only become great by a co-operation of men and ideas in the interest of humanity. Relegating to the past all selfish motives, Australia is looking to the return of the heroes with wild enthusiasm and glad anticipations. Much is expected of us. Shall we prove as stalwart as custodians of future rights as we have been in fighting for them? The monument of the future will be the condition of our country, and that can be erected by the great family of the A.I.F.

The Shropshire Blimp, April 1919

Let us take up civil life determined that over the wreckage and misery of war we will build up an Australia that shall be famed as widely for its Righteousness and Equity as it is for its valour. Only then can we meet the liability we owe to those who fought beside us but will never return.

The Ocean Echo, 14 August 1919

Colored Labor Or Stagnation?
The universal cry today with regard to Australia is production.

Everyone is extremely anxious that the millions of acres of fertile land, at present lying idle, should be opened up; that the productiveness of the country they live in should be mightily increased. . . .

But for every acre of ground in Australia which is being successfully tilled, how many are lying idle?—And what is the reason? In a large percentage of cases it is cost and difficulty of obtaining labour.

For many years now we have upheld the 'white labor' policy, and fought strenuously against the importation of colored workers. The result has been that we have very large tracts of land which might easily have been opened up but which are at present utterly useless. All this simply because the white man refuses to work where his less intelligent colored cousin flourishes. Is it advisable to follow a policy which is a direct bar to National Progress?

A colored race amongst a white population is, if allowed, we know, likely to be detrimental to the community. But surely sufficiently definite steps could be taken to practically prevent the mixture of the races!

The fact remains that while our country persists in her policy of a 'White Australia' she is doomed to failure in the commercial world of tomorrow.

Karmala Kuts, 2 August 1919

That's All
Don't want no fuss when I come home,
Don't want no crowds to cheer,
Don't want to visit all the pubs,
Nor mop up all the beer.
Don't want no blessed band to play
'The Conquering 'ero Comes',
Don't want to hear the trumpets blare,
No beatin' of the drums.
Just want the place I calls me 'ome
—the folk I love the best,
A decent job at a decent screw
And a decent bit of rest.   'Sling'

The Boomerag, 23 August 1919

(Australian War Memorial Printed Records)

EXPERIENCE OF WAR

As the sun neared its western goal, we moved from our rough-and-ready bivouac on our steady approach to the front line. We were to attack at midnight. Our road lay over hill and vale; the walking proved heavy, dusty.

It was our first big stunt; we marched with hopes high, hearts high; brave with that peculiar quality due to ignorance.

As we came abreast the rear field guns we broke into single file. Wondering, curious, elate—we passed the close-packed cannon that made of Sausage Gulley a Field of the Cloth of Steel.

We entered the long communication sap. It was now dark. Wires lying across the trench, sudden dips, the straightness of the way,—all these made progress an art. In certain places a strange sponginess of the ground soon apprised us of what lay beneath.

Throughout one stretch we saw,—well, we took them to be fellows resting in their little "funk-holes"; none of them spoke—Concussion. Later, as we got fairly close, we proceeded along a sunken road strewn with decomposing forms and stray limbs, of friends and foes in ghastly melee.

The last part of the sap was torn and broken. A little before we reached our lying-out ground, we had several men killed by 77s.

Not long had we to lie there waiting for the signal to commence crossing No Man's Land. Shells had been bursting in our immediate rear; we scarcely objected to moving. But we had gone only a short distance, when our movement was detected. Our increased fire on his trench told him "what was doing". He opposed with machine gun rather than artillery fire (though that wasn't scarce), and, on account of the gradual nature of the slope, wrought deadly havoc. The sky lit up with intermittent rockets, the forms of men silhouetted against the searching light, the fall of a comrade. These things impressed themselves vividly on us.

First their outposts. These offered feeble resistance.

Soon after, their front line—many reached it, only to find the barrier of wire in most places intact. The rare and narrow gaps, where seen, were used; the few that passed through were slain on the parapet. At places other than the gaps, men strove to effect a way through those wire entanglements. Machine guns, fired at a murderous short distance, hand grenades and rifles, mowed down these men rapidly surely; many fell and lay dead, over the wire they had, in despairing agony, striven to pass.

After a temporary occupation and consolidation of a sunken road (a very death-trap, where we lost man after man), we retired as ordered.

Six hours after we "hopped off", some fifty per cent of us returned. For several days men kept coming in; some had waited till their strength came back; some had watched for the darkness to escape from a shell hole, which may, perhaps, have been very few yards from the enemy line.

All on their return from the deadly slope of Pozieres looked haggard, wild of eye, infinitely weary; they were silent—silent with the sense of some dread thing evaded they knew not how; avid of sleep. For some hours there had been toil and danger in an encounter surpassed by few in the heaviness and utter gratuitousness of resultant casualties.

And some people still wonder why iron enters into the souls of men.   *Eric H. Partridge*
The Bakara Bulletin, December 1918–
February 1919

Any Soldier To His Son
What did you do, Daddy, in the great World War?
Well, I learned to peel potatoes and to scrub the Barrack floor,
I learned to use the shovel, and a barrow, and a pick;
I learned to "Get a jerk on" and I learned to "make 'em click";
I learned the road from Aussie, and I looked my last on Home
As I heaved my beans and bacon to the fishes and the foam.

At last we got to Europe and the harbour hove in sight,
And they landed us and sorted us and marched us by the right.
"Quick March" along the cobbles, by the kids who ran along
Singing "Appoo—Spearmint—Shokolah" through dirty old Boulong.
I learned to ride a soldier's ride from Base up to the line
For days and nights in cattle trucks packed in like droves of swine.

I learned to curl and kip it on a foot of muddy floor
And to envy cows and horses that have beds of "beaucoup" straw,
I learned to wash in shell holes, and to have a shave in tea
While the fragments of a mirror did a balance on my knee.
I learned to dodge the "Whizz-Bang" and the flying lumps of lead
And to keep a foot of earth between the sniper and my head.

I learned to keep my haversack well filled with "buckshee" food,
To take the army issue, and to pinch what else I could;
I learned to cook maconochie with candle ends and string,
With sardine oil, and four by two, and any Goddam thing.
I learned to use my bayonet according as you please
For a broad knife, or a chopper, or a prong for toasting cheese.

I learned to gather souvenirs (that home I hoped to send)
And lumped them round for months and months and dumped them in the end.
I learned to hunt for vermin in the lining of my shirt,
To crack 'em with my finger nails and hear the beggars squirt.
I learned to sleep by snatches on the fire step of a trench
And to eat my breakfast mixed with mud and Fritz's heavy stench.

I learned to pray for "Blighty ones", and lie and squirm with fear
When "Jerry" started straffing and the "Blighty ones" were near.
I learned to write home cheerful with my heart a lump of lead
With thoughts of you and Mother, when she heard that I was dead;
And the only thing like pleasure over there I ever knew
Was to hear my pal come shouting "There's a parcel, Mate, for you".

So much for what I did do, now for what I did not do.
Well, I never kissed a French girl and I never killed a Hun.
I never missed an issue of tobacco, pay, or rum,
I never made a friend, and yet I never lacked a chum,
I never used to grumble after breakfast in the line
That the eggs were cooked too lightly or the bacon done too fine.

I never told a Sergeant just exactly what I thought.
I never did a pack drill for I never quite got caught.
I never stopped a "Whizz-Bang" tho' I've stopped a lot of mud,
But the one that Fritz sent over with my name on was a dud;
I never played the hero and walked about on top,

I kept inside my funk hole when the shells began to drop.

Well. Tommy Jones's Father must be made of different stuff,
I never asked for trouble; the issue was enough.
So I learned to live and lump it in the lovely land of war
When all the face of nature seemed a monstrous septic sore;
When all the bowels of earth hung open like the guts of something slain,
And the rot and wreck of everything was churned and churned again.

When all is done in darkness, and when all is still in day,
When living men are buried, and the dead unburied stay;
When men inhabit holes like rats, and only rats live there;
When cottage stood, and castle once, in days "avant la guerre";
When endless files of soldiers thread the everlasting way
On endless miles of duckboards through the endless walls of clay;
When life is one hard labour, and a soldier gets his rest;
When they leave him in the daisies with a puncture in his chest.

You'd like to be a soldier and go to France some day.
By all the dead in Devil's Wood; by all the night I lay
Between our line and Fritz's before they brought me in;
By this old wood and leather stump that once was flesh and skin;
By all the lads who crossed with me but never crossed again;
By all the prayers their Mothers and their Sweethearts prayed in vain;
Before the things that win that day should evermore befall
May God in common pity destroy us one and all.   *F.M. Upton.*
                                                    Ocean Echo, July–August 1919

Now the storm at last is over, and the war clouds 'gin to lift,
And we glimpse the silver lining, shining brightly thro' the rift;
We have farewelled all our comrades, Tommy, Yankee, Belge and French,
And we're proud of every Ally who ere glorified a trench;
We are facing to the Southland, homeward turns our every thought,
As our wake streams white behind us to the shores of Devonport,
And the cables bear the message, speeding fast beneath the foam,
That the boys are on the water, Coming Home, Coming Home.

It's a long, long trail they've followed, from the land where they were born,
Where they bluffed the Turks at Anzac, on that fateful April morn,
Through the fertile Hells of Passchendale, of Pozieres, Boullecourt,
Till they stemmed the time at Villers Brett, they've done their share and more;
In the valley of the Jordan, in the streets of Nazareth,
They have rolled their fags and smoked them, in the very face of death;
But from dugout, hut and billet, clear from Flanders to Siloam,
See, the serried ranks are mustered, Coming Home, Coming Home.

You scarce can claim that modesty's their great besetting sin,
But always they made good their boast, and played the game 'all in',
And they stood beside their cobbers with a mateship staunch and true;
If they cracked 'em also, sometimes, well, that's just like Aussie's do.
Be it trench, or leave, or rest camp, put it anyway you can,
You will never find them wasters, but you'll always find them man,
And in every town or hamlet, wherever they may roam,
They'll leave someone sad to see them Coming Home, Coming Home.

There are some we'll leave behind us as we steer across the waves,
And the crosses glimmer whitely over countless comrades' graves,
And our thoughts go out in sadness to the mothers and the wives
And the sweethearts with the sorrow pressing darkly on their lives;
Little use for us to tell them that they died like heroes there—
Their's alone the awful sorrow that no other heart can bear;
But the thought will live eternal, shrined within our memory's tome,
Of the mates we leave behind us, Coming Home, Coming Home.

Homeward Bound, July–September 1919

LEST WE FORGET

A Billjim Epitaph
No chaste white marble vault for him,
They laid him 'neath the poplars in the golden afterglow;
The Padre and a file o' men, to hear the bugles blow.
Somewhere in Flanders tired arms nailed his Cross,
'Sundowner Bill' lies very still.
At last he's found a 'doss'.

Flanders
There—where the Angelus from some old sun kissed spire
Has brought a toil worn Pierre to his knees,
Old 'Cobbers' lie—in stagnant trench and reddened mire,
Where once the lilting lark rose on a lilac-scented breeze.   W.B.H.

The Karoolian, September 1918

Let us drink a toast,
   To that vanished host
Who've crossed the front trench line,
   And the rendezvous
With the proven true
   While the stars as sentries shine.
They surrendered joys
   For the battle's noise
But never in courage did lack,
   So just a silent prayer
For the lads out there
   The Boys who will never come back.   J.M.G.

The Nest of News, 31 May 1919

COMRADES GONE WEST.

Sing we a song of our comrades gone West,
West down the long, long, lone trail.
Fell they defending, or charging the crest;
Great though the odds they stood up to the test,
Faced it, though faces were turned to the West,
Westward, where youth's red cheeks pale.

. . . .

Toast we the memory of comrades gone West,
Toast we in silence deep;
Round some crushed heart, a sorrow-torn breast,
Weeping at home for some comrade gone West,
"Missing" p'rhaps — only God knows the rest,
Memories like tendrils creep.

. . . .

Peace to the souls of our comrades gone West,
Peace, and a sleep deep and sweet;
After the fury of battle, calm rest;
After great daring at duty's behest
Sleep they where foemen no longer contest,
Nor wardrums of Nations beat.

Padre
25·4·1919.

Though returning soldiers looked to the future those who would not return were remembered.
Our Homeward Stunt: HMAT Port Macquarie April–May 1919. (*Australian War Memorial Printed Records*)

Comrades Gone West
Sing we a song of our comrades gone West,
West down the long, long, lone trail.
Fell they defending, or charging the crest;
Great though the odds they stood up to the test,
Faced it, though faces were turned to the West,
Westward, where youth's red cheeks pale.

Toast we the memory of comrades gone West,
Toast we in silence deep;
Round some crushed heart in a sorrow-torn-breast,
Weeping at home for some comrade gone West,
"Missing" p'rhaps—only God knows the rest,
Memories like tendrils creep.

Peace to the souls of our comrades gone West,
Peace, and a sleep deep and sweet;
After the fury of battle, calm rest;
After great daring at duty's behest
Sleep they where foemen no longer contest,
Nor wardrums of Nations beat. 'Padre'
Our Homeward Stunt, March–May 1919

Do Not Forget
When you're dreaming in the moonlight,
   Of the days which now are past,
When you're back in dear Australia;
   And you've been 'Demobbed' at last.

When you're thanking your Creator,
   That you've seen the horror through;
Give a thought to those who started,
   But did not return with you.

Think of little, shattered Belgium,
   Where the 'Iron Heel' was set,
Think of France's crucifixion,
   DO NOT LET YOURSELF FORGET. C.H.R.
The Borda News, 21 May 1919

The shadows gently fall where they are sleeping
The moonbeams dance,
About their graves, for they are in God's keeping
Somewhere in France.
The Diggers' Pie, 9 August 1919

Our Gallant Dead
The pregnant fire of nationhood
That burned within their breasts;
While valiant in youth they stood
Upon the war-flames crest,
Died not, when o'er them surged the wave
But evermore from out the grave shall spur their kindred on.
Their deeds adorn th' immortal scroll,
Their glory ne'er shall fade
But onward—as the ages roll
Thro' every dark'ning shade,
Shall guide to higher realms of light
Till Honour's child sees darkest night
By Heaven's morn outshone.
The Denison Quoter, October 1919

VISIONS OF HOME

Looked forward to be[ing] returning Aussies as John Bunyan's Pilgrim looked forward to the Delectable Mountain. Like Biblical Canaan, a land flowing with milk and honey. Rich in minerals, wheat, wool, fruit, dairy produce *and* beautiful girls.
The Bremen Babbler, 11 June 1919

(*Winner of the competition for an additional verse to the National Anthem*)
Australia, grand and free,
Queen of the Southern Sea,
   Land we adore;
Grant us, O God, that we
Worthy of her and Thee
Through all the years may be,
   Come peace or war.
Homeward Bound, July–September 1919

Homeward Bound
We've said "Goodbye" to the girls we've loved
   We've said "Goodbye" to the Mall
We've had our day and we're sailing away
   To the land that holds us all.
To the Land where the Bush smells sweet and strong
   Where the open spaces call;
And the Jacky laughs so loud and long
   In the great gum trees so tall.

Where the sun shines bright on the beaches white
    And the surf breaks white in foam;
Where the curlews cry in the clear still night
    And the bell bird bells us home.
We're counting the days as we pass them by,
    The days and the minutes too
And the weeks that die as we homeward fly
    To the hearts so fond and true.   W.L. Duncan
           The Denison Quoter, October 1919

An Aussie Soldier's Dream
Along the old bush track
I'm riding in my dream,
Out once more—far outback—
Down by old Lachlan stream.

Out by the boundary fence
Bounds Old Man Kangaroo,
To distant scrub-land dense
Where dwells the Wallaroo.

Resounding with the dawn
Loud crack of stockman's whip,
Upon the breeze is borne
From down the clover strip.

In distant view I see
My dear old home out-back,
The old folks waiting me
Down by the old bush track.
           Homeward Bound, 1919

The Loves of Yesteryear
I am leaning o'er the deck rail, the night is bright and clear,
Pond'ring sadly o'er the memories of the loves of yesteryear.
Oh! Ninette, are you heeding far away in gay Paree,
As my restless thoughts go speeding o'er ten thousand miles of sea?

Marie, are you weeping back in Charleroi?
In memory are you keeping your wayward, wand'ring boy?
Do you ever stop to ponder o'er the mem'ries of the past,
The follies, joys and promises too fanciful to last? ...

As like a feather in a blast my truant fancies roam,
They stray expectantly at last back to my Southern home.
And Nell is at the sliprails where she stood in bygone years,
And though the land is parched and dry her eyes are filled with tears.

And I recall her girlish trust, with a keen pang of remorse,
For like a submarine-chased ship I've steered a wayward course.
Yet her sweet forgiving smile is beckoning to me,
Her kindly voice it seems to rise from out the lisping sea.
How it banishes my sorrow in my conscience-stricken plight,
Brings the brightness of tomorrow to the sadness of tonight!
           Homeward Bound, November–December 1919

GOOD-BYE-EE!

Good-bye to trenches, rats and mice,
To rotten billets, chats and lice,
To bully stew and boiled rice.
    Good-bye-ee!

To bully beef and pork and beans,
Plum-apple jam, and never greens—
I've indigestion still in dreams—
    Good-bye-ee!

To Anzac wafers and rum issue,
The little lot that often missed you,
When other blokes got double issue.
    Good-bye-ee!

Good-bye to going in the line,
To minnies, to the weird shell whine,
To whiz-bangs and the damned five-nine.
    Good-bye-ee!

To gas guards and to Boche air raids,
Reveille, piquets and parades,
Estaminets and chic French maids.
    Good-bye-ee!

Good-bye to mumps and boils and scabies,
To war-time leave and war-time ladies,
To issue sox and war-time babies,
    Good-bye-ee!

To sick parade and iodine,
Sulphur ointment, chloride of lime,
S.A. parade and Number 9.
    Good-bye-ee!

To night patrol and Boche white flare,
To wiring stunts and "who goes there?"
To strombos-horns, P.H., gas scare.
    Good-bye-ee!

To mounting guard, fatigues and drill;
Of dull routine I've had my fill,
Na-poo! I've lost the lust to kill.
    Good-bye-ee!

To dug-out, shell-hole, and shell-crater,
That brought me near the heart of nature;
O! what a yarn I'll tell the mater!
    Good-bye-ee!

And then good-bye to my tin hat
That saved my life when splinters spat;
Thanks to the bloke who thought of that!
    Good-bye-ee!

To red tabs, red tape—Ack—Ack—Ack!
To tons we carried in our pack,
Adieu! I'm never coming back.
    Good-bye-ee!

To cold-footers and red-caps too,
Bonjour! I touch my nose to you;
Henceforth, you've got to earn your screw.
    Good-bye-ee!

My fond adieux to friends known well—
To Abdul, Willie, Kaiser Bill;
I hope they'll feel at home in hell.
    Good-bye-ee!   *'Digger'*
    Our Homeward Stunt, March–May 1919

Australian troops parade past Buckingham Palace. (*Australian War Memorial, Neg. no. D00554*)

APPENDICES

Listed below are the trench and troopship publications examined during the preparation of this book. All the titles are held in the archive of the Australian War Memorial and the extracts in each chapter are reproduced with the generous permission of that institution.

I
PUBLICATIONS OF TROOPSHIPS LEAVING AUSTRALIA 1914–1918

Title; vessel; issue(s), date.

Aeneasthetic; *Aeneas*; Nos 1–4 & Souvenir, Oct.–Nov. 1916.
Afric Echoes; *Afric*; 1915.
Ananias; *Aeneas*; Nos 1–2, Nov. 1917.
Armadale News; *Armadale*; Aug.–Sept. 1916.
Armadillo; *Armadale*; n.d.
Ascanian; *Ascanius*; Souvenir, 1916.
Ayrshire Furphy; *Ayrshire*; Nos 1–7, July–Aug. 1916.
Ballarat Beacon; *Ballarat*; 1917.
Ballarat Lyre; *Ballarat*; No. 14, Aug. 1915.
Bandage; *Kyarra*; Dec. 1914.
Barambah Souvenir; *Barambah*; Souvenir, Sept.–Oct. 1918.
Beltana Bugle; *Beltana*; Souvenir, July 1917.
Benalla Sun; *Benalla*; Nos 1–9, Nov. 1916–Jan. 1917.
Berrima Souvenir; *Berrima*; Souvenir, Jan. 1917.
Billjim At Sea; *Ormonde*; Souvenir, 1918.
Blue Funnel Trooper; *Aeneas*; Nos 1–3, Dec. 1915–Jan. 1916.
Book of the Ballarat; *Ballarat*; Souvenir, 1917.
Boonah Buzzer; *Boonah*; Souvenir, Nov.–Dec. 1918.
Camouflage; *Borda*; Nos 1–2, 1917.
Clan News; *Clan Macgillivray*; Nos 11–18, Feb.–Mar. 1915.
Devil's Own Rag; *Willochra*; No. 4, June 1916.
Dixie; *Medic*; Nos 1–4, Jan.–Feb. 1917.
Dragropes; *Shropshire*; Souvenir, 1916.
Dryarra Wail; *Kyarra*; No. 5, n.d.
Euripidean; *Euripides*; Souvenir, 1917.
Euripides Ensign; *Euripides*; Nos 2–3, 1915.
Expeditionary; *Hororata*; No. 1, Nov. 1914.
Fair Dinkum; *Nestor*; Nos 1–3, Mar.–Apr. 1918.
Furphy Times; *Medic*; Jan.–Feb. 1917.
Geelong Racer; *Geelong*; Oct. 1914.
Heavic; *Suevic*; Nos 1–10, July–Aug. 1917.
Innocents Abroad; *Port Nicholson*; Nov.–Dec. 1916.
Kan-Karroo Kronickle; *Karroo*; Nos 1–11, Oct.–Dec. 1914.
Kangaroo; *Afric*; Nos 1–26, Oct.–Nov. 1914.

Kangaroo Out Of His Element; *Afric*; Oct.–Nov. 1914.
Kangaroosilite; *Wandilla*; Jan. 1916.
Kanowna Lament; *Kanowna*; Nos 1–2, July 1915.
Khiva Nursery; *Khiva*; Souvenir, June 1917.
Kyarra Truth; *Kyarra*; Nos 3–7, Jan. 1915.
Limber Log; *Port Sydney*; Souvenir, 1917.
Limelight; *Runic*; July 1916.
Lincoln Lyre; *Port Lincoln*; Nov. 1915.
Log Of The Lunatic Ship; *Borda*; Nos 3, 5, Dec. 1916–Jan. 1917.
Makarini Cyclone; *Makarini*; Sept. 1915.
Maltameter; *Malta*; Souvenir, Oct.–Nov. 1918.
Miltiades Lyre; *Miltiades*; 1916.
Moultan Memories; *Moultan*; Souvenir, 1917.
Orvieto Chronicle; *Orvieto*; Oct.–Nov. 1914.
Osteralia; *Osterly*; Souvenir, Feb.–Apr. 1917.
Osterly Keystone; *Osterly*; Jan.–Feb. 1916.
Pepper Box; *Malwa*; Souvenir, Dec. 1915.
Persique; *Persic*; Nos 1–11, Mar.–May 1918.
Pink'un; *Kyarra*; Nos 2–4, 1916.
Port Darwin Magazine; *Port Darwin*; May–June 1918.
Port Lincoln Lyre; *Port Lincoln*; No 2, 1916.
Reveille; *Euripides*; Oct. 1916.
Rising Sun; *Kyarra*; Nos 1–5, June–Aug. 1916.
Rising Sun; *Themistocles*; Nos 1–7, Aug.–Sept. 1916.
Runic Rhymes; *Runic*; Aug. 1916.
Seang Bee Sea Breezes; *Seang Bee*; Souvenir, Sept. 1916.
Seang B-Liar; *Seang Bee*; Oct.–Nov. 1915.
Sea Spray; *Star of Victoria*; Sept. 1917.
Shrapnel; *Marathon*; Nos 1–6, May–July 1917.
Shropshire Signal; *Shropshire*; June 1917.
Shropshire Tatler; *Shropshire*; Nos 1–3, May–July 1917.
Silver Track; *Field Marshal*; Souvenir, 1918.
Spasms; *Anchises*; Mar. 1917.
Sports Company Gazette; *Suevic*; Jan. 1916.
Squeak Of The Bally Rats; *Ballarat*; Oct. 1915.
Suffolk Slosher; *Suffolk*; Nos 1–5, Oct.–Nov. 1916.
Sunday Times; *Runic*; July 1916.
Times Of Orontes; *Orontes*; Souvenir, 1916.
Transport Scraps; *Orontes*; July 1918.
Vestalian Gazette; *Vestalian*; Aug. 1916.
W.A.S.A Weekly; *Borda*; July 1917.
Wallaby Chronicle; *Megantic*; Mar. 1916.
Wandilla Wonder; *Wandilla*; Nov.–Dec. 1914.
Weakly Effort; *Orontes*; Jan. 1917.
Wyreemian; *Wyreema*; Nov. 1918.

II
FIELD PUBLICATIONS 1914–1919

Title; subtitle or unit; theatre; issue(s), date.

A.M.C. Weekly News; Medical Corps; Gallipoli/Egypt; 1915.
Abroad With The Fifth; 5th Field Ambulance; Souvenir; France; 1917.
All Abaht It; 10th Field Ambulance; England & France; two issues, 1916 & 1919.
Anzac Argus; Gallipoli; June 1915.
Anzac Bulletin; Issued to Australian Forces; England; Nos 1–129, Jan. 1917–June 1919.
Anzac Records Gazette; Egypt; 4 issues, Nov. 1915–Mar. 1916.
Astra; 3rd Divisional Train; Australia, England France; 3 issues, May–Oct. 1916.
Aussie: The Australian Soldiers' Magazine; France; Nos 2–9, 12, Jan. 1918–Mar. 1919.
Australian At Weymouth; Westham, Littlemoor & Monte Video Camps; England; Nos 1–3, June 1918–June 1919.
Australian Corps News Sheet; War Records Section; Nos 1–18, Sept. 1918–1919.
Barrak; Imperial Camel Corps; Egypt; July, Sept. 1917, Feb. 1918.
Battalion Buzzer; 1st Battalion; France; May 1917.
Battery Herald; 14th Field Artillery; France; Nos 1–3, 1916.
Bostall Boshter; Abbey Wood Convalescent Hospital; England; Jan. 1916.
Brain Wave; 2nd Battalion; England; Aug. 1918.
Bran Mash; 4th Light Horse; Gallipoli; June 1915.
Burnished Bits; 5th Divisional Signal Company; Belgium; No. 2, n.d.
Ca Ne Fait Rien; 6th Battalion; France; Nos 1–65, 1917–1919.
Cacolet; Camel Field Ambulance; Egypt; No. 3, Sept. 1917, No. 4, June 1918.
Coo-ee; Bishops Knoll Hospital; England; Nov. 1916–Oct. 1917.
Deesweet Despatch & Walcourt Argus; 18th Battalion; Belgium, France; Nos 4–11, 1919.
Derniere Heure; G.H.Q.; France; Souvenir, 1919.
Desert Dust Bin; 3rd Light Horse Field Artillery; Egypt; Nos 1–5, April–June 1916.
Diamond; 24th Battalion; France; Nos 2–8, Oct.–Nov. 1918.
Digger; Base Depots; France; Vol. I, Nos 1–26, Vol. II, Nos 1–16, Aug. 1918–May 1919.
Dinkum Australian; No. 1 Command Depot; England; Jan.–Feb. 1918.
Dinkum Oil; Gallipoli; Vol. I, Nos 1–8, n.d., Vol. 3, No. 1, June 1916.
8th Infantry Brigade; June–Dec. 1917, Mar.–Nov. 1918.
First Aid Post; 2nd Field Ambulance; Gallipoli; Nos 1–9, July 1915.
Fiveaustra; Education Service; England; Nos 2–5, 1919.
14th Company Magazine; Camel Corps; Egypt; June 1918.
Gamrah Weekly Wail; Mechanical Transport Services; Egypt/Palestine; Vol. 1, No. 4, n.d.
Ghutz; 1st Field Ambulance; France; Nos 1–3, 5, 1918.
Harefield Park Boomerang; 1st Auxiliary Hospital; England; Vol. I, Dec. 1917, Vol. II, Dec. 1918.
Honk; 5th Corps Ammunition Park; At Sea, France; 1915–1917.
Hurdcott Herald; Hurdcott Camp; England; Nos 1–12, 1917–1918.
Jackass; 1st General Hospital; France; Sept., Dec. 1918.
Kia Ora Coo-ee; Official Magazine of Australian & New Zealand Forces; Egypt, Palestine, Mesopotamia; Nos 1–10, Mar.–Dec. 1918.

Kia Ora Coo-ee News; News Bulletin; Egypt, Palestine, Mesopotamia; Nos 1–19, Aug.–Dec. 1918.
Kookaburra; Motor Transport; France; April, July 1917.
Kookaburra; 3rd D.A.C.; France; June 1918.
Kookaburra: Dinkum Oil Edition; 1st Divisional Base Depot; Egypt; July 1916.
Latest Australian News; H.Q.; Egypt; Nos 1–16, Jan.–Apr. 1919.
Local News; Gallipoli; 3 issues, Aug.–Sept. 1915.
M & H Magazine; Hospital in Melbourne; Australia; Dec. 1918–Aug. 1919.
Midnight Oil; 3rd General Hospital; Aug. 1918.
Mirage; 2nd Light Horse Brigade; Egypt; Nos 1–2, June 1916.
Mud Lark; France; n.d.
No. 5 A.G.H.; Hospital in Melbourne; Australia; Aug.–Sept. 1918.
Noreuil Noose; 14th Brigade H.Q.; France; May 1917.
Palestine Prattle; 3rd Field Troop A.E. Engineers; Palestine; March 1918.
Passed By Censor; A.N.M.E.F.; German New Guinea; Dec. 1918.
Peninsular Press; G.H.Q.; Gallipoli; Nos 1–91, 1915.
Rabaul Record; Occupation Force in German New Guinea; Dec. 1915–July 1918.
Remnants From Randwick; 4th General Hospital; 2 issues, 1919.
Rising Sun; Journal of A.I.F.; France; Nos 1–19, Dec. 1916–Mar. 1917.
Second Brigade Monthly News; 2nd Infantry Brigade Comforts Depot Melbourne; Australia; Dec. 1917, Jan.–Aug., Nov. 1918, Feb., Apr., 1919.
Sixth Brigade Magazine; 6th Infantry Brigade Comforts Depot Melbourne; Australia; Feb.–Dec. 1918, Jan., Mar., May 1919.
Sportsman; A Company 1st Battalion; France; 2 issues, May, July 1917.
Stretcher; Camel Brigade Field Ambulance; 2 issues, Mar., Apr. 1917.
Tassie Times; 40th Battalion; Australia, France; 1916, 1918.
Tattoo; 8th Field Ambulance; Australia, Egypt; Nos 1–7, 1915–1916.
Tenth Brigade News; Australia; Apr.– Dec. 1917, Jan.–Nov. 1918, Mar. 1919.
Third Battalion Magazine; 3rd Battalion; France; Souvenir, Aug. 1918.
Torque; Auxiliary Mechanical Transport Column; France; 3 issues, Dec. 1916, Feb. 1917.
Twenty-Fourth Battalion Journal; 24th Battalion; France; 2 issues, Sept. 1918.
Twenty Second's Echo; 22nd Battalion; France; Nos 1–21, 1918–1919.
Twenty-Third: The Voice of the Battalion; France; Vol. I, Nos 1–5, Sept.– Dec. 1917, 6–24, Jan.–Oct. 1918, Vol. II, 5–11, Jan.–Apr. 1919.
Two Blues; 13th Battalion; Sept., Nov., Dec., & 3 undated issues, 1918.
Waiting Times; 17th Battalion; Belgium, France; Jan.–Mar. 1918.
Walcourt Argus; 18th Battalion Education Office; Belgium; Nos 1–3, Jan.–Feb. 1919.
Yandoo; 7th Field Artillery Brigade; At Sea, England France; 1916–1919.
Ye Chatte; 3rd Field Ambulance; France; Feb., July 1917.

III
PUBLICATIONS OF TROOPSHIPS RETURNING TO AUSTRALIA
1916–1920

Title; vessel; issue(s), date.

Aeneas Times; *Aeneas*; June 1919.
Aussiegram; *Ceramic*; Nos 1–30, Mar.–Apr. 1920.
Austramic; *Ceramic*; Aug.–Sept. 1919.
Back To The Bush; *Durham*; Souvenir, 1918.
Bak-Ara; *Bakara*; Nos 1–7, Aug.–Sept. 1919.
Bakara Bulletin; *Bakara*; Souvenir, 1919.
Balmoral Boomerang; *Balmoral Castle*; Feb. 1918.
Benalla Bulletin; *Benalla*; Souvenir, Oct. 1919.
Berrima News; *Berrima*; Nos 1–6, Sept.–Oct. 1919.
Bill-Jim; *Balmoral Castle*; Mar. 1918.
Boomerag; *Ulysses*; Aug.–Sept. 1919.
Boomerang; *Aeneas*; Dec. 1919–Jan. 1920.
Boomerang; *Devon*; Oct.–Nov. & Souvenir, 1919.
Boomerang; *Orontes*; June 1919.
Boomerang; *Soudan*; Nos 1–3, May 1918.
Boonah Boomerang; *Boonah*; July–Sept. 1916.
Boorara Wave; *Boorara*; July–Aug. 1919.
Borda Bugle; *Borda*; Nos 1–2, Jan. 1920.
Borda News; *Borda*; May–June 1919.
Bremen Babbler; *Bremen*; Nos 1–5, June–July 1919.
Cape Verde Clarion; *Cape Verde*; Jan.–Feb. 1920.
Ceramic Times; *Ceramic*; Nos 1–2, Feb. 1919.
Ceramican; *Ceramic*; Nos 1–6, Mar.–May 1920.
Coming Back; *Port Napier*; Souvenir, June 1919.
Demosthenes Souvenir; *Demosthenes*; Souvenir, Jan.–Feb. 1919.
Denison Quoter; *Port Denison*; Nos 1–2, Oct. 1919.
Digger On The Deep; *Balmoral Castle*; Nos 1–3, Mar.–Apr. 1919.
Digger On The Durham; *Durham*; Souvenir, 1919.
Digger's Doin's; *Valencia*; 5 issues, 1919.
Diggers Ocean Weekly; *City of Karachi*; Nos 1–7, Aug.–Oct. 1918.
Diggers Pie; *Argyllshire*; Nos 1–4, Aug.–Sept. 1919.
Dinki-Di Gazette; *Friedrichsruh*; Mar. 1920.
Dinkum Furf; *Rio Pardo*; Nos 1–4, July 1916.
Dinkum Gazette; *Osterly*; Feb. 1919.
Dry Tak; *Takada*; Nos 1–2, July 1919.
En Voyage; *Rio Negro*; Nos 1–6, June–July 1919.
Final Objective; *Takada*; Souvenir, Dec. 1918–Feb. 1919.
Going Home; *Anchises*; 1 issue & Souvenir, Sept. 1919.
Headin' South; *Chemnitz*; Aug. 1919.
Home Trail; *Borda*; Souvenir, Oct.–Dec. 1918.

Homeward; *China*; Souvenir, 1919.
Homeward Bound; *Argyllshire*; Souvenir, Aug.–Sept. 1919.
Homeward Bound; *Dunluce Castle*; Souvenir, 1918.
Homeward Bound; *Friedrichsruh*; July–Sept. 1919.
Homeward Bound; *Kanowna*; Souvenir, Aug.–Oct. 1919.
Homeward Bound; *Nestor*; Nos 1–2, Nov.–Dec. 1919.
Homeward Bound; *Plassey*; Nos 1–3 & Souvenir, 1919.
Homeward Bound On H.M.T. A 14; *Euripides*; Souvenir, Mar. 1918.
Homeward Trail; *A 30*; n.d.
Homing Aussie; *Euripides*; Souvenir, Sept.–Oct. 1919.
Hororata Special; *Hororata*; Souvenir, May 1920.
Imshi; *Karoa*; Nos 1–4, Apr. 1919.
Kanowna Times; *Kanowna*; Nos 1–3, Sept. 1919.
Karagola Critic; *Karagola*; Nos 1–5, May 1919.
Karmala Kuts; *Karmala*; Nos 1–4, July 1919.
Karoola T.S.S. No. 1 Australian Hospital Ship; *Karoola*; Souvenir, 1919.
Karoolian; *Karoola*; Sept. 1918, Aug. 1919 (two voyages).
Katoomba News; *Katoomba*; Souvenir, Aug.–Sept. 1919.
Khyberian; *Khyber*; Nos 1–13, Apr.–May 1919.
Last Post; *Friedrichsruh*; Nos 1–4, July–Aug. 1919.
Last Ridge; *Miltiades*; Nos 1–2, June 1919.
Lytteltonik; *Port Lyttelton*; Nov. 1917.
Main Issue; *Main*; Aug.–Sept. 1919.
Main H.M.T.; *Main*; Souvenir, 1919.
Maltese Roller; *Malta*; Souvenir, Aug.–Sept. 1918.
Marathonian Double Number; *Marathon*; Apr.–June 1919.
Morvada Magazine; *Morvada*; Souvenir, July–Aug. 1919.
Mystic Leaves; *Themistocles*; Jan. 1920.
Nest of News; *Nestor*; May 1919.
Nevasa T.S.S.; *Nevasa*; Souvenir, Mar.–Apr. 1919.
Norman News; *Norman*; Nos 1–3, July–Aug. 1919.
Nuntius Neptuni; *Argyllshire*; Souvenir, Mar. 1918.
Ocean Echo; *Wiltshire*; July–Aug. 1919.
Orsova News; *Orsova*; Nos 1–9, Aug. 1919.
Orsova Souvenir; *Orsova*; Souvenir, Aug. 1919.
Oster-Wave; *Osterly*; Sept.–Nov. 1919.
Our Homeward Stunt; *Port Macquarie*; Nos 1–4 & Souvenir, Apr.–May 1919.
Persic Pickles; *Persic*; July–Aug. 1919.
Pip's Paper; *Pakeha*; Souvenir, 1919.
Port Lyttelton Gazette; *Port Lyttelton*; 1 issue & Souvenir, June–July 1919.
Prodigal Sun; *Mahia*; Nos 1–4, June–July 1919.
Prodigal Sun In Chronicle And Caricature; *Mahia*; Souvenir, 1919.
Rag Bag; *City of Exeter*; Nos 1–3, July 1919.
Roto Gazette; *Rotomahana*; May 1919.
Round The Map; *Berrima*; Souvenir, 1917.
Runic Herald; *Runic*; Dec. 1919.
Runic Rag; *Runic*; Souvenir, 1918.

Sardine; *Sardinia*; Aug. 1919.
Saxon Sentinel; *Saxon*; Jan. 1919.
Ship's Rag; *Suevic*; Nos 2–3, Aug. 1919.
Shropshire Blimp; *Shropshire*; Souvenir, Apr. 1919.
Sixty-Eight: Journal of Quota No. 68; *Raranga*; Souvenir, 1919.
Southern Cross Gazette; *Themistocles*; May 1917.
Southward-Ho; *Suevic*; Souvenir, 1917.
Strewth; *Indarra*; Nos 1–3, July–Aug. 1919.
Struth: The Medic Medium; May 1919.
Swakopmund Gazette; *Swakopmund*; Nos 1–4, June–July 1919.
Takadaussie; *Takada*; 1 issue & Souvenir, Aug. 1919.
Two-Up Topics; *Durham*; June 1919.
Vie Ormondaise; *Ormonde*; July 1919.
Wahehe Boomerang; *Wahehe*; 1 issue & Souvenir, Nov. 1919.
Wahehe Times; *Wahehe*; May–July 1919.
Warwickshire Wangler; *Warwickshire*; 1919.
Windhuk Times; *Windhuk*; Nos 3–11, June–Aug. 1919.
X-Press; *Llanstephan Castle*; Mar. 1918.